A Most
Unusual
Life

A Most Unusual Life

DORA VAN GELDER KUNZ
CLAIRVOYANT, THEOSOPHIST, HEALER

KIRSTEN VAN GELDER AND FRANK CHESLEY

This publication has been generously supported by
The Kern Foundation

Theosophical Publishing House
Wheaton, Illinois * Chennai, India

Quest Books
PO Box 270
Theosophical Publishing House
Wheaton, IL 60187-0270

www.questbooks.com

Frontispiece photograph: Dora van Gelder Kunz, most likely in 1975 when she took office as president of the Theosophical Society in America.

Photo credits: Grateful acknowledgment is made to Sally Blumenthal, Dr. Michael McGannon, Dr. Martin and Mary Proudfoot, and the Archives of the Theosophical Society in America for providing photographs that appear in this book. The photo of Dora van Gelder Kunz that appears on the last page of the photo insert was taken by Dot Salogga.

Cover design by Drew Stevens
Photo insert design by Kirsten Hansen Pott
Typesetting by DataPage, Inc.

Library of Congress Cataloging-in-Publication Data

Van Gelder, Kirsten.
    A most unusual life: Dora van Gelder Kunz: clairvoyant, theosophist, healer / Kirsten van Gelder and Frank Chesley.
        pages   cm
Includes bibliographical references and index.
ISBN 978-0-8356-0936-4
1. Kunz, Dora, 1904–1999. 2. Occultists—United States—Biography.
3. Clairvoyants—United States—Biography. 4. Theosophists—United States—
Biography. I. Title.
BF1408.2.K86V36 2015
130.92—dc23
[B]   2014040911

5   4   3   2   1   *   15   16   17   18   19   20
Printed in the United States of America

Contents

Photo insert follows page 50.

Foreword

Dora van Gelder Kunz was my aunt, my father's sister, and so I knew her very well. Dora was at once a simple and a complex person. She was simple in living a frugal life, paying no attention to haute couture. In later life she dressed mostly in her favorite blue blouse and nondescript skirt (she rarely wore slacks). At the same time, Dora was complex in the strength of her extremely rare type of clairvoyance that gave her insight into psychological, physical, and intellectual functioning as well as the spiritual development of human beings. I, unfortunately, have never seen an angel or a fairy, but I have no doubt that she could.

Dora's greatest passion was to help everyone suffering from any type of illness. She spent her whole life doing so, though she was pragmatic enough to realize that some conditions were beyond her abilities to heal. She was a private person but loved to socialize, particularly with doctors and nurses. Perhaps unconsciously, she viewed these health professionals in a kind of hierarchy: male doctors, female doctors, psychologists, nurse practitioners, and finally, but not least, registered nurses. The RNs were actually her strongest adherents because they were on the front line of physical care.

Even though Dora was brought up as a Theosophist, she rejected the sycophancy of some of the members of the Theosophical Society as well as some of the Society's literature during the early years of the twentieth century. She thoroughly disliked Jinarajadasa's *First Principles of Theosophy* and Leadbeater's *Man: Whence, How and Whither: A Record of Clairvoyant Investigation*. Both authors she knew well, yet she sought to prevent the republication of those particular works. During her terms as president of the Theosophical Society in America (TSA), she worked hard, following her husband, Fritz Kunz, to develop a greater focus on modern science and to reinvigorate theosophical research.

I once asked her whether the TSA should have disenfranchised the TS lodges in the southern United States that took a "white's only" position. She pursed her lips in a frequent gesture and replied, "You're right. They should have been expelled." Dora may have seen the colors of the aura, but she was adamantly opposed to any racism. Having grown up among Javanese, Chinese, Malayans, Indians, and people of mixed races, she was truly color blind.

Everyone who attended her workshops was bewildered and enthralled by her sudden bursts of gleeful mirth. The context did not matter; the audience was carried along. Still, Dora was almost tight lipped when treating HIV and cancer patients. Her concentration was so acute, and she dismissed both negative and positive predictions. What counted were the results. Dora assessed those who requested her help with her inner faculties, not as invasion of privacy, but only to discover their existential wellness of being.

Few people can claim to have spent their entire lives in altruistic commitment to the wellness of human beings and nature. Dora van Gelder Kunz was one of them, as I'm pleased to say the present volume shows.

—Nicolas van Gelder
January, 2015

Acknowledgments

Many people participated in this exploration of Dora's life. The immediacy of Dora's own words was made possible by the many volunteers throughout the years who transcribed and taped her talks and archived her works. Frank Chesley's extensive interviews with Dora and her associates and family members provided the basis for this book. I'm very grateful for a grant from the Sellon Charitable Trust, support from the many staff members of the Theosophical Society in America in Wheaton, Illinois, and a grant from the Kern Foundation. Betty Bland, past president of the TSA, championed the book, and Tim Boyd, the current president, patiently guided its completion.

Most authors thank their editor, but in my case it takes a village of editors: my husband, Nicolas van Gelder; Ananya Rajan; Richard Smoley; Ed Abdill; Sharron Dorr; and Nancy Grace.

A Most Unusual Life bears testimony to the strength of friendliness and the willingness of those who knew Dora to give their time and share their perspectives and memories. A tremendous creative energy still emanates from the nucleus of friendships that began in Rye, New York with Dora's first visit to the United States in 1925. John A. Sellon and his wife, Emily B. Sellon, were not the only generation of Sellons to befriend Dora and Fritz. Since John's and Emily's deaths, their sons, Peter, Jeffrey, and Michael, continue to support their parents' efforts as Theosophists. Their grant allowed me to bring Frank Chesley's vision of this biography to fruition.

Were it not for Dora's nephew and my husband, Nicolas van Gelder, the book wouldn't have been published. To use Dora's phrasing, "He brought Frank Chesley." Nicolas contributed his own considerable experience as a writer and editor as well as his integrity, friendliness, and iron perseverance.

John and Aino Kunz provided support for the book as well as the remarkable collection of Dora's photos and access to Fritz and Dora's library. Dora's many friends and associates participated in interviews. Margot Wilkie didn't mince words; she spoke with a hearty, New England accent, served tea in pink china cups, and provided gems of insight. Dr. Renee Weber, one of Fritz's star students, and Dr. Janet Macrae, one of Dora's star nurses, are my true friends and continue to inspire my own writing and research. Janet encourages and cajoles through many phone calls. Similarly, Dr. Erik Peper, another of Dora's star students, reminded me that he continues to include elements of Dora's ideas and practices when he teaches in the United States, Asia, and Europe. Susan Loeb broke my heart when she phoned consistently to cheer *me* up even as her own health declined. Marie Jenkins reminded me that there are regular healing groups based on Dora's meditation and Therapeutic Touch scattered throughout the United States. Cookie Jurgens and Dr. Nelda Samarel demonstrated good storytelling and the important role of anecdotal evidence. Jack Samarel and their son, Adam, allowed their stories about healing to be included. Despite multiple surgeries, Dr. Sue Wright shares her enthusiasm for continuing Dora's healing group and insight into Dora's summers at Pumpkin Hollow Farm. I appreciate Peter Michel's generosity in allowing me to benefit from his interviews with Dora. His questions about Theosophical areas of interest and his perseverance introduced lines of enquiry that were omitted from later interviews. And I'm grateful to Sue Wright for transcribing those interviews and to Janet Kerschner for locating them in the archives.

Janet Kerschner, the archivist at Olcott Library in the headquarters of the Theosophical Society in America, steadied my first tentative steps into the Fritz and Dora Kunz archives. Since then she has provided energetic support and immediate answers to all kinds of questions. Marina Maestas, the head librarian at Olcott Library in Wheaton, and her staff and volunteers provided open access to the library as well as expertise. In addition to the book's readers and editors, Jessica Salasek cheerfully directs its marketing and publicity. Kirsten Hansen Pott designed the cover and touched up photos for the interior. Nancy Grace was instrumental in selecting photos and ensuring their quality in the reproduction process.

At Olcott, Elisabeth Trumpler shared her expertise as a research librarian. Because her involvement in the TS began over half a century ago, she was able to provide insights into Dora and Fritz's work at Pumpkin Hollow and in the Northeast Federation. During my stay at headquarters, other of Dora's long-time associates—including Jeff Gresko, Clarence Pederson, Floyd Kettering, and Diane Eisenberg—provided support and encouragement for the book. Govert Schüller shared his own scholarly writing on theosophy and his healthy cooking. Dr. Ralph Hannon shared his journals about the activities at the TS headquarters, including the years Dora was president. His insights and excerpts of discussions and readings were particularly helpful in understanding Dora's interest as president of the TSA in integrating modern science and theosophical enquiry.

Guru Prasad and Shirley Nicholson graciously allowed Nicolas and me to stay at Krotona Institute for five months to research and write. Lakshmi Narayan, the head librarian at the Krotona School of Theosophy, shared memories of Dora in Wheaton and in India. Joy Mills shared her contagious enthusiasm and her recollections of Dora's years as president of the Theosophical Society. While in Krotona, I appreciated the insights of second-generation members of the Theosophical Society, Richard Ellwood and Carol Nicholson, who both knew Dora for decades. Many other residents welcomed us and encouraged the "Dora book" by taking us to the beach and repairing our car when ground squirrels chewed through wires. Marcia Markey, whom I met when I was in my early twenties, remembered Pumpkin Hollow Farm when "campers" dressed for dinner in floor-length skirts and suit jackets. On the drive back to the Northwest from Krotona, April and Jerry Hejka-Ekins welcomed me into their home. They introduced me to their extensive library of Theosophical material and to their efforts to bring Theosophists from various organizations together.

Susan Brown allowed her parents' story to be shared and donated family letters to the Kunz archives at Olcott Library; Carol Bee shared early letters and notes from Dora that provided counseling based on Dora's clairvoyant assessment. Similarly, Adam McDougall, his parents, his brother, and his oncologist participated in a series of interviews with Frank Chesley. They pioneered the combination of conventional and complementary health care in Tacoma despite many obstacles. Ed Alden, president of the Seattle TS lodge, provided several years of valuable computer assistance; he shared transcribing software and provided instructions to Susan Loeb and me. He kept my laptop functioning, helped me tidy my files, and set up a digital library of transcriptions. Also in Seattle during the book's beginnings, both Willamay Pym and her daughter, Linda Jo, were stalwart supporters. Edith Karsten, like Fritz and Dora, had been raised by parents who were members of the TS. She and her husband and sons supported Indralaya for decades, as did Austin and Phoebe Bee, John and Dorothy Abbenhouse, Mary and Alastair Taylor, and John and Margaret Toren. I'm grateful to have known the people who worked side by side with Fritz and Dora.

Loren and Carolyn Wheeler at Pumpkin Hollow Farm graciously answered questions and located recordings of Dora's lectures. Michael Gomes, librarian at the Emily B. Sellon Library at the New York Theosophical Society, welcomed me back to the lodge after twenty years and provided support for the research and writing process.

I also gratefully acknowledge Dolores Krieger and the Nurse Healers Professional Associates; those at Wainwright House in Rye, New York; and those who provided photos, including Sally Blumenthal, Dr. Michael McGannon, Dr. Martin and Mary Proudfoot, and Dot Salogga. Without the patients and "Dora's nurses" and "her doctors," there wouldn't have been Therapeutic Touch. I'm honored to have been involved with the many people who knew Dora and who work now to bring this biography to press; her work remains vital. Her efforts to "live and experiment with the philosophy behind Theosophy . . . as an integrating force" may inspire others who read about her life of many realizations.

Introduction

/

After many years and dozens of interviews with Dora and her family members and colleagues, the initial author of this biography, Frank Chesley, became too ill to continue writing. He entrusted me with a wooden box of cassette tapes, a box of research documents, and four completed chapters. Fortuitously, and because of the generosity of Sellon family members, a grant from the Sellon Charitable Trust allowed me to turn Frank's gift into this volume.

A number of synchronicities and dogged perseverance on the part of many people are present in the pages of this book. Foremost is the inspiration of Dora van Gelder Kunz herself, my first precious guide to the spiritual aspects of life and professional nursing practice.

To begin near the end of her story, in her early nineties Dora was living in an apartment in her son and daughter-in-law's home in Seattle. At age ninety-two she gave that apartment to her grandson and came to live with my husband, Nicolas van Gelder, and me a mile and a half away. She arrived with two suitcases; a small desk from her life back in Portchester, New York; and a wooden image of the Buddha that a representative of the Indian department of education had presented to her husband, Fritz Kunz.

Dora's work after her retirement at age eighty-three had focused on ways to help health-care professionals develop compassion, altruism, and awareness of the spiritual aspects of helping and healing. Therapeutic Touch, a healing technique she and others developed during the early nineteen-seventies, attracted positive attention in the United States and other parts of the world. Not only patients but also nurses and other health care professionals sought to balance the increasingly mechanistic, technological, and sadly impersonal approach to health care. Dora, having lived the first decades of her life in Java and Australia, knew that the world consisted of myriad cultures and many religions. As a result, she taught healing so that it could be practiced in clinical settings and offered to patients as an adjunctive therapy by people of diverse religious backgrounds. Dora's motivation had been to contribute during a time when refugees, largely Jewish, from Europe continued to resettle in New York City in large numbers and in the United States in general.

At about the time Dora moved in with us, Frank Chesley, who was a friend of Nicolas's, found a quiet house to rent on Exeter Avenue, just down the street from our home. The owner of the house had been a Theosophist before she had died and left it to her son, who lived fifty weeks a year in British Columbia. Her carved rosewood tables from Asia and her son's hand-loomed carpet provided a warm welcome for Frank, who traveled with little more than a laptop and a fancy Japanese cassette recorder.

Nicolas and Frank habitually met every few weeks in Frank's living room overlooking Lake Washington or in the second-floor library of our home to natter. Since Dora's sitting room and bedroom were at the front door of our house, no one could visit without her noticing. Quite likely, Frank interested Dora with his hard-boiled appearance as a veteran journalist, and he began interviewing her two years before her death. She wanted to share her life with Frank, who had a newspaperman's enquiring mind and a broad range of experience. He had lived in Paris for many years and sailed and traveled in Mexico and Asia. Having started his career with a degree in journalism from the University of Washington, at the time he worked with Dora he was semi-retired. He lived as simply as she did and, like her, remained concerned for international relations as well as "the beat" in the local area. They were both slim and walked in long strides, though Dora had a quick, purposeful walk and Frank had the gentler walk of someone who suffered from emphysema. At first glance, he seemed an unlikely candidate to work with Dora on her life's story. Before he served in the Army on *Stars and Stripes*, he had grown up in a Massachusetts mill town. Dora's more privileged life with servants and a governess had ended when she was thirteen, but the bearing of a Dutch colonialist remained with her. Frank angered quickly but was patient and persevering by temperament and profession. Dora, on the other hand, suffered from impatience as she aged, even though with nurses and those who sought her help she had the patience of a saint.

If Frank harbored stereotypical thinking about "little old ladies," it was short-lived once he got to know Dora. I occasionally heard them talking as I came home from work as a hospice nurse. Usually I only noticed the tone of conversations, but sometimes I heard Dora say emphatically, "This is *my* life. This book is *not* about CWL [Charles W. Leadbeater]." Her recorded interviews with Frank indicate that she repeated that statement in regard to Frank's questions about Krishnamurti, Geoffrey Hodson, and a number of scientists she knew well.

The direction of this book changed after Frank got to know Adam, a young man who had survived two kinds of cancer by the time he was twenty years old. Originally a patient of Dora's brother, Harry van Gelder, Adam began receiving Dora's help after Harry moved to Australia. Though Frank loved his solitude, he agreed to give his spare room to Adam. Since Frank was reckoning with his own brother's colon-cancer diagnosis at the time, Adam's arrival sparked Frank's interest in healing.

When research revealed that so-called "difficult" patients tend to progress better in treatment, Frank explored further. What he learned was that, when Adam had been a teenager, after his surgery for his second cancer diagnosis his parents had initially refused chemotherapy and radiation. A struggle ensued over Adam's care plan, the medical team deciding that his parents' choices threatened his safety. Rather than be removed from his parents' home and live in foster care during the course of treatments, Adam had undergone the recommended therapies and survived the cancer. He had also seen Dora intermittently over the course of several years, during which time Adam's parents had driven him an hour and a half north to Dora's home for treatments. Adam's participation in her healing group in Seattle likely contributed to his sense of himself as more than a "cancer patient."

By the time Adam moved into Frank's house, he was seeking to save money to complete his education as a veterinary technician. He no longer needed regular treatments from Dora but occasionally still visited her. Adam eventually left Frank's to marry a woman he met while attending the veterinary-tech program. His wife became a veterinarian before he did and then helped put Adam through college. He graduated quite recently, and now they both work as veterinarians. They have two children, and their daughter's name is Dora.

When Dora lived with us, most of her patients came from within the state of Washington, though from time to time she saw patients

from outside the region, including one who travel
from Sweden. Each person sat fully clothed in a chai
small, strong hands kneaded the tight muscles of the
She joked and pulled faces; she concentrated on much m   ..han a
physical assessment. Sometimes she gazed off into the distance in a
distracted way, indicating to me that she was looking clairvoyantly
at the person's aura, habit patterns, and physical problems. She also
assessed the patient's degree of understanding and acceptance of
the illness, or, in some cases, approaching death.

Just when her patient beamed in a relaxed way, Dora often dramatically and jokingly gave firm orders. "Go lie down and rest. You
aren't to talk with anyone until you have thoroughly rested!" When
Dora worked at her own home or in more private settings than a
healing group, her counselling reflected direct patient concerns
and issues. For those who were interested, she often suggested a
simple meditation that she also led in group settings. One of the
benefits of the meditation, she said, was to expand emotionally so
as to overcome the self-absorption that often accompanies illness—
and depression in particular.

Dora van Gelder Kunz lived a most unusual life from 1904 to 1999,
during a century known for violence and bloodshed and massive
dislocations of people from family, community, and homeland.
She encouraged change on the part of each of us. She insisted that
we *can* adopt positive, life-sustaining actions and forego negative,
destructive, divisive ones. Many of us not skilled in logic or learned
in modern physics weren't thoroughly convinced, as we listened to
her, that we live in a dynamic world of interrelatedness. But Dora
applied reasoning and what she had learned from a community of
modern scientists to gain certainty that what she perceived clairvoyantly wasn't madness. Instead of perceiving the aura as just a

bright, ovoid light infusing and extending beyond each living being, she analyzed its patterns, textures, shapes, images, and colors. She sought the help of clinicians and researchers; and then, after several years, they began to seek *her* help to understand human psychology and the patterns of health and disease. Dora became one of the most highly developed clairvoyants in the United States, with a specialty in what became known as medical clairvoyance.

Dora "the Theosophist" began her lifelong meditation practice at age five. At age thirteen, when she left Asia and became immersed in a Christian culture and education, she continued to read and study texts such as the Bhagavad Gita and the Dammapada. Inspired initially by her parents and grandmother to help others, she engaged in active service when she and other young Theosophists in Sydney raised money to help those suffering following the Russian revolution. She helped family members who grieved for soldiers and others who died or were missing as a result of World War I. Since early childhood, Dora had learned that humans could attain a state of spiritual development in which brotherhood exists among beings. She and—particularly during her lifetime—other members of the Theosophical Society sought to develop a nucleus of universal brotherhood without distinction as to race, creed, sex, caste, or color. With such a far-reaching goal, Dora's perspective of change was vast. Yet she didn't expound on such lofty topics but chose instead to be what she called "practical." For example, she sought "harmony" or "unity" among members of her healing groups rather than speaking about "oneness." She taught what she realized for herself, and, even then, she taught very little of what she knew.

As a Theosophist, Dora didn't expect agreement on a single worldview. Differing philosophical views prevail among people of the same religion, and Theosophical Society members represent a diverse number of religions as well as those who have no religious affiliation. Dora's view of human beings supported equality in terms of the inner potential, the wholeness, of each being. Even when spiritual goals are similar, paths to salvation or enlightenment differ. For Dora, compassion was a unifying force. When working in small group settings, as she often preferred, she cultivated altruism, compassion, and the unity of the group. She modeled logical analysis and, at times, taught how more subtle mental development gives rise to intuition and leaps of logic.

More remarkable than the sense of inner stillness one felt when near Dora were the number of personal obstacles that she herself surmounted during her lifetime. The adjustment she made must have been tremendous in moving from Java to Australia with a guardian when she was only thirteen, leaving a life with servants to room in a boarding house in Sydney. At the time, she spoke very little English, and in order to participate in the experimental Theosophical curriculum in Sydney she lived there for two years before her family joined her. Her early achievement of a degree of meditative quiescence and her disciplined meditation throughout her life imbued her with an extraordinary perseverance to develop her positive potentials, not in a dour way but out of devotion to her "master."

This master, Koot Humi, was the reclusive Indian associated with the formation of the Theosophical Society in 1875. It was he who first inspired Dora that the vast stillness of the inner self is ever-present and boundless. She could live in such a way that her own integration with that tremendous and uplifting field would help her change radically; she, too, could realize nondual awareness and become capable of facilitating brotherhood.

Dora's inspiration later in life came from other great teachers about whom she didn't speak. Hers was a life of many realizations; she tested their validity and learned to discern them from mere wishful thinking and thought forms. She gave credence to her realizations as necessary in the development of wisdom. Always motivated by compassion, Dora became a harbinger. In this turbulent time, will spring be far behind? "It depends," as Dora often said. It depends upon each of us and the ability of human beings to think of themselves as part of a greater whole.

Dora's courage to overcome the sense of privilege that colonialism spawned helped her become resolute in reaching her audience members and students who were primarily in the United States. She said to me several times, as though still shocked, that in parts of the world "people are born and live and die on the streets." And of course, people without shelter are often also without adequate food and water. Despite a modicum of wealth during her later life, Dora lived simply.

She discovered intellectually and then clairvoyantly that each person's positive change can be potentiated by his or her own altruistic actions. Dora's was a life of service directed toward healing, toward changing the way we view the world and ourselves as solid and stolid. We need to change and we *can* change—not just our outward appearance but our very consciousness. "The spiritual is primary." Through meditation, when change occurs at subtle levels, the emotions calm and the thoughts quiet. We feel better physically. We can watch our thinking, and when the old, negative habit patterns prevail, we can say no to them. We can observe our changing emotions and feel joy, as participants often did during Dora's healing groups when, for instance, a patient with advanced neuropathy took several steady steps. More positive than sympathy for the patient is to feel joy for a seemingly simple accomplishment. How powerful is compassion, built from recognizing our common suffering, whether rich or poor, cancer patient or nurse, man or woman, adult or child.

The force for change is not beyond us; the very nature of our inner self is wholeness and optimal wellness. Spiritual traditions, religions, and philosophies provide guidance to overcome obstacles and realize this wholeness. But, as Dora would say, "Life is complicated." Perseverance is required because philosophical concepts and sacred verses can usually be interpreted in many ways. Discernment in study and meditation are required to unlock the discursive mind so that it yields wisdom realizations.

Dora avoided religious terminology and even the words *prayer* and *blessings*. Yet, in her own shorthand, she guided students away from materialistic secularism; she taught that, through reverence for life, we can assist and receive support from positive forces in nature called, in her own tradition, angels and devas. In my view, Dora served as an ambassador for the many creative beings of the natural world.

If Dora was a harbinger, then this is the century of dialogue, healing, and understanding. It all depends on whether we persevere—joyously or doggedly. If we never walk outside and notice the tiny flowers and plants, then, according to Dora, it is our loss. If entire communities sleep through winter, will spring continue to be a long way off? Dora's extraordinary life, beginning with her childhood in Java, is the story of someone who yearns to fully awaken. She is like the snowdrop that pushes through the snow long before the grass greens. I hope her life inspires others the way it inspires me.

—Kirsten van Gelder
Stoughton, WI
January 16, 2014

Chapter One

Coming of Age in Java and Australia

Theodora Sophia van Gelder, known to most people simply as Dora, was born on a sugar estate on April 28, 1904. On that day her tiny fist pushed through the birth caul that surrounded her as though willing her emergence from ignorance into light. In her mother's view, the partial encasement in fetal membrane signified the potential for clairvoyance or other extraordinary qualities. Dora's mother, Melanie, is said to have known from the time of conception that her infant would have special abilities, and indeed during her early childhood Dora exhibited clairvoyance. Fortunately she was not ridiculed, because both her mother and grandmother had similar faculties. Besides, such abilities were not viewed as particularly unusual in early twentieth-century Java.

Krebet, the sugar plantation where Dora and her three younger brothers were born, was in the tropical yet temperate uplands of east central Java. The most populated and prosperous of the islands in what were then the Dutch East Indies, Java is one of the more than 17,000 islands that now comprise Indonesia. The verdant, rolling hills were slung like a hammock from a rough rectangle of four volcanic peaks. At just under 1500 feet, the estate was high enough in altitude to escape the enervating heat and humidity of the lowlands.

Dora's mother, Melanie van Motman Schiff, was the youngest of four children who had spent their early years amidst wealth and splendor unimaginable to most people. The van Motmans were a prominent Dutch colonial family that first arrived in Java in 1797.[1] Through stories, the children and grandchildren were regularly instilled with a sense of pride in their ancestors. Melanie spoke proudly of a relative, centuries earlier, who married one of the Hapsburgs, then the ruling family in the Austro-Hungarian Empire.

Melanie's father's and mother's family included some of the most wealthy and powerful Dutch landholders in Java. Some grew coffee or tea on huge plantations. Many relatives, including Melanie's brother and brother-in-law, worked in the Dutch colonial government in Batavia—now Jakarta—and the administration's summer government in Buitenzorg.

Melanie's father, Hendrik Pieter van Motman, was the second child born to Frederik van Motman and his mistress, Tan Kang Nio, who was ethnically Chinese. In another culture, Dora's illegitimate, biracial grandfather would likely have been socially shunned. Instead he was raised as a son from the age of seven months by his paternal uncle, Cornelis van Motman, and his wife, who had no children of their own. In Java at that time, as long as the paternity was Dutch and the child a male, social acceptance of blended families and attempts to ensure an heir were relatively common. Colonial Java included a social safety net for children of concubines that allowed Dora's grandfather to be raised in splendor. Hendrik was educated by European tutors, as was the custom among both the Javanese and European upper classes. He studied business management in London and traveled throughout Europe.

Van Motman family photos include Dutch, Javanese, and Chinese relatives and a photo of young Dora, probably in her early twenties, in an elegant traditional Chinese silk dress with her hair braided and pinned up. Knowledge of her grandfather's beginnings may well have contributed to her pragmatism and to her awareness of social conventions that include and exclude individuals based on birth, race, class, and wealth. During the late twentieth century, when couples in the United States experimented with open marriages, Dora expressed concern for children of those relationships. Lack of knowledge about her biological great-grandmother, Tan Kang Nio, resulted in family tales that the woman had been a Chinese princess. Whatever Tan Kang Nio's family background, in Javanese society a concubine did not fare as well as the mother who adopted Hendrik as the heir to the family fortune. And however well-educated and well-traveled he was, Dora's grandfather would have had challenges as a Buddhist and a Dutch-Chinese man in the colonial society of his time.

In fact Hendrik married into a Dutch family that was esteemed in Java. His wife, Theodora Elizabeth Schiff, after whom Dora was named, developed significant knowledge of botanicals. She knew herbal lore and, because they were far from Dutch physicians, she treated the injuries and illnesses that occurred on the tea plantations. More significantly, Theodora was an experimentalist, a stance that Dora would also adopt. Theodora kept records of the botanical preparations and their effects and compiled a handwritten manual of the remedies she had learned from others and developed on her own. She shared this knowledge with a Dutch doctor who was posted to areas of the island where medicines were scarce, and he reported his own observations to her about the efficacy of her botanicals. In addition, Theodora developed expertise in their use as dyes for hand-woven and batik textiles and was internationally known for her designs.

Theodora's husband, Hendrik, loved his home and the parties he hosted regularly. He expanded the house, furnished it lavishly, and increased the number of servants necessary to maintain it according to their lifestyle. A wing was added to the house to accommodate large parties, which required no less than one hundred place settings of monogrammed china, ordered in Paris during his travels.

According to Melanie's sister, known to Dora as Tante (aunt) Bet, at one time the family owned thirty-six horses. When they were children, Melanie, and Dora's aunts, Bet (Henriette Elisabeth van Motman Schiff) and Cotty (Frederique Henriette Jacoba van Motman Schiff), along with her uncle, Pieter (Pieter Cornelis Theodorus van Motman), received equestrian lessons and instructions in driving the horse carriage.[2]

But that grand lifestyle ended when Dora's mother, Melanie, was ten years old. Blights harmed the plantations' harvests. Moreover, financial mismanagement, combined with European trade issues, put an end to any extravagances. During the last years of the nineteenth century, Dora's grandparents were financially ruined. The Nanggoeng estate, which had been in the family for four generations, was sold at public auction. The family then moved to Buitenzorg and adjusted to city life in a smaller house. Nevertheless, they maintained their place in society and within a decade were able to host grand engagement parties for Melanie and Cotty. (Dora's uncle, Pieter, and aunt Bet never married.)

Dora said once that her *Oma* (grandmother), at the end of her life, was "a tough old lady," a statement of affection and admiration. When financial setbacks occurred, Theodora had not, in Victorian fashion, taken to a fainting couch. Instead, she and her daughter Bet, who studied traditional Javanese batik designs, established a factory for hand-loomed textiles; a school for traditional dying methods, design, and weaving; and a successful export business. After the family's financial reversal, Theodora was given instructions during her nighttime dreams by a woman she described as indigenous Javanese. Theodora was taught the methods of preparing specific dyes, and she included what she learned at night in the development of the textile arts. Tante Bet's and Oma Theodora's efforts popularized traditional batik and hand-woven Japanese patterns that previously had little recognition outside the islands.

Dora was sensitive to the effect of her grandfather's business losses and the social obligations that remained. As a young child, she was impressed with the value of frugality and the importance of contributing to one's family, community, and country. Despite their changed circumstances, each of her aunts and uncles found ways to contribute. For Dora, the adage "Dutch thrift" had little to do with ethnicity. Instead it involved an awareness that change is part of life and that overcoming adversity is part of a creative life.

Dora attributed her pragmatism to her father, Karel van Gelder, who, aside from being "near genius," according to one of his grandsons, had a penchant for engineering and project management. David van Gelder, Karel's father in Amsterdam, imported and exported cigars. Karel had three brothers. His older brother, Louis, expanded the business and opened an office in Brussels, where he and his family continued to live. Karel's other brothers, Max and Abraham, stayed in the Netherlands.

Born in 1875, Karel left Holland at nineteen to study at the world's foremost sugar institute in East Java. After several years in the country, he met the van Motmans, including Melanie, who, at seventeen, was too young to marry. Karel, who had made considerable money from the invention of a sugar manufacturing device, left Java and earned a chemistry degree in Holland. He then toured sugar mills in Hawaii and Japan on the return voyage. He was a manager at Djamboe sugar mill when he and Melanie met again after a two-year hiatus. By the time they married, Karel had gained quite a reputation in the sugar industry, and he was offered a position as general manager of a brand new sugar mill and estate in central East Java. He was also involved in the work of the Theosophical Society at that time.

Karel joined the Theosophical Society (TS) in 1900, and Melanie joined two years later, the year they married. There was growing interest in the Society in Java at that time. Melanie's mother, sisters, and brother-in-law also joined the Society. Because of the Theosophists' interest in comparative religion, philosophy, and science, Dora recognized, perhaps more than most Dutch girls of a comparable age, the complexity of life. Through her family's participation in the TS, Dora also learned to respect and appreciate people from diverse cultures. Because of her family's social status, she learned the etiquette of how to treat all people as being one's equal. Dora learned to mix socially with the Dutch, Javanese, and Chinese and was at ease in high society.

Melanie became the president of the lodge in Malang and held the meetings in their home, while Karel was the president of the lodge in Surabaya. Members of the Society were mostly male, though it was common among the Dutch for husbands and wives to join the Society and attend meetings together. The Theosophical Society's objective of creating a nucleus of universal brotherhood—without respect to caste, class, sex, religion, or creed—meant that members tended to be educated Dutch colonialists and upper-class Javanese who conversed variously in Malay, Javanese, and Dutch. Some members sought to foster brotherhood through study of the ancient wisdom traditions—the philosophies, not just of ancient Greece and the Middle East, but of India and other rich but lesser known cultures of the world. Some members, Dora's mother among them, sought experience of the underlying oneness of the universe through meditation.

Dora credits her mother with teaching her to meditate as part of her daily life when Dora was about five or six years old. Each of her brothers at about that same age also began simple meditation and visualization practices. There was a room in the house set aside for meditation, and since her mother meditated regularly, it was quite natural to be invited to sit quietly. They were quiet together, sometimes for only a few minutes, but increasingly longer as she grew older. When Dora was very young, her mother's lessons were more like play or exploration. Later, part of the learning process involved introduction to drawings of the spiritual Masters, associated with the Theosophical Society, to whom her parents were devoted. After she had been sitting quietly in the room, Dora's mother asked her if there was one she resonated with in particular. What did she feel when she looked at the image of the Master to whom she felt drawn?

Other times the object of meditation might be a statue or a holy relic. Dora said that her mother gave her a variety of things to meditate on and left her alone in the meditation room. She was later encouraged by her mother to discuss her experiences during the short meditation sessions; her mother would ask her what ideas or realizations she had discovered. On one occasion Dora's mother said, "Let's sit here and think how much we love one another." Years later Dora would begin meditations in that way. After saying, "Let's feel harmony together," she would say, "Think of someone you really love and send out love to that person."

Other times Dora's parents provided subjects for her to contemplate that were more difficult for her. When she was older, her mother introduced her to a meditation that involved visualization of colors, each linked to qualities and the beings who helped cultivate those qualities in the world. She was encouraged to meditate at the same time each day and also to meditate on the Master she considered special to her. She was to pay attention to any intuitions, feelings, or thoughts that arose during meditation sessions. She brought her questions to her mother as they arose and was encouraged to read widely on related topics.

Dora referred often to an important ingredient of her education in meditation: "Never did I miss."[3] She joked that her mother did not care whether Dora ate meals or not, but, as busy as she was, her mother made sure Dora meditated every day. Aside from managing all the household staff, planning the menus, and hosting the many guests, Melanie sat for hours at a small desk in her study. She managed all the correspondence for the Malang lodge in her neat, flowing handwriting. She also wrote articles and verses that conveyed a mystic's view of the universe and a deep understanding of the cosmology Helena P. Blavatsky articulated in *The Secret Doctrine*. Unlike Dora's father, Karel, Melanie had not yet met Annie Besant, who was then president of the international Theosophical Society, but Melanie was devoted to her and to her work in India. Dora's mother was very often the hostess for traveling speakers at the Malang lodge who traveled from other parts of Java and occasionally other countries. Dora recalled that there was a steady stream of guests in their house at Krebet.

Tante Cotty, Melanie's oldest sister, married Dirk van Hinloopen Labberton, who was as voluble as Cotty was quiet. He had sailed from Amsterdam to Java on the same steamer with Karel and attended the same sugar institute. While there, the two struck up a friendship that was to become lifelong. *Oom* (uncle) Dirk discovered that he wasn't suited for the sugar industry. Because of his earlier education at the lyceum, he obtained a position in the Dutch government in Batavia. Karel was best man at Dirk and Cotty's wedding. A year later Dirk in turn served as best man for Karel and Melanie.

Dora and her family also attended the *Wayang*—the traditional Javanese shadow puppet theater—and during the early twentieth century those performances often lasted throughout the night. In 1912 Cotty wrote *Wayang or Shadow Play as Given in Java: An Allegorical Play of the Human-Soul and the Universe*.[4] The booklet continues to be recognized by contemporary scholars for its Theosophical perspectives on one of the most popular shadow plays, the Indian epic known as the Mahabharata. Much like Tante Bet and Theodora, Cotty brought positive attention to traditional Javanese arts.

For Dora, it was Cotty's husband, also known as Labberton, who was the real scholar in the family. Dora said that she never met another person as gifted in language as her uncle. He was said to have known nearly forty languages and dialects. As a linguist he identified the relationship among Nippon, Malay, and Polynesian as a family of languages. He was a leading proponent of the notion that, except for those on Papua New Guinea and North Halmahera, the Indonesian peoples shared the same race. He is also credited as the first person to use the term *Indonesia*.

Dirk van Hinloopen Labberton was instrumental in the growth of the Theosophical Society in Java and the other islands. When Dora was a young child, her uncle was the first general secretary of the Dutch East Indies section, which was large, multiracial, and very active. Because he could lecture in the people's own dialects, he introduced hundreds of people across Java to Theosophy.

The van Gelders had a considerable library in their home in Krebet, and there were many books that captivated Dora as a child. In addition to Blavatsky's *Voice of the Silence*, on which Dora meditated for many years, there were many books by Annie Besant. Besant and C. W. Leadbeater produced several books based on their research on clairvoyance, and many were translated into Dutch. One of these, *Thought Forms*, included color plates of an artist's rendition of the physical forms created by certain thoughts and emotions.

19

For the first time Dora could compare the images in the book with what she herself saw clairvoyantly.

Because Dora was allowed to attend the Theosophical Society meetings in their home, she learned to appreciate the different worldviews expressed by various visitors. If not for those gatherings, she might have had a somewhat sheltered and provincial upbringing. It was not until much later that she learned just how much her worldview differed from that of others of her generation in other parts of the world. Altruism was emphasized during Dora's early years, and throughout her life she continued to introduce it as an antidote to egotism and individualism. Had she attended the Dutch school, altruism would likely have been introduced as selfless service to God, family, and country. Theosophists, because they seek universality, allow altruistic action to encompass all of humanity, and some Theosophists include other sentient beings as well.

From the age of seven or eight, Dora listened as a shy, quiet child to discussions during Theosophical Society meetings. The broad goal among members was to develop wisdom and knowledge of the Divine in order to uplift humanity. For Dora, service included the natural world, and one of her unique insights was that of the interdependence of human beings and what Theosophists called the "angelic kingdom."

In an age when people were imploring angels for help, Dora insisted that, on the contrary, human beings can be of great benefit to these unseen beings. As an adult, she used Albert Schweitzer's words "reverence for life" as the key to opening a door to those realms.

On the estate, Krebet, along with daily lessons, Dora swam, played games with her brothers Harry and Lucius, and amused the baby of the family, Arthur, who was seven years younger than she. Despite the activity around her, Dora later stated that she experienced life on the large sugar plantation as lonely. She was only three years older than Harry, but girls' lives were very restricted even during the last years of the Victorian era. Only much later in her life did she wear slacks, for example. "My brothers ate early and I ate alone, by myself at night. I had some good friends among my father's employees, and they came and kept company with me, so I had some grown-up people among my friends. I had no children to play with. I had no girlfriends. I was brought up surrounded by males." Some of her governesses were highly educated European women, but they could not be considered playmates.[5]

Consequently, at a very early age Dora began to study the natural world, not just through books but by using her special abilities. She observed *nature spirits* in the wilder areas of the garden, in streams and waterfalls, volcanoes, and mountains, in the air and in the fire. One evening during her early childhood Dora received what she considered a special mind-to-mind message from the great angel of the mountain across the valley. He told her that if she developed her abilities, she would one day be able to communicate and understand his vast and subtle consciousness. Evening after evening she sat quietly and watched the sky change above the mountain as her younger brothers had their supper.

Dora continued to refer to that angel with a masculine pronoun even after she learned through observation that angels and the entire kingdom of related beings are without gender: unlike the animal kingdom, they have no need for procreation. She also used masculine pronouns out of deference to cultural expectations, although she remarked that those angels who have discernible facial features usually appear androgynous. Other angels, she said, appear as vibrant striations of light and luminescence, with little human form.

Similarly she adopted the term *angel* out of respect for common parlance. *Devas*, a Sanskrit word she used among friends and

21

family, refers to beings from the god realm, according to Indian thought. Among Theosophists she used the term *angelic kingdom* to connote a wide variety of those higher order beings as well as the thousands of types of fairies, gnomes, elves, sylphs, salamanders, and so on. According to Dora, there are devas associated with mountain peaks and great canyons, with vast regions of forest and small inland bays. She distinguished those devas from the "healing angels" that act as sources of energies associated with spiritual healing. These appear on battlefields, near bedsides of the dying, around hospitals, prisons, and other places where people suffer and yearn for help.

In addition, Dora recognized the special role of religious angels, and even as a young adult was asked to ensure that a new priest's mass effectively consecrated the host. Many people in Christian cultures are familiar with cherubim, seraphim, and the angelic hierarchies. But Dora also discovered that angels are part of the Muslim culture in Java, where she grew up, just as surely as they were part of the Christian culture she entered as a teenager. She said that the angels who help with Muslim practices appear slightly different from those who help in Christian services.

Dora discovered that fairy tales were usually told by people who couldn't see fairies, so these stories tended to either exaggerate their importance or trivialize them.

On the other hand, some people in cultures around the world learn to communicate with the beneficent beings of the "unseen" world. According to Dora, the angels, fairies, and other beings live alongside, and often in spite of, the vast majority of people, who are oblivious to them and often indifferent to the natural, nonhuman world. Nonetheless, human beings, animals, and those of the angelic kingdom are all interdependent. Dora discovered that by talking openly about fairies, she could contribute to the ecological movement that burgeoned during the twentieth century. She taught about angels and fairies for over eighty years and emphasized their role in the natural world. While she disliked being a bearer of bad news, she would point out that when a habitat is harmed and made inhospitable, not only animals of all kinds, but the unseen beings of the natural world also disappear. Her concern extended beyond humans, animals, and even the towering teak forests. It also included the tremendous biodiversity of beings both seen and unseen.

Dora's unusual upbringing prepared her to speak for some of those who were unable to speak for themselves. As a young child, she was encouraged to explore her interest in fairies and angels. "My mother and father never laughed at me, nor told me I imagined things, nor spanked me because I told lies. My worst punishment was to be kept in and told I could not go to play with my fairy friends for a half-day. You know, most children see fairies and talk about them until they get spanked and laughed at, and they stop talking and begin to believe they don't see what they really do; and then they lose the inner light and forget the little folks."[6]

Dora played with the various kinds of fairies that populated the lovely gardens at Krebet. They liked the wild parts of the garden, even though she preferred the high branches of "her" tree, where she didn't have to worry about snakes. The garden fairies were at first very shy, but she made friends with them easily and considered them her only playmates. She explained, "I talk to them by making a very strong mental picture. They used to tell me stories when I was a little girl by showing me pictures something like the way children see moving pictures. . . . Sometimes they tap me on the hand or forehead, just as a leaf touches me in falling; that is when they want me to play with them or to look at their flower or bush."[7]

Unlike angels, garden fairies are not highly developed; Dora claimed that they are no more or less spiritual than most cats and dogs. *Fairies* was the name Dora gave to a host of beings of varying sizes, shapes, colors, and temperament. She also called them nature spirits, the term "spirit" conveying something of the transparency and lack of substance associated with them. To the vast majority of people, they are invisible. To others, they are visible briefly out of the corner of one's eye. But to Dora they held fascination. She studied their mannerisms and various habitats and functions in much the way some children make detailed studies of butterflies or dinosaurs. Setting aside the insipid children's stories about fairies, Dora developed nearly encyclopedic knowledge of fairies from the many parts of Java, and, later, from many parts of the world as she traveled.

Dora could perceive events that occurred at a distance and in one instance "saw" that her governess abused her own child. What surprised Dora was that the governess disciplined her emotions while she was with Dora but not with her own child. In later life Dora was asked if she could really have perceived the governess's violence when it had occurred out of range of her sight and hearing. Dora responded, "I knew what I was picking up—other people's feelings. Sure I did. Children are not so dumb."[8]

Dora's father's insistence on debate and reasoning disinclined her from forming emotion-laden judgments. As an adult Dora did not moralize about child abuse. Instead she searched more deeply for the habit of anger in all imperfect human beings and the mistaken view that contributes to abuse. She posited that the tendency toward attachment to "me" and "mine" contributes to excessive concern that one's child will not succeed or will reflect badly on the family. One remedy she suggested to anxious parents was to view their child, not as "their" child, but as just another sentient being.

Similarly, when students complained of conflicted relationships with their parents, she suggested that the parent be viewed, not as "their" mother or father, but as another human being.

When Dora was nearly seven years old, she accompanied her mother to visit her family in Buitenzorg. Dora's brother Harry was two years old, and her mother was pregnant with Lucius at the time. Dora's grandfather, Hendrik, suffered from throat cancer, had a large bandage on his neck, and could no longer speak. It was likely a somewhat frightening experience for a young child, but Dora remembered the visit as her first experience of "going out" to another person in what she later understood as compassion. She sensed that her grandfather was comforted by her quiet presence next to his bed.

Oma, as Dora and her brothers called their grandmother, had as a teenager married a man much older than herself, so she was widowed at a young age. After her husband's death, Oma came to live with the van Gelder family in Krebet, where there were rooms for her in the large house. She was without adequate resources, but Dora's father ensured that his mother-in-law had a home with Melanie and him for the remaining thirty-six years of her life. According to Dora, her father had a special bond with Theodora, as did she. Dora's mother was very loving and friendly "in an emotional way," but her grandmother was able to link with Dora at a deeper level. It is likely that Oma had time for Dora and her brothers that her parents lacked and that Dora, as the only girl, had special access to Oma's rooms. One of Dora's favorite times was when Oma let her come into her bed in the early morning and have a cup of coffee made with extra sugar and milk.

Dora's mother said of Oma, "My mother was interested in the people and she knew all [the local medicinal] herbs. They came to her and she cured the people from all kinds of illnesses. We were very far from a doctor, and so she had to cure us, too, when we were ill. So she had a very useful life."[9] Dora emulated her grandmother's qualities of practicality and helpfulness. Oma's ability to compile her herbal knowledge into a book and compare research with a Dutch physician did not go unnoticed by Dora. Oma also conveyed a sense of incredible stillness. She tested details from her nighttime dreams that contributed to her color-fast botanical dyes.

In many ways, Dora had a charmed life as a child. Because she was raised in colonialist Java, she had advantages that are unimaginable to most people. Occasionally as an adult, a shadow of her privileged childhood would suddenly appear and disappear just as quickly. She would brusquely wave away a waiter at a restaurant with a demeaning gesture or announce, "This is not hot. I won't have it." Nevertheless, Dora was not arrogant by temperament. She was helpful and genuinely interested in people, but nonetheless, she was more likely to express her impatience toward someone she considered socially inferior. That negative habit pattern was created very early in her life, although she did manage to temper it by recognizing the incompatibility of universal brotherhood and colonialism. As a result, Dora was not among the Theosophists who criticized Annie Besant for her participation in the Indian independence movement; she mentioned Besant's role with respect.

During Dora's childhood, it was not unusual for her mother to be away from home, because she made frequent visits to her family in West Java. In both Javanese and Dutch upper-class families, it was common for girls of about twelve years of age to prepare for marriage by gradually learning to manage the kitchen staff. So Dora often assumed some of her mother's responsibilities, such as selecting the menu and carrying the keys to the house's food storage room.

Dora's father worked for one of the wealthiest Chinese men in Java. On at least two occasions, at about age eleven and twelve, Dora acted as hostess for two wealthy Chinese businessmen who came to visit when both of her parents were away from the house. After the two men had been served food, she sat demurely at the table with them as hostess. Her family was vegetarian, but she had arranged for a meat dish to be prepared for her guests. She also asked the servant to serve them alcohol from the stock that was kept in the home for guests. As they waited for her father to return, they conversed with her in Dutch, and Dora said that the men teased her about being vegetarian. Perhaps she announced, as she would throughout her life, that she had "never tasted any meat, chicken, or fish." In any case, she remembered that at their urging to try a little of the tasty meat dish she burst out, "I will never eat any meat!" Her story speaks to her outspokenness despite her shyness as well as her firm resolve. She remained vegetarian throughout her life.

Dora and her brothers joined the Theosophical Society and later, as young adults, Dora and at least one of her brothers joined the Esoteric Section (ES).[10] Dora was private by temperament, and the ES emphasizes the necessity of privacy on the path of spiritual development so as to avoid judgment, criticism, and expressions that lack compassion and understanding. Those disciplines from her years as an active member of the ES helped Dora to abstain from gossip and to maintain confidentiality later in her life when she counseled people.

Leadbeater was a prolific writer and a man of immense energy and leadership ability. He was to become a central figure in Dora's early life. She met him in 1911, during his first tour of Java, when he stayed with the Labbertons in Buitenzorg. She recalled, "He seemed to me a giant of a man. He absolutely terrified me because the first time I ever met him, I remember that he picked me up and

27

threw me up in the sky. And I was terrified because, I think, of the difference in our size. What I think very few people realize is that he really was a big man."[11] At just under six feet tall, Leadbeater would have towered over seven-year-old Dora. He was about five inches taller than Dora's father and nearly a foot taller than her mother. In addition, he had a full beard, an uncommon sight in the heat and humidity of Java, and he was very broad-chested.

During Leadbeater's second visit to Java in 1914 he stayed at Krebet and was introduced to Dora's clairvoyance. He was also impressed with her shyness, because he commented later that she was the shyest person he had ever met. Until his visit, Dora had been known as "Dotty" to family and friends, but Leadbeater took exception to it because he did not think it suited her. It was he who suggested the name "Dora."

A photograph remains of Leadbeater's 1914 visit to Krebet. He is seated in the center of a group of children. Dora stands behind him holding what looks like a feather between her fingers, a solemn expression on her face. The photograph amused her because Leadbeater had tremendous fondness for cats but loathed dogs. In the photo, Dora's dog, Blommie, is lying at Leadbeater's feet.

World War I erupted shortly after Leadbeater left Java. Since he was touring Australia at that time, he decided to settle in Sydney for the duration of the war. He was determined to start a school for gifted children from Theosophical families, and Dora was one of the children he selected as a potential student. After meeting her during his two visits to Java, he wrote to Melanie requesting Dora's assistance. He had received a letter from grieving parents whose daughter in Java had died, and Dora was asked to report how the girl was adjusting to the after-death state. She was apparently able to "locate" the child, and what Dora communicated by letter rang true for the child's parents. Dora commented that she had been terrified by the experience, but it is unclear whether she was frightened by Leadbeater's test of her abilities or because the astral plane "wasn't always pretty." Dora overcame her feelings in order to help him respond to the Dutch family whose daughter had died. As a result, Leadbeater determined that Dora had the requisite focus, concentration, and maturity for an extraordinary education. He wrote to Dora's parents and advised them to allow her to move to Sydney, where he intended to start teaching young gifted students. Her clairvoyant abilities were such that she would benefit from the educational opportunities he hoped to develop for a small group of select students.

Like other parents who recognize a child's unique interests and abilities, Karel and Melanie saw the potential benefits of the innovative curriculum Leadbeater proposed. Though Leadbeater had been a member of the clergy in England, he had served as headmaster at one of the Buddhist schools in Ceylon started by Henry Steel Olcott, one of the Theosophical Society's founders. Leadbeater had lectured on Theosophical topics in various countries around the world, conducted clairvoyant research, and published articles and books related to the mission of the Theosophical Society. He was credited with clairvoyant recognition of the spiritual potential of a young Jiddu Krishnamurti when he saw him at the Society's headquarters in Adyar, India. And Leadbeater had tutored him and his brother, Nityananda (Nitya), until they were old enough to be sent to England for education. Leadbeater offered to Dora and a handful of other students her age a British education designed to help develop future leaders of the Theosophical Society—and perhaps of society as a whole.

Dora was twelve years old at the time, and her parents trusted her to decide whether or not to study with Leadbeater in Sydney. She recalled, "Both of them said, 'We're not going to do anything.

You're going to meditate and stay there an hour and whatever you decide, we'll do it." Dora described her qualms:

> I was going alone; I didn't want to go because I was frightfully shy, didn't know much of the English language, and [on the other hand] I was just going to enter a Dutch high school. I was just preparing for the examination [as] I wanted to be a doctor. . . . I thought about it and I decided I wanted to go. Part of me didn't want to go at all, but I thought—I felt inside—it was the right thing for me. . . . That was tremendous—I was the only girl—for me to make that decision. They believed that if my "inner self" told me it was right to do, that they would make it possible. That was remarkable of them; not many parents would do that.[12]

At another time she elaborated:

> But I decided that's what I should do—and I did—and my parents backed me up. You have to say that they stuck to their principles, didn't they? My parents made all the arrangements and I went. I grew up then. At twelve I went to CWL [as she referred to Leadbeater], and I was on my own. And I have been really on my own the rest of my life. . . . I've made my own decisions.[13]

Dora understood that even the process imposed by her parents helped her develop intuitive abilities. "I would have to go and be quiet and meditate and then find out—in that quietness of mind—what my decision should be. If you feel that you have done that, even if you make a mistake, I think you get a sense of self-confidence. Because it isn't about what you do, but this inner sense of experiencing it—this inner certainty."[14] That process became easier as Dora matured and relied on meditation for help in decision making. She explained to students that intuition from a level deeper than the personality is accompanied by a sense of resolve.

In late 1916, accompanied by Tante Bet, Dora sailed for Sydney. She may have felt certain about her decision, but once she realized the difficulties and the expectations for her there, she wondered how her parents could have allowed her to go there without them. In any case, her journey to Australia changed the course of her life.

Chapter Two

A Young Theosophist in Australia

Since the Netherlands, and thus the Dutch East Indies, remained neutral during World War I, Java was less directly affected by the war. Australia, on the other hand, as part of the British Empire, was deeply involved in the fighting in Europe. From the time of Dora's arrival in 1916 ships containing the bodies of soldiers returned to the country through Sydney's harbor. The war was to affect her deeply. But during her initial visit at the age of twelve, Dora remained relatively unconcerned with war issues. With the help of Tante Bet, she concerned herself with trying to understand the English language and a new culture.

Tante Bet introduced Dora to a different way of relating to others as an independent woman in a man's world. Bet was a suffragette. She owned and managed her own business. Since her teenage years she had dressed in trousers and suit jackets and kept her hair cropped short. That style, about fifty years ahead of contemporary fashion, likely sent shock waves through drawing-room gossips. She buffered Dora's culture shock, and her example helped Dora to largely ignore sexism and adjust to a school with male tutors and an all-male student body. When Dora arrived, she was the only girl among seven students she admiringly called "CWL's boys." They had mostly come from Australia and Britain, had already begun their studies, and did not have to grapple with a new language.

Australian Theosophists were pleased to have Leadbeater residing in their midst and providing leadership to the Sydney Theosophical community. Thomas H. Martyn, a wealthy stockbroker and a leader in the Sydney lodge, invited Leadbeater to quarter with his family and even named his son Thomas Leadbeater Martyn. With Leadbeater's leadership and vitality, within five years the Theosophical lodge in Sydney numbered over eight hundred and was the largest in the world. In turn, Leadbeater liked Australia. He escaped the growing nationalist movement in India, in which Besant played a very significant role. A self-governing India may have been Besant's dream, but it was not his. As Dora explained, "He had totally no interest in politics. He was brought up to vote the Conservative ticket; he continued it. And of course during that time, Mrs. Besant was completely in the opposite direction."[1] She was heavily involved in politics both in England and in India. According to Dora, Leadbeater was a resolute monarchist who assumed that Britain was the pinnacle of civilization. Australia was overwhelmingly British, though not as repressively class-conscious as the United Kingdom, where Leadbeater, who was of lower middle-class origin, would have been considered not quite the right sort.

Dora's resolution regarding her experimental education was tested soon after she and Tante Bet arrived in Sydney. Leadbeater seemed to have suffered a heart attack. "The first time I was there, he really got ill," she later recalled. "It was the first time he fainted—a man who never in his life had to stay in bed. He had the first symptoms of two illnesses—a leaky valve in his heart, and he developed diabetes." In addition to the crisis created by Leadbeater's health problems, he had not formally created a coeducational boarding school. There were no facilities for a female student, so Dora required a foster parent if she were to remain there to study.

Tante Bet had a business to manage in Buitenzorg, and Dora had no other family in Sydney to care for her. After several months, Dora and Tante Bet returned to Java. She would later say, "He couldn't have me [continue as a student] then because there was no woman, he said, to look after me."[2]

Dora was not back in Java for long. Leadbeater "got so sick that Mrs. Besant sent a woman doctor, Dr. Mary Rocke, and he cabled me that now there was a woman that could keep some sort of eye on me." In addition to the doctor, tutors had been hired to replace Leadbeater during his recovery. Dora's parents were willing to allow Dr. Rocke to provide guardianship for Dora, so she decided to return to Sydney. Her decision to return to Sydney without her family, however, contributed to the end of her childhood. She later said:

> That was a very decisive moment. My God, it changed my life, totally. It must have been very hard for my parents. I always have appreciated it and learned it was as hard for them as it was for me, because, not that I knew then, I was never a child again in one way—I learned independence. I mean if you're alone in a foreign country you either break or fall [apart] if you don't get in the [new] patterns. Isn't that true? . . . I don't know what my life would have been or not have been; I can't tell you, but I chose it, not my parents. I have not to blame them for anything.[3]

Being the only female student, Dora helped prepare the way for more girls to follow. By the end of the decade, the girls at the school outnumbered the boys. But Leadbeater, according to Dora, preferred the company of male students to girls. Like many Englishmen of his generation, he had been educated in all-male environments, and as a result, he claimed that he could better predict how boys would respond to teachings, particularly in meditation practices.

Dora's guardian, Dr. Rocke, was fifty-two in 1917, when she sailed to Australia to help the growing community that was coalescing around Leadbeater. Dora laughingly recollected that "Rocky Doc," as the students called her, "didn't have a motherly bone in her body."[4] But Dr. Rocke cannot be overlooked as a tremendous influence during Dora's teen years. Like Tante Bet, she was a suffragette. She had earned her medical degree in London and worked there initially. She eventually moved to India to work as a Christian missionary doctor and to study Theosophy. She later contributed considerable resources to the movement that coalesced around the hope for Krishnamurti as World Teacher. The amphitheater built for him in Sydney was largely due to her inspiration and efforts.

Dora was introduced to the role of nurse as she assisted Dr. Rocke, who was responsible for the medical care of the students as well as Leadbeater. "I have three brothers," she recalled, "so I was used to it even before I came there. They're all younger than me so I was conditioned to accidents. If the boys [in Sydney] got hurt—and did they get hurt; they got in every accident—I learned very early to wash lots of dirty bandages, which I didn't like. I had to stand by while she did all sorts of operations and hold the basins and all that. That was the girl's role. If anybody got hurt I had to be, automatically, her assistant. Maybe that got me interested; I don't know. Well, I'm not a nurse. I didn't like it at all!"[5]

Dora studied Latin and gained an understanding of the rudiments of medical terminology and of anatomy and physiology. Dr. Rocke, who was quiet and circumspect by temperament, was no doubt careful about personal confidences and how she communicated to Leadbeater and the community. This was to prove helpful to Dora, who would be asked the following year to expand her clairvoyant abilities and contribute in a small way to the war effort.

Teenaged Dora had to reorganize her life according to her radically changed circumstances. When asked if she had missed her family during the two years she was in Sydney without them, she responded, "Completely." Dora transferred her affection for her brothers to her schoolmates, and as she ran a little faster and swam a little farther to keep up with them, her homesickness faded. "I had CWL and all the boys—they were my family. . . . I was raised with them. The boys were my family and that's what they remained. For the truth of it, they remained my family for all my grown-up days too."[6] They traveled together around Sydney by ferry, explored the lovely parks, sailed, went to the beach, and had fun together. Though Dora did not play tennis, cricket, or soccer, all the students hiked and swam and participated in picnics and sight-seeing expeditions.

Though Leadbeater showed affection for his young students, he valued and insisted upon what Dora called "meticulousness." For example, because he emphasized punctuality, the door to the meditation room was closed at exactly the minute the session was scheduled. Students who were just a few paces too late were left standing in the hall. As an adult, Dora also maintained adherence to punctuality: a helper who was tardy too often would be replaced by one who was conditioned to be on time. During classes and meditation sessions, Dora often asked one of her students to close the door to the meditation room, but for her it was a reminder and not a barrier.

Leadbeater, though unwell and in great pain at times, had what Dora called "an iron sense of duty."[7] While Leadbeater's public demeanor could be imperious, within the intimate circle of his students he evoked joy and had a sense of warmth that delighted his young charges. Dora said that he was not at all solemn, and that was why the children liked him so much. Once he had convalesced and was healthier, he met with students regularly and told wonderful stories of his travels and the Masters. His "preachments," as Dora referred to morality stories, were balanced by his wonderful sense of humor, a dry British wit, that when combined with a straight face, could evoke laughter even in the most pious listeners. In addition to telling funny stories, he loved to be told jokes. He had "a huge laugh," according to Dora, who was well-known as an adult for her own infectious laughter.

Like Dora's parents, Leadbeater influenced Dora to think for herself and to act independently from social mores. He cultivated future leaders who were more apt to influence change than merely "go along to get along." Leadbeater tended to take risks and act on principle, no matter what the consequences, and that contributed over the course of the following decade to a growing backlash against him.

Dora was also an independent thinker, but she carefully considered the consequences to herself and others before she acted on principles that made her stand out from the opinions of others. She cultivated patience and, as with the publication of her books, often waited decades for public opinion and interest to change before presenting ideas. She pragmatically accepted that few people are guided by the inner authority of their Higher Self; many are passively manipulated, often misguided by public opinions. Later in life, as a teacher, Dora remained cautious about what she shared with her own students; she would not entertain questions about sexuality in group settings, and she largely avoided the topic in individual interviews as well.

Leadbeater's tendency to confront challenges despite public disapproval probably contributed to Dora's circumspection about emotionally charged issues. She very likely learned from Leadbeater's mistakes. During teaching sessions, she often addressed an issue through stories that seemed tangential rather than confront the matter directly. While she did not ignore real concerns raised by students, she sometimes waited and analyzed more information about the issue before responding. Other times she acted quickly and quietly, for example, when she informed a camp manager that a student or a patient who exhibited prurient interest or aggression be asked to leave a residential workshop and be excluded from future workshops. In her later work to help health care professionals understand healing dynamics, she advocated the transformation of sexual desire through compassion and affectionate friendliness. She encouraged students to attempt to resonate with the Higher Self and function from the area of the heart.

In general, Dora exhibited reluctance to expound certain teachings, particularly if misinterpretation would likely result. As an adult, she taught nonattachment to outcome, but not as it relates to a more subtle philosophical view or to the emptiness doctrine of Buddhism. More than a few students who knew her over decades complained that she seemed to share very little of what she knew even regarding meditation. She occasionally refused to discuss controversial issues or answer questions on topics of concern. Sometimes she said that she hadn't researched an area sufficiently; at other times, she seemed more concerned with avoidance of conflict. "If you don't know, go slow" was one of Dora's aphorisms—helpful in a world where telecommunications were creating a fast-paced world.[8]

Dora described Leadbeater as politically conservative, but he was unconventional in the ways he tested his students. As an adult Dora laughed about one of the exercises in nonattachment to others' judgment that Leadbeater imposed on his first courageous group.

He insisted that the students go barefoot year round. Dora described going barefoot on the ferries and in the posh downtown area. Since Leadbeater's clairvoyance was highly respected, few people questioned his recommendations. "I think nobody but us had to go through this ordeal of dressing differently," Dora later said. "First of all, his theory was that [through] the barefootedness, we contacted the earth's current; but secondly, to do what was in front of one and be totally unselfconscious. I'm not saying this is the right thing to do, but this was his theory; you had to learn to do things and completely forget yourself, and that this was really a very small thing to do for the Master's work. This is why he used to require this sort of thing from us."[9]

Sydney was a modern city, and Dora's appearance evoked sympathy and ridicule. She was even mistaken for a Belgian refugee from the war. "Because this wasn't summer; this was winter; we wore no shoes at all—and so many people, particularly because I was a girl, came and offered to buy me a pair of shoes out of pity. I think we did create rather a sensation when there were all these seven boys and I marching down [the street] without any shoes, without any stockings. I must admit we really were brought up in a very hardy way. Not only did we wear no shoes and stockings in the winter but we wore very few warm clothes. A sweater is all we ever wore."[10]

Another way that Leadbeater tested the mettle of the students had to do with the mail boat that carried post to other parts of the country and the world. Leadbeater maintained a massive correspondence and depended on secretaries to take dictation in shorthand and type letters for his signature. One particularly difficult exercise occurred on a regular basis when Leadbeater and a group of students were talking amiably in his chambers. He would select one of them—never Dora or one of the other girls—to carry the day's correspondence to the mail boat before it left the harbor.

Under normal circumstances the task required a considerable walk through the streets of Sydney to the harbor. In this case, tremendous ingenuity and fleetness of foot became necessary, because Leadbeater had a habit of engaging the boys in conversation, then looking at his watch with some surprise as though to say, "Are you still here?" At the last possible moment, the hapless boy ran toward the harbor with the satchel of letters. "And remember," Dora said, "the boys ran through the streets of Sydney with the mail barefooted."[11]

Leadbeater was even-handed, and Dora had challenges of her own. He had a large white cat that hunted for mice near the coal bin and got covered in black dust, so he insisted that the cat be bathed regularly. "Being a girl among the only boys," recalled Dora, "I was supposed to look after the cat." Of course the cat would screech and put up a terrible fight, and Dora had to overcome her shyness about the noise and the ordeal. After many years of that task, Dora told Leadbeater that she would no longer do it. Leadbeater, she said, accepted her decision without question.

Leadbeater's health remained unstable, and there were times when he required additional help to manage his many responsibilities to Theosophists around the world. One responsibility Dora accepted was, as she herself said, "a very peculiar one." At the time of his illness, Leadbeater had lectured and published on topics related to life after death for over fifteen years. Letters of enquiry often regarded the well-being of a loved one following death. They came from Theosophists and others who shared the perspective that there is continuity of consciousness. After World War I started, the number of letters increased from people who sought information and solace regarding those who were missing or killed in war. Because Leadbeater's health remained precarious, he could no longer respond to all the letters. That is how Dora, at the age of fourteen, became involved with difficult work related to the Great War.

Her task was to clairvoyantly "locate" in the after-death state those who had died and to then share something of what she discovered in letters of response. Her research required a combination of clairvoyance, telepathy, interview skills, sensitivity to grief issues, and tact. She dictated a response to Leadbeater's secretary, and when it was completed, Leadbeater would then read the letters and sign them. "It was the Great War, you know; CWL was very sick, frightfully sick," she recalled. "He was terribly ill. I couldn't say no. He was lying in bed and they thought he might die. He picked me. I never felt elevated; I felt overburdened very often."[12]

There was much death, particularly from the Gallipoli battles, in which Australian troops played a major part. In all, World War I claimed nearly 62,000 Australians through military death and left another 152,000 wounded.[13] The war virtually wiped out a generation of Australia's young men, as it did throughout Europe. The flu pandemic killed millions worldwide, including soldiers. Under those circumstances, Dora felt that one must do one's duty for the war effort; besides, she could return to Leadbeater any letters that were especially troublesome to research.

The assignment helped Dora in many ways; she developed her clairvoyant abilities, interview skills, and grit. Because those who wrote were largely members of the Society, Christian and Australian, she learned to perceive death from other cultural and psychological perspectives. She was also forced to improve her English and had the expert help of Leadbeater's secretary to do so. All that opportunity came with many challenges. When among the other students, she casually referred to her work with "the deaders," as though to make light of the difficult task. However, it was emotionally heavy work. She had to learn how to assess the varying needs of the recently deceased, how to avoid distractions in the astral world, and how to describe sad events in ways that helped rather than overwhelmed grieving family members. At no time, Dora later emphasized, was she under Leadbeater's control. In fact, she was largely on her own and had little guidance apart from the many books Leadbeater and Besant had published on the subject. Neither Leadbeater nor the other tutors gave any instruction in how to "locate" a person in the after-death state. But Dora occasionally asked Leadbeater questions about some of the things she experienced.

The work taught Dora to be tactful and to avoid details of the circumstances of deaths and the unpleasant aspects of the after-death state. It also taught her pragmatism. In an article called "Messages from the Unseen," Leadbeater shared a glimpse of the approach Dora took in her work when he wrote, "It must be your common sense which is your final guide in all occult matters, as it should be in all matters of the physical plane."[14]

Leadbeater was not well enough to review Dora's work with her. But she perceived that as an indication of his trust in her, which gave her confidence. She said, "At first I only [dictated] letters and after that I interviewed them; I had mastered the English language by that time. I interviewed quite a few people, not, I think, the first year. I was fifteen or sixteen [before] I interviewed them. I didn't write one letter; the secretary wrote them all, so the English, everything was correct."[15]

Unlike doctors, nurses, or clergy, Dora could not hide behind a uniform or title when she interviewed soldiers who had died. She learned to be calm and caring and to keep from drawing back at the sight of injuries and violent deaths. Because Leadbeater's secretary was confident that Dora's observations and advice were tactfully stated, she learned to manage correspondence herself, an ability she diligently maintained throughout her lifetime. She also learned to keep confidences and not to divulge the names of people who asked for help.

> I did a lot of clairvoyant investigations. And goodness, how many people lost their sons, their husbands. I had to write letters to a lot of people in different [countries]—but I interviewed the ones who died [from] Australia and all that. A lot of perfect strangers I had to interview, so I learned that early in life. Sometimes I shrank from it, because I was very young to interview some of the soldiers who came from Gallipoli. That, I think, was pretty hard on somebody young— but maybe it was good training. Interviewing those people was very, very hard for me.[16]

After nine years, Dora refused to help Leadbeater with any more correspondence about "the deaders," and he again accepted her decision without question.

Since Dora's letters were all signed by Leadbeater, identification of them may prove difficult for future researchers. However, a series of Dora's letters were preserved from correspondence she maintained with a member of the Theosophical Society beginning when Dora was forty-eight years old. The letters, which span a twenty-year period, demonstrate how she communicated to the bereaved woman and what interested her about the experiences of the man who had died. They also provide some insight into the clarity and lack of detail of her descriptions. What is missing are communications of emotional longing, and that remained an aspect of Dora's counseling style. She perceived the emotional complexities, but that wasn't her focus.

"Nadine Butler" (not her real name) knew Dora personally and wrote to her in 1952 following the death of her husband, "Fred," when his private plane crashed. In those letters, Dora pragmatically conveyed her view that there are subtle aspects of the person that cohere for a period of time after death. When she wrote about Fred, her handwriting changed slightly, and her sentences became longer, as though she were sharing her thoughts without editing them. Four months after Fred's death, Dora's letter to Nadine included simple observations.

> He comes and is with you every time when you think of him and you don't know how he tries to get you to see him and he says some day when you are not expecting it probably will be the time. But he is also doing something very positive and so he is in a happier frame of mind. He says that we don't realize in what a fright of tension the world is in now from the inner point of view with regard to war and so he is really working with people in bands who are trying their best to help this. He now is a fully fledged "invisible helper,"[17] and he and a group of people work together helping individuals, and also they go to places where feeling is high even to the U.N. and they try to really think and help. But he also is still with you and the kids especially in the evenings.[18]

In order to contact the deceased, Dora merely shifted the focus of her awareness while writing a letter or speaking with someone who requested counseling. She worked from a state of waking consciousness and not in a state of trance or sleep state. Such communication with the dead requires concentration without emotional distraction. Dora had to learn her way around, in terms not of physical locations but of subtle states of consciousness through mind training and mental projection. She learned that fearlessness was necessary to avoid the lower, coarse aspects of the after-death state that are attracted by strong emotions. If she harbored idle curiosity, she could find herself drawn into all kinds of dramas; focus and concentration were necessary. She knew about impish tricksters among the fairies and could easily avoid similar impish or negative beings and thought-forms on the astral plane. Projecting stillness and peacefulness helps those who have recently died, and Dora had already developed those qualities.

Dora once counseled the wife of a man who had committed suicide five years earlier, a process that sheds light on her simple style of communication. Unlike death in wartime combat, suicide is considered a negative action in most cultures, and often grief is complicated by feelings of shame and other emotions. Dora told the woman that her husband immediately regretted his suicide: regret was considered, according to the couple's religion, a factor that mitigates negative karma to some degree. Dora told the woman that her husband had difficulties in the beginning but that "after a time he found a modern lama" and was very happy with his new studies. Her straightforward tone and reassuring manner conveyed a sense of normalcy as much as her words did.

In 1919 there was a feeling of relief among citizens at the end of the long war, but reminders of death and impermanence continued as ships brought soldiers back to the country. That same year a ship from Java arrived carrying Dora's parents, three brothers, and her beloved grandmother. Her family had survived the flu pandemic, which had been particularly severe in Java, and moved to Sydney. Though she was only fifteen, she described feeling that her relationship with her parents, her father in particular, had unalterably changed during the two years she had been away from them. She said that her father noticed her self-reliance but that neither she nor her father spoke about the effects of their separation. She had become fluent in English and, to a certain degree, acculturated.

Even though she and her brothers shared many activities related to the Theosophical Society, she communicated her sense that she was different from them. "I never went to school with my brothers. It sounds funny, but I 'belonged' to CWL. I belonged to CWL's group; we had a private education and private tutors. My brothers went to ordinary high school."[19] Dora said that she and her brothers loved Sydney, and their parents were quickly involved in the vital and promising Theosophical center. Karel and Melanie bought a house in Cremorne that they named "Suryastana," and Melanie gained a reputation as a warm and loving hostess. The van Gelders hosted visiting Theosophists from near and far. Both Dora's parents became members of the board of Morven Garden School, the first coeducational school in Australia. (Leadbeater's program of education, which was coeducational after Dora's arrival, was regarded as private tutoring guided by a specialized curriculum; it was not considered a school as such.)

Leadbeater was consecrated a bishop by James Ingall Wedgwood in 1916, who had himself been consecrated in an Old Catholic line. (Old Catholics believe that their bishops hold a valid line of apostolic succession—going back to Christ's first disciples—but they do not hold any allegiance toward the pope or the Roman Catholic Church.) Together Wedgwood and Leadbeater organized the Liberal Catholic Church (LCC), a new denomination that employed versions of Catholic rituals while espousing Theosophical teachings. The entire van Gelder family joined it.

Leadbeater used his clairvoyant powers to investigate the effects of Christian sacraments such as the Eucharist and crafted the rituals on the basis of his findings. During her first years in Sydney, Dora and the boys assisted Leadbeater and others with what she referred to as the "invention of a new religion." They served as acolytes while Leadbeater clairvoyantly investigated the various aspects of the service to ensure that the host was consecrated and that any changes heightened the power of the sacraments. They walked in the processional in a specific direction while the religious rituals were performed; then it was tried in another direction, and so on. Leadbeater observed what created the greatest "opening to" or "resonance with" the spiritual forces and the subsequent "downpouring" of blessings.

Leadbeater emphasized the important part that human beings play in making uplifted forces available to angels, who can spread their benefits more widely. Dora emphasized the mutuality between human beings and the angelic kingdom when, forty years later, she developed her mode of healing in much the way Leadbeater and his associates developed the LCC. She relied upon the uplifted energies created by harmonious groups of people who consciously attempted to be of help to others. Although she was taciturn about the fact, she relied on those she called "healing angels." Leadbeater influenced her tremendously in that respect and provided her with a sound, though unorthodox, Christian education.

When teaching people who were not united by a shared religion, Dora avoided religious terms such as the "invocation" of angels and resulting "blessings" and "miracles." Instead she encouraged students to be centered in the "subtler consciousness of the Higher Self" with "reverence for life" so that they, too, could act as instruments of what she called "healing energy." She emphasized that intention is critical; the intention of individuals to be of benefit to others facilitates the "harmony of the group." That unity of consciousness then helps the healing angels, just as the devotion and intention of members of the clergy and the congregation help the religious angels.

Dora was only thirteen years old when Leadbeater and his associates first involved the students in clairvoyant investigations of the sacraments. From Dora's perspective, their utter seriousness of purpose created some hilarious situations. For example, Leadbeater prohibited the students from wearing their everyday clothes, believing that they interfered with his clairvoyant observation. So during the beginning months, when the church had not yet acquired surplices, Dora and the other students paraded solemnly around an empty church in their white nightgowns. All the while Dora, the only girl and a shy one at that, did her best to stifle giggles.

Though she had fun, Dora did not waste the unusual opportunity. While Leadbeater clairvoyantly observed the religious rituals, she, too, investigated clairvoyantly, and in 1924 she described some of her insights in an article for an LCC publication.

> We are generally accustomed to think of our Lord the Christ as our own especial Lord, as being the Teacher of humanity only, or even sometimes as the Teacher of Christianity only; and we are apt to forget that He is the Teacher of Angels as well as of men. . . . There is a particular aspect of His Nature which is manifested to them, an Ideal of Angelic perfection, even as there is an aspect of Him which is the Ideal of Human perfection and into the likeness of which we are expected to grow. . . .
>
> Among these Archangels are many of various, scintillating colours; but some of them are of that wonderful, glowing, delicate rose which is so especial a characteristic of the Lord of Love Himself. They are tall and mighty, these Great Ones;

their eyes are shining with His compassion; their whole presence breathes serenity and love and peace. They stand so close to the Lord that they are actually centres, as it were, in His Consciousness, channels for that wondrous power which they are ever pouring upon the world in His Name. Under them are Hosts of lesser Angels of their Order who obey them implicitly and carry out their commands. . . .

All members of the Angelic Kingdom have a sense of unity in consciousness; and because of this unity they are channels of great power. For the work of the Church, the Angels draw down the power of their Superiors through their union with them, and so offer an additional channel of blessing and strength quite apart from the links with Our Lord conferred upon every Priest at his Ordination, or from the Sacred Host Itself Which is His very Presence. Although human devotion is an essential factor in the building of the Eucharistic form through which spiritual power is called down and distributed, in many Churches this devotion is not sufficient. In that case the Angels will draw upon their own sources of power to supplement our deficiencies in this respect.[20]

During the course of study, Leadbeater expected each student to choose an organization to serve. Dora participated in the LCC for several years but gradually stopped attending the services, choosing instead to devote herself to the Theosophical Society. Asked why she did not remain with the LCC, she replied that she was "active" by temperament. Like the Roman Catholic Church, the LCC did not accept women for ordination. She did not want to watch as a member of the congregation while her classmates progressed from subdeacon to deacon and so on to become priests and bishops.

Photo taken at Djamboe, the estate of Dora's grandfather, Hendrik Pieter van Motman, in West Java, 1905. Dora's mother, Melanie van Gelder, holds Dora on the top row, left.

Photo taken during C. W. Leadbeater's visit to Java in 1914. Dora stands behind him holding something between her fingers. The dog at his feet is Dora's pet, Blommie. Top row, second from left is Dora's brother Harry van Gelder. Top row to right of Leadbeater is Dora's brother Lucius, and next to him is her youngest brother, Arthur van Gelder.

Dora with C. W. Leadbeater in Sydney
during her first visit to Australia, 1916.

The Manor in Sydney, Australia, where Dora and her family and many other Theosophists
lived beginning in 1922. She left there when she immigrated to the United States in 1926.

Dora van Gelder in Sydney, Australia, 1919.

Oskar Kollërstrom and Dora in Sydney, Australia, 1920.

Left to right: Byron Casselbury, Dora, and Fritz Kunz, Sydney, 1924.

Dora van Gelder, 1925, in Sydney, Australia. "Bet" is Dora's maternal aunt, Henrietta van Motman Schiff.

Dora and Oskar Kollërstrom aboard the S.S. Ormuz from Naples, Italy, to Adyar, India, for the Jubilee Celebration of the Theosophical Society, 1925.

Dora in Los Angeles, California, 1925.

Dora en route to Adyar, 1925.

Dora, who was one-eighth Chinese, is seen here in traditional dress in Holland, 1925.

Rukmini Devi Arundale and Dora at the Manor in Sydney, Australia, 1926.

Young Theosophists camping in Australia, 1926. Left to right: Helen Knothe, Dora, Queegly, Rukmini, and Hely Labberton.

Dora van Gelder in Hollywood, California, 1926.

Fritz Kunz and Dora van Gelder picnicking in Ojai, California, 1926.

Dora Kunz with her son, John, ten weeks old.
He was born February 22, 1928, at Providence
Hospital, Seattle, Washington.

John Sellon, John Kunz, Peter Sellon, Emily Sellon, and Dora. Rye, New York, 1935.

Fritz, John, and Dora Kunz at the headquarters of the Theosophical Society in America to attend the 1935 convention.

Dora, John, and Fritz outside their new home in Portchester, New York, 1937.

Left to right, seated: Helene van Gelder; Dora's mother, Melanie van Gelder; Dora's brother Arthur van Gelder; Dora's maternal grandmother, Theodora van Motman; Dora's son, John; and Dora. Standing: Dora's first cousin, Martin van Gelder; Dora's aunt, Bet van Motman; and Fritz Kunz. The photo was taken during a family reunion in Doorwerth, Holland, 1936.

Dora, John, and Fritz at Indralaya, Orcas Island, 1937.

John and Dora Kunz at their home in Portchester, New York, mid-1940s.

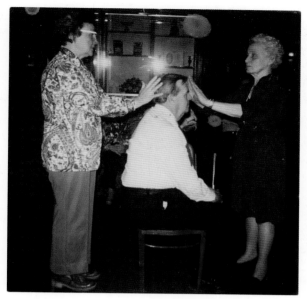

Beverly McNiece and Dora providing a classic Therapeutic Touch treatment at the Theosophical Society in America, Wheaton, Illinois, 1977.

Dora is seen here in the center of the circle at an Invitational Healers' Workshop, Pumpkin Hollow Farm, early 1980s.

Dora in her office at the national headquarters of the Theosophical Society in America, Wheaton, Illinois. She became president of the Society in 1975.

Dora, as president of the Theosophical Society in America, presenting a Tibetan ceremonial scarf—or khata—to His Holiness, Tenzin Gyatso, the Fourteenth Dalai Lama, Wheaton, Illinois, in 1981. On her left is Radha Burnier, then the international president of the Theosophical Society.

Dora at an Advanced Invitational Healers' Workshop, Pumpkin Hollow Farm, August 1985. Dr. Otelia Bengtsson sits behind her.

Dolores Krieger and Dora at Pumpkin Hollow Farm, 1985.

Dora at an Advanced Healers' Workshop, Indralaya, Orcas Island, 1997.

Through her work for the Theosophical Society, she quickly engaged in challenging new endeavors.

Dora seemed to live Theosophy; it was far more than a source of intellectual challenge. Koos van der Leeuw, a brilliant Theosophist whom Dora knew during her late teens and early twenties, articulated a view that likely influenced Dora. He said that Theosophy is the realization of life by each person. Theosophy is not defined according to dogma or creed put forward by the Theosophical Society; nor is it a religion or conditioning by family or culture. One person may realize it most fully through the Christian church, another through a different religion, another through purposeful effort in medicine, science, the arts, childrearing, or any number of avenues. Theosophy is reverence for life along with the realization of wisdom that allows one to develop compassion and active altruism.

The year Dora turned eighteen coincided with one of the most tumultuous years in the history of the Sydney Lodge, and the events tested the commitment of the most stalwart members. In April of 1922, the annual convention was held amidst conflict due to allegations regarding immoral conduct by Leadbeater toward two of his young charges. Although the allegations were eventually dropped for lack of evidence, the damage was irreparable. Mrs. Besant was unable to attend the convention, but several leaders of the Theosophical Society arrived to mediate. In addition to the charges against Leadbeater, Mr. Martyn and others voiced concerns about the Liberal Catholic Church and its relationship to the Theosophical Society. By the time Mrs. Besant arrived in May, the turmoil had reached a boiling point. Even her presence and her skills in mediation and public speaking were not enough to bring resolution to the conflicts. The community split, with the majority of members following Martyn, who formed a new Theosophical organization that was not affiliated with the Theosophical Society in Adyar. As a result, Mrs. Besant promptly revoked the charter of the Sydney Lodge. The two hundred members who supported Leadbeater and the Liberal Catholic Church quickly organized, formed a new board of directors, and rented a hall. Dora and her family members were part of that group and instrumental in the formation of the new Blavatsky Lodge.

During those tumultuous months Dora met many people who influenced her life enormously. They included Mrs. Besant, of course, as well as Krishnamurti and his brother Nityananda (often called Nitya). She got to know A. P. Warrington, past president of the Theosophical Society in America, and Fritz Kunz, the man who would become her husband, when they stayed with the van Gelder family for six weeks.

Dora had already met C. Jinarajadasa and his wife, Dorothy, in 1920. "CJ," as Dora affectionately called him, had chaired the rancorous 1922 convention in Sydney. Born in 1875, the same year as Dora's father, Jinarajadasa was recognized by Leadbeater as an exceptional child when the latter was the headmaster at Ananda College in Ceylon. Jinarajadasa was sent to England, where he took a tripos in oriental languages at St. John's College, Cambridge, and later learned Italian, French, Spanish, and Portuguese.

Jinarajadasa's wife, Dorothy, who was from England, dedicated her life to the cause of women's education. Along with Annie Besant and Margaret Cousins, they founded the Women's Indian Association.

According to Dora, during Jinarajadasa's visits, he took it upon himself to educate her about classical music. They attended many concerts, and Dora said that she felt "terribly embarrassed" on one occasion when they were hushed by those seated nearby. Jinarajadasa keenly impressed Dora as a teenager, and she later said that the brilliant Theosophical leader had high levels of realization and devotion.

To hear Dora tell of the events of 1922, one would think that the luminaries arrived from afar just for her eighteenth birthday. Despite the unrest in the Sydney lodge, one of Dora's main concerns was her birthday party at the end of April. Aside from Mrs. Besant, who would arrive a few weeks later, they were all there: Fritz, Krishnaji (as Krishnamurti was called by those who were close to him), Nitya, and Warrington. Dora was relieved that a quiet party at her parents' home meant that she would not have to endure the usual fanfare that Leadbeater insisted upon with all the students. Even as an adult, after she had overcome shyness, she claimed that she never liked birthday parties. In the end, she had to graciously accept two parties in her honor that year: Leadbeater and the students also stood by their tradition.

The uppermost thing in Dora's mind at that time was her first meeting with Mrs. Besant. She would later recount that Mrs. Besant was not even five feet tall.

I'm little but she was littler. But she had such a tremendous presence when she spoke that you felt that she was a big lady. The power of her expression made you feel that here you were in the presence of a great person but also much bigger than she actually was.

There were some very difficult times at that time in Australia. And what I remember then, I always associate with Mrs. Besant, is that when there was tremendous uproar she was a very, very quiet person. A person can be a great orator and yet convey the presence of quietness. When she talked, she talked in a very quiet voice and she projected really— quiet, peace, and strength—and no excitement whatsoever.

She never responded in a violent way; with all the waves of opposition, none of that ever appeared. Whatever she said was firm and at no time was ever antagonistic. She just stated the facts and I was enormously impressed by her quiet strength.[21]

Dora would hear Mrs. Besant again in England, the United States, and in India, but at no time was the contrast between social unrest and her peaceful presence more evident. The qualities that she recognized in Mrs. Besant were ones that she emulated. Dora, too, could be said to have had "quiet strength" and to have responded to violence with inner stillness.

Dora began to teach meditation when she was about eighteen years old. By that time she had meditated daily for twelve or more years. She started with small groups of Theosophists and then taught meditation at retirement centers in Sydney. "I don't know how I started my 'old people's home' meditation group," she later said. "It must have been started before I was eighteen, and how I got them I don't know. I must have just said I was going to have it. In that first group, I think I looked at their auras and told them how they were wrong in what they were doing in meditation. I don't do it now."

In addition, she taught what she called a "special course on clairvoyance," which she described as an "additional sense." As an adult she would explain that one of the types of clairvoyance she exhibited relied on the subtle mind more than on extraordinary sense perception. It did not involve the use of her normal sight at all. The two-page handout she prepared goes into some detail: "Just as a blind man would have little understanding of the glory of the sky, so the non-clairvoyant moves about in a world which brings to the seer an immense expansion of experience difficult to convey to others. We shall call this super physical realm, the astral, for brevity."[22]

In describing her many astral experiences, Dora made a helpful distinction between "two classes, first those things and beings which exist in the physical world and have astral counterparts, and, secondly, those things and beings without physical body, which exist in this invisible world altogether." According to Dora, the second class—without physical bodies visible to most people—included "forms of life such as angels or devas, fairies and nature spirits, emotional or mental forms (thoughts and feelings) thrown off by different beings, elemental forms, the hosts of the dead in various states, and superhuman men. A catalogue of the fairy forms alone gives some idea of the variety and interest of these creatures. There are hundreds of quite definitely different varieties. Whether they are as numerous as physical animals, birds and insects is a question: but certainly the genera and species are as varied as are birds, reptiles, amphibians, mammals and the like among us physically."[23]

A few years after that class on clairvoyance, Dora wrote a regular column for the journal *Theosophy in Australia*, and more than one article was devoted to fairies. Theosophists in Sydney were more interested in her clairvoyant investigation of fairies than were members in Java, who took them more as a matter of course. In addition, the long, dark war seemed to inspire interest in light-hearted stories about the unseen world. Sir Arthur Conan Doyle, the author of mysteries featuring the eccentric and brilliant Sherlock Holmes, had lost a son in the war, and his new interest in Theosophy soon led him to investigate the Cottingley photographs—alleged photographs of fairies done by two young English girls. Doyle's book *The Coming of the Fairies* described his investigation of their photos and their claims. The girls later confessed to their prank of masquerading stiff paper cutouts of fairies as real fairies in the photos.

Dora remained nonplussed about the Cottingley photographs and referred to the statement by the Theosophist E. L. Gardner in Doyle's book. He wrote that if fairies appear to have human form, this is due to humans' beliefs about how they are supposed to appear. Dora wrote:

> We must not think of fairies as having a perfect human form. There are few fairies who are clever enough to imitate the human form perfectly, although a great many nature spirits do try to copy and imitate the human form, as it is the perfect form. . . . All of us must have seen those most interesting fairy photographs in Sir Arthur Conan Doyle's book, *The Coming of the Fairies*, but I myself have never seen fairies like those; they look somewhat too perfect, and the suggestion that they might be fairies who took that shape because the children were accustomed to think of them in such a form sounds most reasonable.[24]

Dora's interests were already beginning to shift from the natural world of fairies to human beings. At around age twenty she wrote about what is now called medical clairvoyance—as though to forecast her later contributions: "There is a rare form of sight which enables its possessor to read the pages of a closed book. This is useful in medical diagnosis, for it is possible to see the organs of the body in action in place, and also the organic structure of the subtle or astral matter of the person, which structure is very important to health. An enlargement of such powers as these has great practical value, and the future will bring much of this experience to many people."

For Dora, clairvoyance was not just an anomaly to be researched; it was part of her life. If it inspired others to develop themselves by knowing something of extended human abilities, then she shared what she knew. Her education with Leadbeater kept clairvoyance, service to others, study, and meditation in perspective. He drew teachings from several religions to impress his young students with the importance of joyous effort on the spiritual path. Dora understood that her clairvoyance and intuitive abilities were helpful to her spiritual development and to her ability to help others in their development.

Oscar Köllerström had been one of Dora's best friends among Leadbeater's students, and some photos of them suggest that if conditions had been different, they might have married. Oscar grew up in Sydney, and he and his father were both very active in the Liberal Catholic Church. Oscar started a Theosophical youth movement in 1922 called The Order of the New Age, with Dora as secretary. The group merged with the Youth Lodge of London a year later, and the new group was called the World Federation of Young Theosophists.

Krishnaji, then twenty-nine years old, and D. Rajagopal, who would become Krishnaji's manager and publisher for many decades, were the president and vice-president of the Federation of Young Theosophists in Europe. America and India also formed federations. When Oscar moved to England, Dora became the president of the Australian Federation of Young Theosophists. There were groups in other major Australian cities: Perth, Melbourne, Brisbane, and Adelaide. She served as the secretary for the Sydney Young Theosophists and wrote a series of articles for the World Federation of Young Theosophists that discussed the need for youth involvement in world issues in order to bring peace to the world. She urged members to join with other youth groups. At age twenty, she wrote with a growing sense of activism: "Many Theosophists do not realize the necessity of bringing our ideas and ideals to the outside world; they live their own lives and do not bother about the world at large. But the mission of our Order is most distinctly to help the world at large and to try and enlighten the ignorant; we young people often do not realize what a great deal of misery there is around us."

Dora helped arrange camping trips to the Australian bush for the Young Theosophists. While she enjoyed being in nature far from the city, the camping trips also allowed her to develop executive ability. There were tents to locate; the waxed canvas type was heavy, so horses had to be hired to accompany the group as pack animals. She helped plan menus, ordered food, and located supplies. Others arranged drivers, mapped the route, and made contingency plans for bad weather. Photos show Dora and other young women in slacks well before slacks became fashionable.

The Young Theosophists in Australia solicited funds on the ferries, hosted concerts, and held other fund-raisers. Some of their fund-raising was part of a larger effort coordinated by the Theosophical Order of Service in London to ship food parcels to members of the Theosophical Society in Russia, where there was widespread starvation in the wake of the 1917 revolution and subsequent civil war. The Young Theosophists drew attention to this situation. One refugee in Switzerland trying to raise money for a soup kitchen said that Russian children received aid while the adults, especially the intellectuals, starved.[25]

As Dora recalled, "I don't know all the things I tried. The first thing is when I became head of the Theosophical Society, the Young Theosophists, we raised money. . . . We started (from afar) the first soup kitchen—Russians were starving—'The HP Blavatsky Soup Kitchen' located in Russia to feed hungry children and we had to raise money for it. So I organized it. I had the school help me and all sorts of people helped. We were allowed to have a begging plate and have a picture of starving children and we raised the money on that one day begging at all the ferries which came in and out of the [harbor]."[26] Dora's efforts in Australia paved the way for her later work with the World War II European Parcel Project.

In her column in *Theosophy in Australia*, Dora wrote about brotherhood and the need to overcome class hatred and national prejudices:

> We must not have a vague desire that there shall be no more war in the future, but we must clearly realize the necessity of peace, understand fully the social conditions of the world today, as it is no good to live in a sort of blissful ignorance of the conditions of the people around us, as I am afraid so many of us do. By knowledge alone will we be able to change the evils of the world. If we really thoroughly realize the horror and ghastliness of war we would be able to work for Peace with all our strength and enthusiasm. But let us not be too serious and feel that the burdens of the world are on our shoulders, as we can do far more good when we radiate joy and happiness. So very few people are joyous. If we were to be called "suns of love and joy" wherever we went, we would do a great deal to lighten the misery of the world.[27]

In another column for the Young Theosophists she declared the motto of the Sydney group: "Laugh at yourself." The ability to radiate joy and laugh at oneself was her tribute to Leadbeater as well as evidence of her cultivation of meditative stabilization. Despite all the difficulties, Dora realized the spontaneous joy that is a sign of those who have achieved some degree of calm-abiding from the practice of single-pointed meditation. Hence her own motto during that time was "Laugh a lot." Dora's three years in Sydney as the head of the Australian Young Theosophists familiarized her with Krishnamurti's teachings as the next World Teacher. The international group included in its objectives "to spread ideas expressive of the spirit of the Coming Age as seen in the light of Theosophy." The realization of world brotherhood was the goal, and it required forward-looking people who could think in longer spans than five or ten years. The words indicated much hope, but Theosophists young and old would be tested in 1929 when Krishnaji relinquished his role in the TS.

The years between the Great War and the Great Depression were full of hope. Dora's father, Karel, had long been interested in communal living as a pragmatic approach to economic issues. Dora's father published his business plan, *The Ideal Community: A Rational Solution of Economic Problems*, in 1922. The van Gelder family had bought a house in Sydney, but Dora's father still longed to move to the United States to create a self-sustaining community in California. The unrest in the sugar industry in Java and strikes in Australia provided the larger inspiration. Possibly a more immediate inspiration came from two houseguests, Fritz Kunz and A. P. Warrington, who stayed with the van Gelders during the crisis in the Sydney lodge. Warrington and Marie Poutz, who also visited Sydney at that time, helped develop Krotona, the Theosophical community that was initially located in Hollywood. Both of them were beginning to research areas outside of Los Angeles for an expanded endeavor.

Karel van Gelder envisioned communities where members shared resources and responsibilities. "Humanity will have to make a choice. Either it must limit its desires, making life more simple, more beautiful, and more happy, or it will continue to increase wishes, which can never be fulfilled, thereby multiplying its worries and damaging its physical and moral health."[28] He foresaw that social conditions would become more problematic during the twentieth century and called for more equitable conditions through voluntary simplicity on the part of individuals and cooperative efforts on the part of community members "who think along the same lines and feel brotherly towards each other. Any so-called solution which does not found its activity on voluntary co-operation is doomed to failure and misery." His writing was both pragmatic and hopeful. "It may be that the science of 'Economics' will become the science of 'Happiness.' Let us build our economic system on the happiness of the human soul, and we shall find that the productive power will enormously increase."[29]

Koos van der Leeuw's unpublished diary entry for July 16 (probably 1924) reflects the growing interest among Theosophists in Sydney in a communal living situation. "Of course, the idea of a 'compound' is already old; Van Gelder has been busy for some time on his community scheme which is to make life more reasonable, cheaper and more useful. Everyone here is at his wits' end financially, so the idea of a 'compound' appeals to all. Van Gelder sold his house a fortnight ago and has been looking for a suitable place."[30]

Dora, however, said that their house was sold because her parents intended to move to the United States with the family. She said that at a Rotary Club meeting her father had heard about the house that became The Manor. He toured the fifty-five-room mansion, which had been empty for many years, overlooking the harbor. Within a short time, Leadbeater toured the house and, according to Dora, agreed to provide leadership to a community if her father assumed the responsibility as manager. Koos van der Leeuw wrote about the events of the next month.

> The end was that the different families met in council and that Bishop Leadbeater invited Mr. van Gelder to assume the most

difficult task of managing the community. He accepted, the rooms in the house were divided amongst the families, the lease signed for three years with two years' optional extension, and on August 3rd, while a howling southerly was shaking the house, the first group of new inhabitants came in, consisting of Walter Hassel, Hely Labberton, Lucius van Gelder and myself.

During the next week Bishop Leadbeater, with the Köllerström family, the van Gelder, Mazel and Vreede families and "those without family" arrived. They were chaotic days those first two weeks of the Manor. Mr. van Gelder certainly had a great task to perform, and, with the help of the whole household, he accomplished it successfully; the community never experienced any serious trouble. This certainly proves the splendid spirit in which all undertook the work and the willingness of all who hitherto had run their own households to fit in with whatever was necessary.[31]

A cook and a few other employees were hired, and students were given work-study scholarships to manage the cleaning. Dora, her parents, and her grandmother each had a room, and Dora's three brothers shared a large top floor room with the boys and children from other families. There were also classrooms, a meditation hall, and an LCC chapel in the basement where services were held each morning. Karel's publicity efforts included the purchase of radio equipment, and he set up an amateur station in the Manor. In 1926, his efforts became the basis for 2GB, the commercial broadcasting station of the Theosophical Society in Australia. (GB stands for Giordano Bruno, in honor of the magus who was burned as a heretic in Rome in 1600.)

The residents ate meals together (though according to Dora, Leadbeater often preferred to have his meals in quiet in his room).

Residents volunteered regularly for certain chores in the building or on the grounds. Initially Dora and the other garden volunteers were instructed by professional landscapers; she credited that experience for her later involvement with gardens wherever she lived. The grounds were not large compared with the gardens at Krebet, but they went right down to the water, and there were no more servants in Dora's life. She was beginning the first of her several experiences with cooperative living.

Mrs. Besant asked Clara Codd to move to Sydney as a lecturer, and she joined the group in the Manor. Miss Codd had been a teacher, a feminist, and a suffragette in London. In her autobiography *So Rich a Life*, she recalled Dora as one of Leadbeater's students from that period.

> Among his girls was the now celebrated clairvoyant, Dora Kunz. Before she married Mr. Fritz Kunz she was a little Dutch girl, Dora van Gelder, born in Java. She was in Sydney with her father and mother, three brothers and her grandmother and aunt. Dora in these days hardly looks any older than she did all those years ago. I remember her so vividly then, a rather wild little girl of eighteen, with very decided views of her own. She had classes for meditation with the young people there, and also what she called her old people's class. Once a week, she would sit cross-legged in a big chair, while we older people sat round. Then she would tell us what to think of and how, and describe to us afterwards what had happened.
>
> Dora taught me some very valuable things. One was that meditation does not only consist in thinking, but that it must evoke vivid feeling, too. She used to laugh when she told us of people who when told to meditate on peace or love, for example, would inwardly keep on saying, "love, love," instead

of really feeling it. . . . we must learn to expand and extend the auric radiations. This last she brought about by making each of us concentrate our thoughts on something or some person we truly and really loved. Then, when our hearts began to glow and expand, we were instructed to use the will and to extend the aura as far as we could.[32]

Eight months after Dora and her family moved to the Manor, Leadbeater requested that Fritz return to Sydney to help him. He and Warrington had accompanied Krishnaji and Nitya from India to Australia prior to Mrs. Besant's arrival during the 1922 crisis in the Theosophical community. Fritz had then accompanied them to Ojai, California, when they left Sydney, because Warrington had suggested that the dry mountain air would benefit Nitya, who was suffering from advanced tuberculosis. Fritz's role during that year was to help them settle in the United States. They rented and then purchased a cottage on the east side of Ojai that Krishnaji named Arya Vihara.

By April 1923 the Manor had nearly thirty residents, including Dora's Tante Cotty, Oom Dirk, and cousin Hely from Java. When Fritz first arrived, he had to live in a nearby rooming house until a room was available for him. Fritz edited Leadbeater's writing, delivered some of his sermons in the Liberal Catholic Church, and lectured and wrote articles for Theosophical publications in Australia. Both Fritz and Koos van der Leeuw, who had a doctorate in psychology, were interested in modern science and influenced Dora's perspective. Dora began to describe the physical body as a "nexus" in energetic fields of greater and lesser density. She eventually gave up the materialistic notion that the astral was a fixed plane, or location, in space. She would later refer to the astral as a "level of consciousness," the "emotional field," or "state of consciousness."

Dora attempted to choose language that would not reinforce dualities. She changed the term "Higher Self" to "inner self" to avoid the notion that the spiritual exists "up" in a distant heaven.

Since she helped start the Young Theosophists, she began to teach many non-Theosophists and made a conscious effort to avoid Sanskrit terms, even though they are more specific and convey richer meaning. She also avoided the use of Blavatsky's terms such as the "monad" and "ego," and attempted to speak in simple language about complex subjects.

About a year after Fritz's arrival in Sydney, Dora experienced a health crisis that would bring her closer to him. In early 1924 the horse she was riding fell or faltered while crossing a wet, slippery bridge. She suffered a severe concussion. At times her head pain was so crushing that she was unable to do anything for hours or even days at a time. She said that during that time in her life, she felt "useless to everyone." If ever there was a period of disenchantment, it was this time, when she was twenty years old. She consulted specialists in Sydney but got little relief. Just as she had observed Leadbeater reorganize his life when confronted with diabetes and heart disease, Dora, on a much smaller scale, had to reorder her life.

Dora worked hard to overcome her own serious head injury. The accident and its aftermath reinforced her awareness of the deep calmness that is necessary when helping the ill. She learned that rhythmic movement and music helped heal neurological problems, and she also learned the importance of rehabilitation therapy. She encouraged patients to look out the window at a "friendly tree" or a large body of water if they were fortunate to have either view. It is also possible that Dora's own healing process contributed to her awareness of small, helpful actions. As an adult working with people who had multiple sclerosis, Parkinson's disease, or AIDS that affected the neurological system, she seemed acutely aware of the focused attention required for the first step in walking. She congratulated patients when they walked, as though she knew the importance of recognition for small steps. Like Leadbeater, Dora believed that daily walks were important; she maintained them religiously throughout her life and insisted that people with head injuries or other similar neurological problems benefited from the rhythmic movement of walking.

The same year she had the equestrian accident, Dora's parents returned to Java, primarily for financial reasons. On July 16, 1924 the steamer left Sydney harbor for Batavia, where Karel accepted the position of port commissioner. As Dora explained, "Some of his shares didn't do well, so he went back to Java to resume a job. He finally went to India and became the manager of another sugar factory, and he stayed there until he retired to the United States. So I lost contact with my parents."[33] Except for a brief family reunion in 1936, this second separation from her family was to last for over twenty years.

Whether it was inspired by the separation from her parents or by the urging of a friend to write during her recovery, Dora turned some of her ideas about the angelic kingdom into a little booklet, *The Christmas of the Angels*. It offers insight into her perspectives at age twenty. In this work, she wrote of the sun as the symbol of "the union of the Christ in heavens with the Christ Incarnate both in Nature and in the heart of man." She also wrote:

> We generally look upon the universe from the standpoint of form, thinking first of the form and only then of the life which energizes and ensouls it—that is the typically human point of view. And even when the inner vision is opened and sight of the invisible worlds is gained, the human observer still looks

first at the form-side of those worlds, and only subsequently at the consciousness playing through the different forms.

The angels' point of view is exactly the opposite; he looks first at the life or consciousness, and then, only as a secondary consideration, at the form in which that life is enshrined—that is the typically angelic point of view. The angel would regard the man from the standpoint of consciousness, would look to see how far God's Life was manifested in the man, how many forces were able to play through him—and only then would he look at the form. This is a fundamental difference in outlook belonging to two separate lines of evolution.[34]

During the last two years of her life, Dora tried to distance herself from this work. She acknowledged that the ideas were her own but said that an unnamed "English gentleman with very proper grammar" helped her and imposed his own language. It's unclear if she took issue with the pamphlet's Christian language or with its Buddhist mind-only view.

Within a year of her parents' departure for Batavia, Dora began what she later referred to as a "traveling life." Before her departure, she had a final year with Oma, Theodora van Motman, who was seventy-four years old by then. Dora spoke of a special quality she learned from her grandmother.[35] She said that Oma exemplified "rootedness," and despite adversities in her life, she "drew people to her. It was her rootedness and friendliness and she was always cheerful. She had a very definite place and attracted people to her. Wherever she went, she was completely rooted in herself."

Dora perceived the quality of rootedness in Oma's aura as "integration in the fields."

In her case she just "was." She didn't have any particular purpose; she was very creative and open. The rootedness was shown in her reactions to adversity. She could pass through it cheerfully. She had a giving attitude. She was never snowed under by adversity. She could accept any civilization. It didn't make any difference where she was. Rootedness has to do with a feeling of destiny or a place in life in which you can give.

Some people are rooted and feel very satisfied and deeply rooted with their Christian background or whatever it might be. They are satisfied with their small part in the universe and fairly content. I think they would have a sense of balance and rootedness. They have a sense of belonging and being in their place where they think they want to be. There aren't many people like that left in the modern world, but there are still some.[36]

Chapter Three

Decisions (1925–1928)

Despite the loss of Karel and Melanie van Gelder, the Manor continued to be a catalyzing agent, with Koos van der Leeuw as the new manager. Koos was engaged in writing some of the books that contributed to his high regard in the world as an innovative thinker.

The annual convention for the Australian Section was held in Sydney in April 1925, so the center saw more visitors than usual as delegates arrived from all over the world. Ernest Wood and his wife arrived from the United States, and Jinarajadasa, vice-president of the international Theosophical Society, arrived to chair the convention, as well as Lady Emily Lutyens from England and Krishnaji and Nitya. Krishnaji's beloved brother, Nitya, suffered more debility from tuberculosis, and his worsened condition cast a pall over their stay. Another delegate was Rukmini Devi Arundale. While Rukmini's husband, George Arundale, was busy with Leadbeater in matters having to do with the LCC and the Esoteric Section, Dora and Rukmini became friends. They were both born the same year and also shared a tendency toward independence of thought and altruistic action. They forged a bond that was to last for the rest of their lives.

Krishnaji spoke at the Manor, but the most memorable occasion of the convention for Dora was when she attended his first and only teaching at the new Star Amphitheater. This arena overlooked Balmoral Beach on land purchased by Dr. Rocke. It was built especially for Krishnamurti, whom Theosophists regarded as the coming World Teacher. Dora's father, along with other Theosophists in Sydney and around the world, contributed finances and skills to the construction project.

An expression common among some Theosophists of this era was, "We proceed as the way opens," and in many ways, that suited the circumspect young Dora. She continued to suffer from intermittent severe headaches, and Fritz suggested that she go to the United States for treatments. He had located an osteopath in the Los Angeles area who had an excellent reputation as a diagnostician and clinician. So Dora decided to go to California.

Los Angeles at that time was relatively small, with a population of only a half million people. Here Dora stayed with the Field family and became friends with their son, Sidney, who was active in the Young Theosophist movement in the United States and knew Krishnamurti and Nitya well. He later wrote *The Reluctant Messiah*, his memoir about his meetings with Krishnaji and Mrs. Besant. Sidney drove Dora to the beach and to her osteopathic appointments. She recollected her visits to the osteopath: "I came to this country because I had a concussion [and] I got the most frightful headaches. I went to a blind osteopath; he was a famous diagnostician and he really did cure me. He told me that he could see energy fields and he could feel with his hands. Through his fingers he could feel and 'see,' with his mind's eye, an energy field which was not in order. He had tremendous success."[1] Within a few months, Dora's headaches were relieved and did not recur for the rest of her life.

The hot summer in Los Angeles inspired Dora to visit the beaches. She recognized the therapeutic effect of the ocean. "Water has a definite healing effect. The sea has a tremendous etheric energy in it."[2] In the gardens, Dora clairvoyantly noticed golden-colored fairies as well as the ones with stripes of pale gold, who were unique to southern California.

Fritz knew many people in Hollywood and Ojai. He had spent a year at Krotona in 1912 shortly after it was started in Hollywood. Warrington, Marie Poutz, and others had successfully moved Krotona to Ojai in 1924, so Fritz and Dora visited with Warrington and his wife in their new residence. Dora met many new Theosophists through Fritz and those of his family members who had relocated from Illinois to Hollywood and Ojai.

They visited with L. W. and Maisy Rogers, whom Dora already knew from Australia, in part because their son, Grayson, had stayed at the Manor. Rogers, as the president of the American Section, arranged for both Dora and Fritz to speak at the convention in Chicago later that summer. During their months in Ojai, Fritz and Dora also visited Krishnaji. Nitya remained gravely ill. Earlier in the year, Krishnaji appointed Fritz as his personal representative in the United States for the Order of the Star in the East. Membership in the organization reached 43,000 the following year and was spread across forty countries.[3]

Fritz and Dora traveled by train across the United States to the Chicago convention of 1925. Dora was warmly received by members; it was the first time she had spoken at a convention, and she charmed the audience. She could not have stolen Fritz's spotlight, since he was a seasoned and excellent presenter. As one attendee wrote about Fritz's lecture, "He certainly burned them up. It was the most inspiring and effective lecture of the convention; an appeal for service." Dora spoke on the Masters during the afternoon session of the Clerical Synod of the LCC. She presented what was described by one of the priests in attendance as "an exceedingly interesting lecture. She spoke from direct and personal knowledge."[4]

Following the convention, Dora traveled from Chicago to the East Coast, where she stayed with Captain Ernest and Barbara Sellon, who lived just north of New York City in Rye, New York. Ernest and Barbara Sellon had discovered the Theosophical Society after they moved from London to Rye about a dozen years earlier, and were very active members of the Society in New York. Dora had a good time staying with them and their two children, Betty and John, who were nearly her age. Ernest Sellon brought them to see movies, and he and Barbara Sellon introduced Dora to many members of the Society in the New York area.

When Dora left New York, she was on her way to Europe and Britain for the first time. She was reunited with Oscar Köllerström in Amsterdam, likely a happy moment for both of them. They traveled together to Huizen for the Star Camp, an annual gathering held at Ommen, usually presided over by Krishnamurti. Ommen was a large estate that had been donated by Baron van Pallandt to Krishnamurti's organization, the Order of the Star in the East. Unfortunately Krishnamurti had not been able to attend the Star Camp that year, which had about 800 attendees. Had Dora been there in subsequent years, she would have been one of 3,000 participants.

Following the Star Camp, Dora went to London and heard Mrs. Besant and Krishnaji speak at Queen's Hall in London. Mrs. Besant spoke that evening about "The Coming of the World Teacher." She was referring to Krishnaji, whom Theosophists believed to be an emanation of the bodhisattva Maitreya, the future world Buddha and the bodhisattva of loving-kindness. Dora said that Mrs. Besant held the attention of the group with her tremendous presence, but what was most impressive was her personal kindness.

Dora recalled that Mrs. Besant "came right up to me and right after the lecture, she looked at me and she was worried about me. She said, 'Do you know how to get back home?' It shows her immense motherly feeling; there I was, alone. I was very young and this is what she had [noticed]; she had this immense caring and enquiring about people. I think all her life she really observed people and she had this motherly caring about her."[5] These were qualities that Dora emulated during her life.

By the time of Mrs. Besant's Queen's Hall presentation, a large contingent had gathered in London from America and Britain. On November 8, they began their long journey to Adyar for the Golden Jubilee, the fiftieth anniversary of the founding of the Theosophical Society. This year's annual convention in Adyar was to be an extraordinary celebratory event. The group left London in a snowstorm and crossed the English Channel. The snow continued as they traveled through Paris and into Switzerland. Finally, as they crossed the St. Gothard Pass into Italy, the storm was behind them, and they continued by train to Rome and Naples in sunshine. Dora and Oscar, along with Hugh Noall and Byron Casselberry, took a side trip to Venice, where they met and had dinner with Leopold Godowsky, the famous pianist and composer. Dora was to remain friends with Godowsky, who lived near New York City. Toward the end of his life, he participated as a subject in her research, which was published as *The Personal Aura.*

On November 8, the group departed from Naples on the *S.S. Ormuz* for India. Six days later, after the ship left the Suez Canal, a telegram arrived with the news that Nitya had died on November 13, 1925, at Arya Vihara in Ojai. He was twenty-eight years old. Mrs. Besant had adopted both Krishnaji and Nitya, so she had known him more than half his life. Leadbeater, with a group of about seventy Theosophists who had sailed from Sydney, received the news of Nitya's death when their boat reached Brisbane.

In the days that followed, Fritz borrowed money from his brother-in-law to pay for the cremation, since no arrangements had been made in the event of Nitya's death. Others helped arrange Nitya's funeral, which was held in Hollywood.

Dora recalled the news of Nitya's death and her perception of Krishnaji's response:

> Nitya died in Ojai from TB and Fritz saw him through his passing over. They cabled this to Krishnaji who didn't think that it would happen—but it did. The moment I heard it, I really felt one thing certain; Krishnaji was bound to leave the Society because I felt that he would have to go his own way. It was natural . . . that a time would come and that he would go his own way because he had to give his own message.[6]

The Jubilee Convention in 1925 was attended by people from all over the world. Through all the social commitments and speaking engagements of the convention at Adyar, Krishnamurti wore a black scarf, but outwardly he and Mrs. Besant showed little sign of grief. Leadbeater's words may have rung in his ears: "Never let yourselves be shaken or depressed, and hold yourselves well in hand, so that whatever service or whatever sacrifice the Lord may require of you, you will be ready to give it."[7]

Before the end of the convention, Dora summoned her courage and told Leadbeater's secretary, Kathleen Maddox, that she would no longer answer Leadbeater's letters. Dora had responded to questions about the dead for seven years, and she was now giving up that work. "I answered his letters. And when I was twenty-one, we all met in Adyar and I said, 'I'm through. I never will write another letter for you.' I was going to stay in the United States."[8]

The most special moment for people attending the convention occurred during the Star Day on December 28. It was then that Krishnaji spoke under the 450-year-old banyan tree and conveyed his clear spiritual realization. To those who attended, he seemed to be emanating Maitreya. Dora did not comment on his realization; she considered spiritual development a private matter. Four years later, in 1929, Krishnaji broke off his relations with the Theosophical Society and asked that all hopes and prayers for him as the World Teacher be relinquished. Dora's view was that Krishnaji remained a world teacher; his teachings influenced people all over the world. She believed that Leadbeater had not been mistaken when he saw Krishnaji's remarkable potential.

In 1926 Dora returned to Australia for a visit. She had made the critical decision to move to the United States, but she never said that her feelings for Fritz were her primary reason for relocating. She had lived under the same roof with him at The Manor for over two years and had traveled with him in California and then to Chicago. Dora never described a whirlwind romance or roses and an engagement ring. She said that Fritz was passionate, though it was not clear whether she meant intellectually or romantically.

Dora arrived in San Francisco by steamer on May 25, 1926. For part of that summer, Fritz and Dora lived at Arya Vihara and were hosted by Frank Gerard and his wife. Dora met Beatrice Wood from Manhattan and Max Wardall from Pasadena, who were also guests at Arya Vihara during that summer. In the late summer Dora traveled with Fritz while he lectured in various cities on Theosophical topics. They then joined three thousand other Theosophists who traveled to Wheaton, Illinois, where Mrs. Besant ceremoniously laid the cornerstone for construction of the new headquarters building of the Theosophical Society in America.

Fritz was a brilliant public speaker, and Dora said that at some point he understood that the ideas he was developing about education were not likely to be realized in a small mountain town like Ojai. "Fritz would have liked to live in California but to me, there would never have been the educational opportunities."[9] She said that he needed to collaborate with scholars from some of the great seats of learning; she mentioned the East Coast and specifically Harvard and Yale. Fritz stopped working for Krishnamurti and the Star of the East at the end of 1926 and resigned in early 1927. Fritz had known Krishnaji since he was eighteen years old and Fritz was twenty-five. There was a falling-out between the two, but neither Fritz nor Dora would disclose the reasons for it. As a result, Dora continued to visit Krishnaji and attend his talks, and Fritz did not.

Fritz continued to travel for most of 1927 with a speakers' bureau; he visited twenty-eight cities in three months that year. Dora also traveled. She went back to the East Coast and stayed with the Sellons in Rye and with Beatrice Wood in New York City. Articles on Dora's clairvoyance and fairies appeared in several newspapers that year, including *The New York Herald Tribune* in April and the *Boston Herald* in June.[10] Dora remarked that her talks and articles about communication with fairies proved something of a disservice to her: people equated fairies with child's play rather than with the complexity and majesty of nature. One article, for example, entitled "Fairies, Real Fairies, Are Playmates of This Little Girl," overlooked the fact that Dora was twenty-three years old and hardly a little girl.[11] *The New York Herald Tribune* ran a similar story in April 1927, and a letter from an editor to Barbara Sellon indicates that Mrs. Sellon had been instrumental in bringing attention to Dora's unusual efforts to educate people about the natural world.[12]

Beatrice Wood, whom Dora met the previous summer, was eleven years older than she and had been a member of the Society for only a few years. She seemed very cosmopolitan, because she had studied art in Paris and was involved in the theater in New York City. That summer, Dora and Wood were at the home of

Robert and Sara Logan near Philadelphia. Wood wrote in her autobiography about her own first meeting with Mrs. Besant and the kind attention she gave to Dora.

Twenty of us were in the Logan's [sic] sitting room when Dr. Besant entered. She was dressed in white, said a few words to the group, then came over to speak to me, "I am glad Dora has a friend who understands her," she said. She was referring to Dora van Gelder, a fascinating young Dutch woman who was visiting me at that time. A tiny creature with a narrow, elfin face and slanting eyes, she was considered one of the finest clairvoyants in the world. In spite of her delicacy, she was forthright and outspoken. Married to Fritz Kunz, she lectured widely and became a president of the Theosophical Society. Many were in awe of her, and many were captivated by her charm. I treated her simply as a friend. If she wanted to discuss the best looking waiter at the delicatessen, I was happy to oblige.

Dora told me that I had a great deal of green in my aura—the color of sympathy—but that it was too light, too diffused. She said that I was not organized enough and must become more hardboiled. Then she added severely: "You also have a great deal of grey in your aura and you must throw it out." It was true, I was grieving over Reginald and grey is the color of grief. I wondered if Dr. Besant, too, could see my grey aura.

At the meeting that morning, she said many of us were ready to be drawn into closer studies and work, but others were not yet serene enough. "Some of you can take the summer for quiet thought and bring steadfastness into your being. We will meet in the fall and see if you qualify."[13]

The following prose poem about Dora was also published in Beatrice Wood's memoir. It reveals that despite Dora's desire to quit "the deaders," the work followed her to her new life in the United States. The scene was quite possibly a hot day during late spring in 1927, when Dora was staying with Beatrice in her fourth-floor walk-up apartment in Manhattan. The poem conveys Dora's sense of humor and the fun she and Beatrice shared. "The Angel Who Wore Black Tights" captures a conversation with twenty-three-year-old Dora.

One hot morning, sitting cross legged on her bed, wearing only a shirt and drawers, she was in the mood to refer to her occupation.

"Beatrice," she began in firm, staccato voice. "I am reading a letter from a man who is distraught over the loss of his son. I have written him that the son is fine, going on with his work and . . . " she paused, observing me wickedly, and continued. "Goodness, do you suppose the son can see me sitting here in my underwear!?"

I moved to the window to pull back the curtain and announced, "A man across the street is peeking at us."

"Stop looking. He'll think you're encouraging him."

"I'm sure he thinks I'm studying to be a virgin."

That made her laugh. "Oh, you naughty girl, why are you so naughty?"

"I like to be," I answered, rolling my eyes around.

"Do you know why?" she said.

"No."

"Come here and sit down. I'm going to talk to you." I obeyed.

She smiled and shook her head slowly. "I'm going to disillusion you, and you're not going to like it. You're not as naughty as you think. You're conventional and somewhat of a prig, and just put on an act to cover it."

"That isn't true!" I cried, my cheeks becoming red.

"I know you are. You try to shock others before they shock you."

"As soon as I'm dressed, I'm going out."

She went on relentlessly. "If you were really free inside, you wouldn't concern yourself with pretending to be the opposite of what you really are. You think that by facing the balance in one direction, you counteract the other."

"What are you going to do with me then? I don't want to be integrated. I don't want to be free of opposites. I want to be naughty and buy possessions for my house."

She came over and put her arms around me, and I felt her warmth. "You're an angel," I said in a low voice, as I rested against her softness.

"An angel who wears black tights," she answered sadly. "The least disturbance and the black shows."[14]

In May of that year, before the summer in New York became as stifling as Wood suggested in the poem, Dora and Fritz had gotten married. There seems to have been no formal engagement; instead of giving Dora an engagement ring, Fritz sold one of Dora's rings, presumably so they could afford her train ticket to Chicago from New York. An entry in Fritz's travel diary on March 1, "Paid $98 for Dora's ticket; Got $70 for her ring and gave her $50."[15]

Unlike Dora's parents' wedding twenty-five years earlier, there was no high-society engagement party with a band and dancing, followed later in the year by a formal wedding with a reception and lavish rice table. They didn't even share the news of their marriage with Fritz's family until several weeks or a month after the event.

Chicago was a convenient spot on the map for Fritz's lecture tour. The date of their wedding was Fritz's thirty-ninth birthday on May 16, 1927. It could not have been a more Spartan wedding. They had a civil ceremony before a justice of the peace at the city hall. Dora was a very petite and shy twenty-three-year-old and Fritz, an obviously worldly older man. Fritz later recalled that Dora "looked very young and apparently not very happy on their wedding day, so the judge stopped and said to her, 'Young lady, are you sure you want to get married?'"[16] Dora must have convinced the civil authority that she was a willing bride, because Fritz's journal entry simply read, "Married 2:40 standard time."

They spent two days in Chicago; Fritz's journal entry two days after their wedding read, "Stopped at Chicago Heights in the cold rain." Fritz lectured in Omaha, St. Louis, cities along the way to their destination: Biloxi, Mississippi. Dora later joked that they had spent their honeymoon in a prison in New Orleans. She described her own experience as no laughing matter for a young bride:

> Fritz was interested in prison work before [and] he had an entrée to talk in federal prisons. Just when we were married, he talked to the New Orleans prison. I never felt so sick inside myself. It was the most gruesome, the most filthy place that I ever was in. And the warden turned to me; I was feeling so sick and he said, "Shall I call the women for you to address?" and I said, "No." But anyhow, that was my first contact with prison. Fritz, after that for some time, spoke to a lot of federal prisons because he felt very strongly and he knew how to speak; he told them jokes. In those times, he talked to those federal prisons and two or three hundred prisoners could come. You can't do it now; they're too afraid of riots. He started by telling them jokes and that made them happy. They thought

they were going to be "sermonized" and then he talked to them about Theosophical ideas.[17]

After hearing Fritz speak about karma and reincarnation, one prisoner spoke excitedly about "the religion of a second chance."[18] The shock of the jail experience may have been modified by the lovely days Dora and Fritz spent on a plantation in Biloxi with members of the Society. But even that was a little unsettling to her:

> I'd never been South, first of all. That was a shock to me. The first thing she asked me, one of the girls I met there, "Have you seen our President's house?" I thought I was nuts because I thought that Washington was where the President was. What they were talking about was Jefferson Davis. I had never, never in my whole life heard of Jefferson Davis and she was talking about "our President." I thought I was living in another world. After that, I thought I was so ignorant. I am now a very, very well read girl on the subject of American history. I have read an enormous amount of books on the subject. I felt I couldn't remain that ignorant.[19]

Dora may have been influenced by her father's idealized view of America as a place where democratic ideals could help brotherhood develop. In Java, slavery gradually ended at around the same time it ended in the United States, and Dora was well aware that the colonial system favored Europeans in terms of access to education, government positions, and professional and highly skilled employment. But in Java the Theosophical Society was one of few places where people of different religions and races met together. That was not the case in the United States. She had read and heard so much about freedom and equality in the United States. During her visit to the South she saw the effects of segregation in the Theosophical Society and among members of the TS and their black servants in Biloxi. Servants at Krebet were not expected to be virtually invisible.

The first year of Dora's and Fritz's marriage was hectic, and when they wrote his family to announce that they had gotten married, Dora said that they were shocked.

> I think the difficulty was for Fritz's sisters to accept me. They never got used to me, really, because first of all, I was a baby in their point of view. I was 16 years younger than Fritz so I was 20, 25 [years] younger than his sisters. And there was this independent girl![20]

Dora said that she never discussed her clairvoyance with Fritz's sisters, but that is unlikely since Dora and Alma Gulick shared a common interest in fairies. Alma had published a children's book about fairies in Adyar in 1918.

> There was not a bad word spoken in my life to them but the age difference was too gigantic. Not one of Fritz's sisters I was close to, but the one who adored him and who had brought him up, she must have been thirty, forty years older than me. They had made up their mind that Fritz would never get married; then he gets married to somebody [so] young. They didn't dislike me, but I was a girl from a foreign country, if you know what I mean.[21]

Fritz's three sisters in California adored him; he was the baby of the family, the last of twelve children. His sisters in California, Litta, Minna, and Alma, considered him almost like their child, and they must have assumed that he traveled too much for the Theosophical Society to provide a stable lifestyle for a wife. Fritz's travels for the Society had begun when he was sixteen years old, and he had only slowed down long enough to finish high school and college.

Like Dora, Fritz had been brought up as a Theosophist from a very young age. And, like her, he had been raised in a family whose values reflected the ethical and philosophical views of both Hinduism and Buddhism. He first gained awareness of the Theosophical Society as a five-year-old-boy. He had been the only one among his sisters and brothers to stay behind at their home in Freeport, Illinois, when his parents brought the rest of the family to the first Parliament of the World's Religions in Chicago in 1893. The presenters that interested his father and mother were not those from the Christian denominations; they were Mrs. Besant and the teachers from Asia, Swami Vivekananda and Anagarika Dharmapala. That same year, Dora's father, half a world away in Amsterdam, also heard Mrs. Besant lecture for the first time. Karel van Gelder was also immediately impressed by the new worldview that she expressed. Thus Dora's father and Fritz's father were both introduced to the Theosophical Society in the same year, and both began immediately to change their lives in accord with what they learned.

Three years after the Parliament of the World's Religions, the Kunz family was inspired by Dharmapala to become vegetarian. Fritz was eight years old when he stopped eating meat and fish. According to a school-aged friend who took it upon himself to protect Fritz from bullying, the bullies did not care so much that Fritz's family members were Theosophists, but they ridiculed vegetarianism. Dora never ate meat or fish in her life; in addition, neither she nor Fritz drank alcohol or smoked cigarettes. At the same time, each of them accepted the different choices other people made for themselves, so that neither of them proselytized or moralized about their way of life.

Fritz lectured in the Pacific Northwest. There were vital and growing Theosophical communities in Portland, Seattle, and Vancouver as well as in many other smaller towns. Ray Wardall, whom Dora knew from the 1925 Chicago convention, and others had expressed interest in starting a retreat center. A place was located on Orcas Island in the San Juan Islands off the coast of Washington state. It appealed to both Fritz and Dora since Fritz needed a place where he could express and develop his ideas.

They took the ferry from Bellingham, Washington, and arrived on the island on July 5, 1927. After a considerable drive down a narrow dirt road, Dora recalled being shocked when she saw, not a flat, open field, as there had been in Ommen for the Star Camp, but a dilapidated farmhouse with a sloping hayfield and an orchard of apple and plum trees surrounded by a forest of fir trees. "You should have seen it when we came," Dora said, laughing, about her first impression of the place. There, that first summer after their marriage, they camped for five weeks. She went on to recall:

> Theosophists are not practical sometimes. To our horror, the grass was in some places taller than I. We had a little [mail]-order tent. This camp was supposed to be open [in only a few weeks]. There was no food in the house; there was no path cut, nothing. You can see what a shock that [was]—but I'd had experience in all those camps in Australia. So we telephoned Seattle and said, "You can't have a camp until you bring some tents." Fritz hired people to cut the grass. We had one wood stove and let me tell you, I never in my whole life had seen a wood stove. We got the water from a well, etc. etc.

Thank goodness the first camp was the younger people. That's how the first camp was started.

Fritz was extremely practical. There's no doubt about [it]. He could do anything in carpentering, plumbing—you name it. And we had a little [tent]; it only fitted a bed, that's all—and a table. We spent the summer there. What we did was to call a meeting. The Canadians came and they evinced that this property would be a nice place for a Camp. . . .

Some of the members paid the back taxes. We bought it by paying all the back taxes and from then on—with a lot of people helping—[the camp on] Orcas was born. We took it in teams; we cooked—on that wood stove which very few of us really [mastered]. We had candles and kerosene lamps and, in teams, we cooked for one another. It was alright. We had absolutely nothing to start with there either but Orcas is an extremely successful Camp right now. My philosophy is "Try it." As I've said, I've often done things I know nothing about.[22]

Fritz named the site Indralaya, which means "the abode of the god Indra," a king of nature in Hinduism and Buddhism. The decision was made to set up a foundation to purchase the property and make improvements. Fritz, Gene and Viva Emmons, Ray Wardall, and others were instrumental in raising money and other resources.

Dora discovered she was pregnant just before she and Fritz organized the first camp at Indralaya, so she spent her first trimester living in a tent, using an outhouse, and bathing in a washbasin or at the lake on the other side of the island. When they left Orcas Island on August 29, she returned to Marysville, Washington, where she stayed with Ruby Griffiths and her family while Fritz toured for the speakers' bureau. Finally, on December 21, Fritz and Dora were able to spend Christmas together and find a small apartment in Seattle.

Just nine months after Dora and Fritz's marriage, their son, John Kunz, was born at Providence Hospital in Seattle, on February 22, 1928. Dora was twenty-three and Fritz was thirty-nine years old when their only child was born. Dora wrote to her parents and grandmother in Batavia. They also wrote Leadbeater with the happy news and asked him not to do any clairvoyant investigation of "Johnny."[23] Leadbeater had used his clairvoyant abilities in the past to investigate the previous lives of Krishnaji, Mrs. Besant, and others. He wanted to determine possible potentials during their current incarnations, but Dora and Fritz chose to have their son's past lives remain private.

Chapter Four

Transitions and Choices
(1929–1939)

As an adult John Kunz commented on the effect of parent-hood on Fritz and Dora. He said that by the time he was eighteen months old he had been to the states at the four geographical extremes of the continental United States: Washington, California, Florida, and Maine. "That's with a little kid; an infant didn't slow them down; they did it for years."[1] Even when John suffered pertussis, they were on the road. It was a remarkable enough event that Fritz noted it in his pocket calendar, which he usually used only for appointments and lecture schedules.

Dora did not tell stories of her adventures in parenting. She had no sisters and, other than Fritz, no family in the country to help her. She relied on his can-do sensibilities and on the kindness of others. Fritz continued to lecture at Theosophical Society lodges and for the speakers' bureau, but the economic news did not bode well for a lecturer with a wife and child. They did not have much money, but at each lecture stop they found temporary refuge with friends.

Still, Fritz sought to inspire people to explore their own world-views and consider new perspectives. He emphasized the neces-sity of serving others, developing one's highest potentials, and creating a harmonious world. He used humor and deftly interwove references of philosophers from ancient Greece and India as well as contemporary writers.

In 1929, Fritz and Dora received an invitation from Barbara and Ernest Sellon to join them in developing the vibrant New York lodge. They gave up their apartment in Seattle and started a new life near New York City. According to Michael, one of the Sellons' grandsons, "intoxicating discussions resulted" when the Sellons met Fritz at the Theosophical summer school in Wheaton.[2] Barbara Sellon had already begun to promote Dora's teaching about angels and fairies, and she later encouraged her to write her first manuscript on the topic. Later the Sellons moved to Adyar for several years, where Ernest served as the treasurer of the Society. Barbara Sellon, a distinguished painter who had studied art in London, ensured that the spiritual aspects of the arts were recognized within the Society. She and the Captain (as Dora called Ernest Sellon) supported Rukmini Devi's efforts in India to revive traditional dance and to establish Kalakshetra, an academy of traditional Indian dance and music, in 1936. Once back in the United States, they hosted Rukmini Arundale and many other visitors from abroad in their large home in Rye. Since Fritz and Dora lived nearby, they were able to join in discussions and help host visitors.

Dora knew John Sellon and his sister, Betty, from her first visit to the United States in 1925. As influential as Ernest and Barbara Sellon were to young Fritz and Dora, John Sellon would eventually play an even more prominent role in their lives. He was six years younger than Dora and almost a generation younger than Fritz. He studied at Princeton University for a year but left, in part because of the economic downturn, and he joined the business world. He joined the Theosophical Society in 1929, the year Fritz and Dora moved to New York, and quickly became a leader in the TSA.

During the early years in New York, Dora and Fritz had an apartment in Bronxville and spent summers at a friend's cabin in New Hampshire before they traveled west to Orcas Island. When they traveled it was still customary for visiting lecturers to be hosted in private homes. Those experiences helped them gain a better sense of the various interests among Theosophists all across the country. They exchanged ideas informally and were introduced to new areas of enquiry. Though Dora spoke occasionally at lodges around the country, their travels were ostensibly Fritz's lecture tours. Still very shy and mastering subtleties of the language, Dora forced herself to speak publicly at lodge meetings and conventions during those years. She also started teaching meditation classes at the Theosophical Society in New York, as she had in Sydney, and spoke occasionally about clairvoyance and about nature from the perspective of fairies and angels.

While holding one of her meditation classes, Dora met Emily Boenke, an intelligent, independent thinker. Emily worked as a secretary and was intent on a career in dance performance. However, after one disastrous concert when her dance partner arrived drunk, she abandoned dance for other interests. Emily's aura, according to Dora, indicated her intense spiritual search, and the two of them struck up a friendship almost immediately.

Dora claimed credit for introducing Emily to young John Sellon, and their relationship became the kind that film stars of that era tried to depict. When they met, he was a lad of nineteen and Emily was a year and a half older. Their romance blossomed quickly. Though one likes to think that the affections were mutual, the story told was that "John fell totally in love with Emily."[3] The elder Sellons insisted that their son spend a year in London on his own, where he would gain experience in banking and have a cooling-off period. John Sellon later said that they were worried that his relationship with Emily was precipitous and had influenced his decision to leave college.[4]

Despite their separation, Emily and John were married in 1931, shortly after his return from England. Their wedding vows were remarkable, not only because they swore to be together for a lifetime, but because they included a vow to follow a vegetarian diet for the rest of their lives. This decision reflected not only the elder Sellons' ethical views, but also the young couple's own interest in the Theosophical Society.[5]

During the summers of 1931 and 1932 Fritz, Dora, and their son, John, spent several months in Taos, a seventy-mile drive from Santa Fe, New Mexico, at the ranch of Mabel Dodge Luhan and her husband, Tony Luhan. Mabel had been a wealthy heiress and social doyenne in Paris, Florence, and Manhattan's Greenwich Village before she renounced that life for a twelve-acre ranch next to Taos Pueblo. The summers in Taos exposed Fritz and Dora to creative individuals outside of the TS. Here Dora befriended a young painter, Dorothy Brett, a member of England's upper class who sought refuge in the simple life of the high desert. Dorothy had arrived at the ranch with D. H. Lawrence and his circle and settled into one of the guest houses and artists' studios. She and Dora shared their love of horses, and because Dorothy was very deaf, Dora could sit quietly with her and young Johnny. The two summers were lovely there, hot and dry, but snow still capped the highest peaks of the Sangre de Cristo Mountains.

The other person who made a lasting impression on Dora was John Collier. Ten years earlier, while a guest at the Dodge-Luhan ranch, he had begun research into Indian land rights among the Pueblos. This, along with other research, served as the basis for a successful campaign on behalf of the people of Taos Pueblo. In 1933, Collier was appointed United States Commissioner of

Indian Affairs in Franklin D. Roosevelt's administration, and he remained an advocate for indigenous peoples of the Americas for the rest of his life.

Their chance meeting was tremendously influential to Fritz and Dora, because Collier's early work had been in the development of communities. Dora saw that Collier extended his reverence for nature to the communities of Pueblos, who lived in harmony with nature. A half-dozen years passed before some of the seeds planted in conversation with Collier began to bear fruit in the Kunzes' efforts to create a supportive community.

Back in New York after a summer in the quiet lands of New Mexico, Washington, and California, Fritz and Dora's lives continued at a faster pace. The Sellons saw in Fritz an American who was firmly rooted in the noncompetitive spirit that drove the early Americans to unite disparate colonies into a union. The Captain needed Fritz's grass-roots organizational skills to unite the three lodges in New York into a federation. Fritz's efforts, along with those of members Pepe Borrel and Paul De Sass, were successful. In 1931 the New York lodge incorporated as a tax-exempt nonprofit organization, with Emily Sellon as the librarian, and by 1934 the New York Federation was also incorporated as a nonprofit organization. John Sellon served as the treasurer for several years; following that, he served as treasurer and then president of the lodge for several terms. Ernest Sellon and Fritz served on the boards of both organizations. Later Emily Sellon and Dora served on the board of the New York Theosophical Society (NYTS) in various capacities.

Dora and Fritz moved out of Bronxville and rented a house in Rye. After their son, John, started school, Dora stayed home with him during the school year while Fritz traveled. She had accepted what she called "self-responsibility" at age twelve, when she left her family to study in Sydney.[6] She credited the sense of independence she gained from that with helping her care for John on her own while Fritz was away. Dora immersed herself in her new roles as wife and mother. She respected the importance of parenthood to society, but she did not view motherhood as the ultimate purpose of her life.

Fritz and Dora's parenting style was conditioned by their views from Java, the Theosophical Society, and Fritz's years in South Asia. They differed from many other American parents of their generation because they accepted the ideas of karma and rebirth, so they did not view genetics and parenting as the only sources of a child's character. Dora did not believe, as some psychologists suggested, that infants are blank slates at birth. Her studies and her clairvoyant observations indicated otherwise. As parents, Dora and Fritz tended to appeal to John's better nature and were somewhat lax when it came to punishment. But they pushed him intellectually and helped him obtain a good education from an early age.

Having experienced the Manor in Sydney, Fritz and Dora participated in a second bold and creative experiment in supportive community. John and Emily Sellon were instrumental in the endeavor. The young couple had their first child, Peter, in 1934 and purchased a parcel of land in an unincorporated part of Port Chester, New York, that is now Rye Brook. They built a large house at the far end of the property. When they moved into their house, Peter was a toddler. The family soon included two more sons, Michael in 1938 and Jeffrey in 1939.

The two families began a closer collaboration when Fritz and Dora acquired adjoining land owned by Katherine Loines's daughter, Barbara, and son-in-law, Ted Dreier. That same decade, Mrs. Loines, an active member of the TS, would later play a major part in founding Pumpkin Hollow Farm, a Theosophical center in

Craryville, New York. In 1933, the Dreiers became involved in the creation of the innovative Black Mountain School in the Blue Ridge Mountains of North Carolina. As a result, they were unable to build a home on their land in Port Chester, so they presented Fritz and Dora with the parcel of land. The property adjoined John and Emily Sellon's land, so when Fritz and Dora built a house for themselves in 1937, the two couples became neighbors.[7] By this time Dora had shared Fritz's traveling life for ten years. He himself had lived most of his life out of a suitcase and a trunk, often relying on his sister's address. Building a house did not change their lives much. "They lived a nomadic life," John said of his parents. He was taken out of school before the term ended each spring and started each new school year nearly a month late. When Dora was asked about John's modified school semesters, she said simply that he was intelligent enough to keep up with his education.[8]

John Kunz, then nine years old, played unsupervised at the brook that ran through the property. He and the Sellon boys got along over the years, sometimes as friends and sometimes as neighbors. Most importantly for Dora, she and Emily became closer friends. They visited more often than just twice a week for the lodge meeting and Dora's meditation class. They became creative collaborators, much like some of the composers, activists, and artists Dora got to know after her summers in Taos.

It was during this time that Dora observed the beginnings of another social movement: Alcoholics Anonymous (AA). Dora initially visited Bill Wilson, one of the movement's founders, during one of his many hospitalizations for alcoholism. Wilson experienced a spontaneous and profound altered state of consciousness that he associated with his own renewed ability to begin healing. During the 1930s similar experiences were often trivialized by medical professionals, who did not understand them, but Dora perceived that, aside from providing energy, his experience of white light and profound peace were powerful symbols of regeneration.

> I know the founder of the Alcoholics Anonymous, Bill Wilson, very well. I was associated with him. He was a stock broker and when he conceived this idea, he was in the hospital with the D.T.s and they said he could never survive another intoxication program. I liked him very much; he had a tremendous sense of humor. He had an experience; I am not going to give the details. He said a lot of alcoholics are in that process when everything is so horrible, the most horrendous that they see. Very often what they suddenly perceive is a light or something like that. This takes them out of all the visions with the spiders and, heaven only knows what else. From that, in thinking about it, he started Alcoholics Anonymous. He talked to me a great deal of what the alcoholics really experience. When a lot of this came out, they never wanted to talk about it because the psychiatrists said this was part of the "nutty" phenomena. Yet, these were the symbols of the beginning of regeneration and change.[9]

Soon after AA's formal beginning in 1935, Bill Wilson and his wife, Lois, moved from Brooklyn to a small town near Port Chester. Lois then helped create Al-Anon, an organization similar to AA but intended for friends and family members of alcoholics.

Dora and Fritz and Bill Wilson had a friend in common, Aldous Huxley, the intellectual, writer, and public speaker. Huxley was part of the circle that frequented the Dodge-Luhan ranch in Taos. One of his areas of research was the use of hallucinogens to treat intractable problems such as alcoholism and chronic depression.

Could such drugs induce transcendent experiences that would radically alter one's awareness and contribute to healing? Though Bill Wilson served as a research subject to test Huxley's hypothesis, his memoir indicates that he did not put much credence in it. Dora did not experiment with hallucinogens, but she knew others at that time who took LSD in controlled situations for therapeutic use. She viewed that approach as inferior to meditation for producing long-lasting changes in consciousness and did not recommend it.

Alcoholics Anonymous and Al-Anon helped people who were considered social outcasts to mend their own lives or at least find a nonjudgmental community. Those who achieved sobriety in turn helped others. The basis for the approach depended on shared search for integration of one's Higher Power or spiritual dimension into everyday life. Much of the benefit occurred in small, supportive peer groups that met regularly. The movement, which did not reject the disease model for alcoholism, reduced the social stigma associated with it as people began to talk about what had formerly been unmentionable.

Huxley wrote that Bill Wilson was "the greatest social architect of the Twentieth Century." The brilliant community-building aspect of AA served as the basis for similar contributions by Dora and her colleagues four decades later, when they founded the healing modality they called Therapeutic Touch. Dora referred to it by its acronym—TT—seemingly a tribute to Bill Wilson's organization. Like AA, Therapeutic Touch was involved with healing and depended upon small, supportive groups that met regularly. Drawing on the AA model, Dora encouraged informality within a structured meeting as well as the use of first names in the group. Anonymity was not the only purpose of this practice. In Dora's view, people who are experiencing a weakened mental state, such as those who are extremely ill or are suffering from dementia, benefit from hearing their names spoken—the names they are accustomed to hearing at home.

The most significant commonality between Dora's later work in healing and AA was inclusivity of people of all religions. People of various backgrounds could wholeheartedly embrace AA. The meeting format and the language Bill Wilson developed were intended to include anyone who wanted help with alcoholism. Dora was emboldened by the way AA was accepted by people of all backgrounds, not only in the United States but worldwide. As a Theosophist, Dora sought to support the Society's mission to create a nucleus of universal brotherhood irrespective of race, religion, sex, caste, and creed. She seems to have adopted elements of AA that supported a sense of social equality among members of the group. She avoided having paid staff and allowing professionals and other experts to dominate the groups. The meeting structure allowed down-to-earth exploration without intellectual discourses or sermons that distracted from the hard work of trying to change negative behaviors and cultivate new positive actions. She later lectured at large conferences, but her educational and healing groups were based on the small group approach. Dora realized that often those who are most motivated to change are those facing imminent death, as was Bill Wilson, by his own admission, when she met him. She realized that every word and symbol is important to a person who has been told that he is in the last stages of a fatal illness. Thanks to her fortuitous meeting with Bill and Lois Wilson, Dora began to form her own ideas of an ideal community that were far different from her father's. John Collier, the activist for Native American rights, helped Dora realize the importance of supportive community in civilized cultures, and Bill Wilson helped her realize the relationship between supportive community and healing.

"I saw a lot of alcoholic patients at one time," Dora later recalled.[10] From those experiences and from her study of the subject, she wrote an article on addiction. Through the years, Dora referred many people to AA groups and often mentioned AA during lectures. She continued to lead meditation classes at the Theosophical Society lodge to help participants find inner quiet and deeper, more subtle levels of consciousness. She emphasized the transformative aspect of the self as immanent as well as transcendent; the spiritual, in her view, permeates the world and everything in it. From her observations, Dora concluded that a person may have a transcendent experience, but it may be so incongruous with his belief system that the profound peacefulness—the still, small voice, the sudden upwelling of the divine—is often ignored and forgotten. Whatever the impetus—religion, intellectual curiosity, the Twelve Steps of Alcoholics Anonymous, or spiritual search—for those who venture toward gnosis or self-knowledge, the subtle inner self becomes a greater and greater force for healing and transformation. Thus Dora was inspired by what became known as the self-help approach. Moreover, according to Bill Wilson's intentions in the development of AA, the spiritual aspects that he called "a Higher Power" are primary.

Dora thrived in the New York region, with its many cultures, races, and ethnic groups all living side-by-side in relative harmony. She encouraged meditation students to extend their practice from their cushions to their everyday lives; she suggested that they respond with compassion to all the jostling in New York City crowds, irritable bus drivers, and those who appeared miserable on the streets. It was easy to turn one's back on the poor and the homeless and to feel overwhelmed by the masses of people who needed help. Dora encouraged students to send thoughts of goodwill to those in need. For example, if someone yells or shouts in a train station, instead of cringing or thinking negative thoughts, she recommended thinking of the stillness of one's inner self and then sending goodwill toward the calm inner self of the disturbed person. She was accustomed to teaching meditation, and that was how she first met the people who would become her best friends and lifelong collaborators.

Around 1932 Dora met Dr. Otelia Bengtsson, and that friendship was to last for sixty years. Dr. Bengtsson came from a Swedish family in Ossining, a town on the Hudson River north of New York City famous for the prison known as Sing Sing. According to Dora, Bengtsson's family had sacrificed to pay for her education until she earned a full academic scholarship to the Cornell medical school in Ithaca, New York.

Dr. Bengtsson was introduced to Theosophy in an unlikely way. As she described it, she was leaving one of the libraries at New York University one evening when the librarian said to her, "I've been noticing the books you check out and think you may also like this one." The librarian pulled a book on Theosophy from under the counter. Bengtsson said that the book started her on a new intellectual and spiritual endeavor. From there she quickly discovered the Theosophical Society, where Dora and Fritz were teaching. She enrolled in one of Dora's meditation classes and said that she was immediately intrigued by Dora's clairvoyant abilities and her willingness to share what she knew.[11]

Dr. Bengtsson was not a great intellectual who could elaborate subtle philosophies, but she was practical. She helped Dora build on what she had learned in Australia from Dr. Rocke. Bengtsson commuted by train into Manhattan, where she worked for thirty years for one of the early allergists, Dr. Robert A. Cooke. In addition to teaching Dora basic anatomy and pathophysiology, Bengtsson introduced her to the rapidly developing fields of allergy medicine and immunology.[12] She also brought Dora her first patients. As a result of their collaborative efforts, Dora accomplished some of her best work as a clairvoyant during those early years and laid the groundwork for her later contributions.

For centuries, Asian medical systems posited that mental and emotional behaviors affect both health and illness. In Europe and the United States, these connections were just beginning to be explored: resentment and anger can contribute to heart disease; laughter and feelings of hope can facilitate the rate of recovery from surgery. The relationship between the mind and the body, apparent in allergy medicine during the 1920s, required another fifty years before it was accepted in mainstream medicine. Dora was intrigued with those areas of research because she said that, as a clairvoyant, she could not discern a clear distinction between the emotions and the physical body. From an energetic perspective, the emotions and the physical interpenetrate. It was common sense to Dora that treating the physical body required cultivating positive emotions as well as providing a supportive environment.

Dr. Bengtsson introduced Dora to her medical community and to hundreds of her patients. When Dora taught, she always called her friend "Dr. Bengtsson" or referred to her as "the doctor." Dr. Bengtsson was open-minded, articulate, and had a wonderful sense of humor. She came across as friendly and unassuming, though not meek. Her family, she said, called her "Moose" even though she was short and slender, spoke quietly, had fair skin and blue eyes, and was decidedly unmooselike.[13]

Over the years, Dr. Bengtsson introduced Dora to key researchers and other colleagues in health care, as well as to more traditional, faith-based healing phenomena. Without that help, Dora's contributions would likely have centered on meditation and the development of intuition. But through her sixty-five-year collaboration with Dr. Bengtsson, Dora became involved in the world of modern health care. In turn, Dora helped Bengtsson understand the emotional and mental obstacles that contributed to her patients' allergies and compromised immune systems. Dora observed select patients and compared her clairvoyant investigations with the doctor's medical diagnoses.

Another of Dr. Bengtsson's contributions was to take notes of Dora's interviews with patients, enabling her to have a better basis of comparison with the medical notes. She also transcribed many of Dora's lectures and class presentations. When asked how she had contributed to Dora's work, Bengtsson said, "I was the scribe," and quickly added with characteristic humor, "Beware of scribes and Pharisees."[14] Before the advent of tape recorders, Bengtsson, Theosophist Shirley Nicholson, and others who knew shorthand transcribed Dora's talks at the New York lodge and made typed copies available. It is unclear what became of the records of Bengtsson's work with Dora, but copies of several of Dora's lectures provide glimpses into the development of her ideas.

Though Dora participated in a lot of research during her lifetime, Dr. Bengtsson was the first person to engage Dora in a consistent research approach to her clairvoyant investigation. At the allergy clinic Bengtsson obtained consent from some of her patients for Dora to assess their health concerns clairvoyantly. Dora sat in the back of the waiting room, where she observed the patient unobtrusively in order to avoid evoking any emotional reactions. After observing the patient clairvoyantly, Dora met with him or her, along with Bengtsson, in one of the treatment rooms. They compared Dora's observations with the medical exams, patient histories, lab tests, and other diagnostics. They engaged the patient in a discussion in order to verify or refute Dora's observations and to add to the plan of care if possible. The patient became an active participant in this unorthodox research and assessment method.

The health care field was an area well-suited to Dora's pragmatism; she contributed to it while developing her clairvoyance and intuition. Dr. Bengtsson opened the door to the world of medicine and offered Dora privileges as a lay consultant. One of the other settings they worked together was the New York Theosophical Society. Prior to the Wednesday members' meetings they regularly helped patients for over a decade. Dora offered her clairvoyant observations along with suggestions for changes to diet or behavior. Bengtsson occasionally wrote a prescription for blood pressure medication, for example, when she concurred with Dora. There were occasions when Bengtsson also paid for prescriptions to be filled for patients who lacked resources.

Dora's motivation to help and to learn forced her to overcome her shyness and to master the English language. Two of her works, *Conscious Use of the Aura* and "Clairvoyance: Its Value and Limitations," appeared before she and the doctor embarked on an ambitious research project together. *Conscious Use of the Aura* is a six-page booklet that begins as though addressing a student and ends with a brilliant summary of the relationship of meditation and the aura to the path:

> It is most important for a student to understand the workings of his own emotional body, as our emotions are always with us. Every time we feel an emotion a vibration is set up in the halo of ethereal matter which surrounds each person—the aura. At the same time color is produced. Thus when a clairvoyant observes us, we appear to be surrounded by a series of colors constantly in motion, which are the result principally of our emotions. This matter around us looks like

colored clouds of light. These colors have a definite meaning and thus, for instance, when the color rose is seen around a person it denotes a feeling of love. The lower emotions are to be seen from the feet to the waist, and produce dark, dense colors. From the waist up the colors become lighter and the material of which the aura is composed appears to be less dense. Each person has a combination of different rates of vibration which is peculiarly his own. The student should aim at having a few steady rates of vibration instead of the many and often jangling emotions which the average person experiences. This is of course achieved by self-control and the proper understanding of the emotional body.[15]

She goes on to describe valvelike structures in the aura that protect the individual from the strong emotions of others. According to Dora, the valves do not affect the expression of emotions, but only regulate the energetic intake and perception of the emotions of others in the environment. Dora wrote that when a person is fatigued, deficits occur in the functioning of the valves so that the "sifting process" alters, and as a result "other people seem to get on his nerves—their vibrations come too close to him."[16] This increased sensitivity to emotions was also apparent to Dora in a small percentage of the population and was the basis for her interest in what she called the "sensitive child"—although adults could have this sensitivity as well.

Meditation should not be neglected. The important thing in meditation is not to have a vague goal before one, but a definite one. To feel a sort of good and friendly feeling is not meditation. It is important to enjoy doing it, but the aim of it all is self-knowledge and thus development of the power within ourselves. The object is service. . . . any person who has succeeded in doing this will find naturally his consciousness centered in the heart.

Find [your] own equilibrium, emotionally as well as mentally, as only after we have found our own center of peace can we get in touch with our higher self and the things of the spiritual worlds. This process is not easy, as most of us are behind prison walls of our own making—those of prejudice and emotional narrowness and dryness. What we all need is to get free of the walls around us, and this we can only do ourselves.

One of the simplest ways is to enlarge our emotional bodies, as they are very elastic. The way to do this is of course by developing emotion within us. The easiest and yet most powerful emotion we can feel is that of love. Whenever I use the word love I want it understood that I do not mean a sickly sentimental feeling. To me love is the greatest power we all have potentially within us; it is the power of our own soul. Also love has a most powerful vibration; it can be as steady as that of the pendulum of a clock. It thus has the ability to calm our less pleasant feelings and at the same time to enlarge our fluidic emotional bodies more than anything else.[17]

As a result of her clairvoyant investigations, Dora claimed that practicing a meditation that included "sending love" would transform the student's aura. She insisted that people confuse love with sentimental passion, so she called the force of love "goodwill" to help students experience nonattachment toward human beings, animals, or any other object of their meditation. That seemingly simple approach remained largely unchanged for the rest of her life.

Love received little attention in scientific circles until much later in the century; it was considered the stuff of poetry and prose and not a force for self-transformation. Dora did not care whether her clairvoyant methodology satisfied the criteria of medical professionals; during the 1930s her primary interest was to determine what her clairvoyant observation could contribute to psychological understanding of the personality. She cut directly to the application of clairvoyance to health care and how to guide students in their meditation practice and spiritual development. A broad scientific paradigm that encompassed her view of the world did not yet exist in the United States, so she assumed the role of a living, breathing anomaly in a positivist scientific system. For forty more years she continued to be a participant observer in her research on the role of meditation and love in what she called "emotional equilibrium."

"Clairvoyance: Its Value and Limitations" was a transcription of a lecture Dora delivered on November 24, 1935. She read widely: in the lectures she recommended books such as *Extra-Sensory Perception* (1934) by J. B. Rhine; *Mental Radio* (1930) by Upton Sinclair, with a preface by Albert Einstein; and *Man the Unknown* (1935) by Alexis Carrel.

In the lecture, Dora made a rough distinction between two different clairvoyant approaches: one that observes the etheric energy associated with a physical object, and the other, which perceives the energies associated with the emotions. The first type of clairvoyant observation of etheric energy requires great concentration. It helped Dora make detailed observations of a myriad of fairies and other nature spirits all over the world, in the sky, forests, lakes, and oceans, and in volcanoes and other parts of the earth.

She described an interesting but extremely rare subset of that type of clairvoyance and offered the example of a boy in Chicago who could read the print on a page of a closed book. Dora herself relied on that same kind of clairvoyance in research with Dr. Shafica Karagulla several decades later, when she described pathologies in the organs of fully clothed subjects. They were able to investigate the relationship between the subtle energy centers or chakras and the endocrine system in human beings.

The second type of clairvoyance, which allowed her to observe the aura, was the basis for her detailed research with Dr. Bengtsson in 1936 and 1937 using case study methodology. A summary of their findings was published in Dora's 1991 book *The Personal Aura*. Dora said that she learned to associate the colors, textures, patterns, and densities of a person's emotional field with specific emotions, interests, and significant psychic stresses and whether those experiences were generally happy or unhappy ones. She said that each color has a definite meaning and that symbols in the aura carry connotations unique to each person.

In this 1935 lecture, Dora had clearly chosen the focus of her work in the world with regard to her clairvoyant faculties—health and disease. "There are an infinite number of things to learn from the use of clairvoyant sight," she said. "What I am interested in is health and disease."[18] Dora also recognized that clairvoyance would remain incongruent with the health care field until professionals could break out of the narrow confines of materialism. She said that clairvoyance must be combined with understanding of the underlying philosophy that supports it. Fifteen years before Thomas Kuhn's research that served as the basis for his classic book *The Structure of Scientific Revolutions*, Dora stimulated the exploration of new paradigms through the data from clairvoyant investigations. She offered new concepts, such as the "sensitive child," to help understand the relevance of clairvoyance, and she recommended a variety of applications of clairvoyance in health care.

Dora purposely or unwittingly acted as a change agent among health care professionals. Her methodology was simple; she presented clairvoyance. She was aware that it was inconsistent with classical physics; it was an anomaly, but she believed that, as Thomas Kuhn posited, science would leap forward to new systems of thought to accommodate and understand the anomaly within a new framework. Dora followed her intellectual curiosity and interest, and she seemed to know intuitively when a good opportunity presented itself. Quantum physics and relativity theory were being explored in scientific communities around the world. New systems of thought supported a less materialistic understanding of phenomena. Of course she hoped that within a span of time clairvoyance would be understood as something other than aberrant and pathological. Those in modern cultures with such abilities should not risk being considered crazy. Dora practiced patience and was astounded at the end of her life with the change that had occurred in areas such as health care. She also practiced perseverance. The world was changing, but slowly, and not without effort on the parts of many people over many years. Kuhn suggested that shifts in paradigms do not occur by "leaps and bounds" as much as by "crawl and leaps."

Concepts such as field theory from modern physics provides tentative support for the interpenetrating and dynamic vibratory frequencies Dora described in her book *The Personal Aura*. She adopted the term "energies" from physics to help others understand her nonmaterial clairvoyant perspective.

Even though the research Dora and Bengtsson did in 1936 and 1937 was not published for over fifty years, it helps us to understand her development in her earlier life. When they started the project, she was in her early thirties and the mother of an eight-year-old. However, she had clearly been developing her ideas for a number of years: she had lectured on the topic at age eighteen in Sydney. She had also been doing what she called "aura readings" for members of the Theosophical Society and their children beginning in the early 1930s. According to Theosophical literature, the dynamic ovoid of colors that interpenetrate the body and surround a person is called an "aura" because of its radiant iridescence as it appears to clairvoyants. Dora further distinguished her observations as the "personal aura" to identify its relationship with the human personality and to distinguish it from the auras of dogs and cats. The aura is a localization of the emotional field and is unique to each person. Not only does it interpenetrate the physical body and the associated "etheric field," it interpenetrates the mental field as well as more subtle fields.

Glimpses of the astral, or emotional, field are common but largely ignored. There are times when people who are not usually clairvoyant experience an altered state of consciousness. Those who are very frail or dying occasionally have heightened sensitivity. Partly as a result of Dora and Bengtsson's research, sick people who hallucinate are less likely to be considered insane. Some of these astral experiences bring comfort to people who are very ill, such as when a loved one, though already deceased, appears at the end of the bed. For those who have frightening experiences, hospice staff can provide medications to block the sensitivity.

Clairvoyance can occur when a spiritual leader gives a sermon or teaching or prays; a halo may become visible to those who experience a degree of meditative quiescence. Those who take hallucinogenic drugs often describe the astral field and can experience its lovely or terrifying aspects. A small percentage of children are thought to be at least minimally clairvoyant and are able to see the personal aura in a very coarse way as a colorful radiance.

In these examples, the perceiver has no control over the experience. As a child, Dora learned to shift her attention in order to turn on and off her clairvoyance and other related abilities. She was educated about the phenomena and was introduced to a worldview that made sense of what she perceived and intuited. She was also encouraged to master her mind so as to avoid being overwhelmed by her perceptions or her own responses.

Dora determined that she did not want merely to teach people to become clairvoyant. Her focus involved self-knowledge and spiritual development to benefit others. Her research with Dr. Bengtsson was intended to help people who were already clairvoyant to understand the phenomena. It was also intended to present a study of personality and human development from an energetic perspective. Dora wrote: "We are living partly within a world made up largely of our own emotional habits. And thus our emotions that surround us all the time affect our point of view and our habits very powerfully. I think that if we could fully realize that we ourselves, from within, can affect the results or circumstances of our emotional habits, it would be much easier for us to change emotional habits."[19]

The aura is very fluid, so the research was designed to produce a portrait of a subject's aura as though it had been photographed. For adult subjects, the sitting lasted several hours because of the details and to ensure valid reproduction of the colors in the aura. According to John Kunz, Dora's approach differed from that of Leadbeater and Besant in their books, *Thought-Forms* and *Man Visible and Invisible*. He said that Dora did not portray the aura as an amalgam of the emotional fields of several subjects she had observed. Rather than describe the way an emotion *commonly* appears in the field, she described the emotional field as though she had cognitively frozen it in a moment in time. With discipline she ignored the constant movement in the aura in order to describe its appearance at one moment to the artist.

Descriptions of auras differ from one clairvoyant to another, so this research provided a basis of comparison, not only with Leadbeater and Besant's early work, but also with that of contemporary clairvoyants. Dora included a remarkable degree of detail in her assessments of various personalities. For example, she often described the approximate age of a subject's childhood emotional difficulties. She observed the degree of resolution, suppression, or repression of "emotional scars":

> Most of us go through a number of difficult experiences during our lives, but we usually get over them after a while, so that very little memory of the experience is left. When the experience has been really traumatic, however, it can leave a very damaging impression which can easily surface again when a comparable situation calls it forth. In such cases, we never seem to be able to escape from the effects of the experience because everything conspires to remind us of it. Thus we fall progressively into a pattern of emotional repetition.
>
> It is this repetition that creates what I call emotional scars, which are whirls of denser energy in the aura—a record which remains even when we are not consciously thinking about the conflict which caused it.[20]

The "scars" are emotional events in the subject's life that may be recent or may come from thirty or more years previously; vortices of dense energy are often accompanied by symbols in the aura.[21] She distinguished between a wide range of emotions in auras and often could identify a subject's vocation and avocations. Another distinction she made was whether a subject tended to be more intellectual, emotional, physical-kinesthetic, or intuitive and whether the person had the ability to bring ideas to life or, on the other hand, was not inclined toward practical action. She attempted to verify some of her observations and extend the research longitudinally by follow-up with subjects after many decades.

Another unique characteristic of the research presented in *The Personal Aura* was that Dora expanded the normative developmental model with what she called "karmic indicators."[22] The key to what might present challenges or opportunities during the person's lifetime can be clairvoyantly perceived. Karmic indicators are potentials; they do not necessarily indicate outcomes. Dora also perceived "the possibility of developing certain emotional qualities"[23] on the basis of the person's ability to reframe the experiences. When working with parents, if Dora suggested something about their child, she did not give details of what she perceived, but focused instead on possible antidotes to potential problems. A child with karmic indicators of impetuous or aggressive behavior might be encouraged to take up sports that develop physical discipline and stamina.

Dora herself experienced very different cultures in Java, Australia, and the United States. One of her karmic indicators may have had to do with the probability that she would experience a "traveling life." She could reframe the experience of immigration and separation to one of travel and adventure. She could emphasize the spirit of independence in the United States as freedom of thought and freedom of speech rather than isolationism.

Another aspect of her later research was to define optimal health from an energetic perspective. She perceived a "wall" of psychic matter around people who were depressed, which, she said, indicated health problems. As a result, she taught people how to expand their auras, including meditation practices to eradicate the psychic wall. Indeed she often spoke about helping patients whose auras indicated chronic self-absorption or related depression. Her main message in *The Personal Aura* is "We can change." By working with individuals in meditation and healing groups for many years, she was able to approximate how long that effect generally took when students practiced daily. She also emphasized that the emotions associated with friendliness, harmonious relations, and altruism also contribute to optimal health.

One portrait in *The Personal Aura* provides an intimate glimpse of a person in the chaos of an emotional breakdown. It evokes Edvard Munch's painting *The Scream* or the drawings of Käthe Kollwitz. The subject was observed in the middle of the Great Depression, and the portrayal is chilling because of the lack of sentiment in the description. Of course the drawing does not portray the subject's facial expression, bowed back, or tears; instead, one sees the aura in all its grays as an imprisonment of chaotic negative emotions. Dora referred to these in *Conscious Use of the Aura* when she said, "Most of us are behind prison walls of our own making— those of prejudice and emotional narrowness and dryness." In the subject's case, financial problems and despair contributed to fragmentation and the creation of mental-emotional walls. The fact that the man died a short time after the portrait was done raises questions much like Margaret Bourke-White's photographs of the Depression era. How did he get here? What could have prevented his collapse?

The personal aura, as understood by Theosophists, is a localization of a universal field known as the "astral plane." Over time, Dora preferred the contemporary terms "astral field" or "emotional field" to designate what she observed. Scientists define a "field" as a nonmaterial continuum that is, by implication, coextensive with the universe. The energetic fields in science include the electromagnetic field, the strong and weak nuclear fields, and the gravitational field. Dora proposed that energy fields, otherwise known as states of consciousness, exist as localizations in space. Her hypothesis was that a human being consists of a system of inter-penetrating energy fields. From this perspective, the human being is a spatial localization of interpenetrating universal fields.

Dora based her descriptions on her early education in the Theosophical Society—much of which derived from ancient Indian Vedic teaching—and the application of the field concept from modern physical science. If there were terms that conveyed the findings in physics that had been brought to the attention of the general public since Blavatsky's time in the late nineteenth century, she chose these. For example, the Theosophical concept of the "etheric body" became the "vital field" or "etheric field."

From an energetic perspective, the "etheric field," associated with the physical body, interpenetrates the body as well as the emo-tional, mental, and more subtle fields that constitute the human being. Some clairvoyants who specialize in this area are known as "medical clairvoyants." Dora did not use that term in reference to herself. She never attended medical school and was careful to avoid accusations of practicing medicine without a license; she almost always worked in conjunction with physicians. She learned profes-sionalism in terms of the ethical doctor-patient relationship from friends such as Dr. Rocke and Dr. Bengtsson. She developed a methodical and scientific approach to her work as a layperson based on her clairvoyant observations and other abilities.

Dora avoided the term "psychic," which has so many different meanings that it confuses rather than clarifies. Used as a noun in early Theosophical literature, the word indicated a person with a range of abilities that included perception of the astral level. Another word, "occultist," according to the early literature, expressed the ability to perceive and work with hidden ("occult") phenomena; today it is considered dated. Dora avoided both terms.

She referred to herself as "clairvoyant" rather than as "*a* clairvoyant," on the grounds that there are many types of clairvoyance.

The mental consciousness is more subtle than the emotional consciousness, according to Dora, and there are even more subtle levels of consciousness associated with intuition and nonconceptual meditative states. Dora discriminated among those levels of consciousness when, during the last decade of her life, she shared her observations of the differences among some of the highly intelligent scientists and other scholars she had known. One of her interests was to observe the various ways some of the scholars she knew remained balanced in personal relationships during periods of concentrated and abstract intellectual efforts. Dora spoke of the states of consciousness associated with intuition "and beyond," because she preferred to avoid the Theosophical terms *higher manas*, *buddhi*, and *atma*.

As mentioned earlier, different clairvoyants perceive the aura in ways unique to each clairvoyant, but there are many commonalities among their descriptions. For most clairvoyants, the aura consists primarily of striations and patterns of colors varying in texture and intensity. In addition to these, Dora visualized symbols and patterns in the aura. She identified particular emotions and their influences based on many factors: exact shade and density of colors, location of the colors in the aura, and the vibrancy of the color.

She made a distinction between her clairvoyant investigations and those of another Theosophist, Geoffrey Hodson, and posited that the age at which one develops clairvoyance influences one's perceptions. "I suppose if you are born with it, you don't go through the same ecstasies as Geoffrey. He learned to be clairvoyant when he was in his thirties. It's much more exciting than if you are completely used to it. There's the difference between us."[24]

The research on the personal aura represented one of the first detailed observations of the human aura outside of Asia. In addition to Dr. Bengtsson, Dora's research assistant, Juanita Donahoo, was an artist who combined various mediums that allowed them to portray the energetic densities and symbols evident to Dora in the aura. She sketched a rather generic, age-appropriate human figure on large white poster paper. With the research subject seated in front of them, Dora described the colors as the artist approximated the shade of color, the size of the various areas of colors, and their location in the aura. She also described specific symbols present and other unique aspects of the aura. Airbrushing was done on the final versions. The entire process was laborious. They produced portraits of twenty auras and an additional image of a group aura during a meditation session.

Dora did not reveal the names of the subjects even after more than fifty years of presentations on the research. They are known only because she penciled some of the names into a transcript. Dora was so careful to maintain confidentiality that only a few people aside from the researchers, such as Emily Sellon and John Kunz, could identify the aura portraits by name.

One of the subjects, Dorothy Brett, came from a very class-conscious British family and was raised with many family expectations regarding her future. Dora said that Brett's aura showed signs of emotional strain in her early life from the cultural constraints as well as from her almost complete deafness. Brett had first visited Taos in 1924, and the austere natural environment provided her with a new kind of freedom. Despite her family's objections, she established herself as an artist. As Dora wrote in *The Personal Aura*,

> [Brett] had a deep love for the mountains and the Indian pueblos
> and the colors of the bare rocks and the sight of horses running

on the open plains. In this environment she became herself at last; it was as though she had been reborn. When she was free to live the kind of life she deeply needed, she became more unified, less complex, and her own inner integrity began to shine through her work. This transformed her art, for when she was free to represent her own self, as well as her artistic insights, her painting came into its own.

This aura is fascinating because there is such contrast between the past and the present. It is hard to imagine a life in which there could have been more radical change, for she exchanged a narrow, conventional environment for one of unrestricted freedom, and a life of wealth and luxury for one that was extremely simple, even Spartan. . . . She lived very plainly, with few possessions, and succeeded in immersing herself completely in a culture that was totally alien to her upbringing.[25]

Dora prized the painting that Dorothy Brett gave her of two people of the Pueblo wrapped in their traditional wool blankets riding on horseback, dogs running beside them. The blankets contribute to a sense of flight as well as unity with the natural environment. The painting hung on a wall in each of the places Dora lived as though a reminder of "unrestricted freedom" and Brett's ability to change.

When not in use for presentations, the large aura pictures were stored in the attic of the Sellons' house in Port Chester. Michael Sellon said that the boys occasionally went into the attic and got them all out, no doubt with wonderment at some of the complex psychological cases. Attic seclusion serves as an apt symbol for the relative silence that followed that burst of creative effort. Though the work generated interest and Dora and Bengtsson presented the portraits to many audiences, many decades passed before their work reached a wider audience.

Before the start of the project with Bengtsson and Juanita Donahoo, Dora and her family made a trip to Holland together in early 1936. It was eight-year-old John's first trip to Europe and his first introduction to Dora's family. Dora's parents and grandmother, along with her brother Arthur, traveled from Java for the family reunion. Karel's parents, David and Sophia van Gelder, had already died, as had the oldest of Karel's brothers, Louis. Fritz, Dora, and John met a number of members of their Dutch family. Tante Bet and her companion, Coos, arrived from Oosterbeek; Tante Cotty, Oom Dirk, and Cousin Hely came from Naarden, where Dirk was the headmaster at the Theosophical Lyceum.

It seems that Dora, Fritz, and John never mentioned to family or friends that Karel and his family were Jewish. Karel may have been raised as a secular Jew and may have shared little with his children. As a Theosophist he may have attempted to overcome identification with nationality, ethnicity, and religion. Their silence more likely existed in response to cultural conditions. Dora and Fritz would have been aware of these conditions even before they made the trip to Holland. The palpable oppression, combined with a sense of uncertainty, contributed to a stark experience of helplessness among Europeans, particularly among Jews. War seemed imminent and inescapable.

Separation was a dominant occurrence, particularly in the first half of Dora's life. After the family reunion in Amsterdam, Dora did not see Karel and Melanie again for eleven years and never again saw many of her Dutch family members. She knew that her father's family might be in danger because they were Jews. As war became more likely, she was also concerned about her mother's family members in Holland including Dora's chaperon to Sydney in 1916, Tante Bet, and her companion. Dora's cousin Nettie Westerman and her family lived in The Hague, and some of them immigrated to the U.S. after the war. Nettie was active in the TSA, and she and Dora stayed in touch throughout their lives.

In any case, Dora began her aura research with Bengtsson and Juanita Donahoo the winter after that visit. "Make progress in the good" was an expression common to Theosophists of her parents' generation. She threw herself into her good work, but she also spoke against the evils of the Nazi regime. After that visit to Holland, she and Fritz turned their attention to the creation of a rural Theosophical community. In that same year, 1936, Dora compiled her observations of fairies and angels in the natural world. One of the most creative periods in her life occurred during a period of worldwide war and tremendous destruction.

Chapter Five

The Real World of Fairies and Pumpkin Hollow Farm

Dora's research in 1936–37 studied the effect of human emotions on health. And in 1937, she wrote a work that the Theosophical press published forty years later as *The Real World of Fairies: A First-Person Account*. Its study encompassed not just garden fairies but the angelic kingdom and the world of nature spirits. Both studies—the first on personality and the second on nonhuman beings—reveal Dora's views on spiritual development. Elements common to angels and humans include love, devotion, and a gradual process of unfoldment. Spiritual realizations aren't granted by God; they are earned with practice, perseverance, and trial and error.

Though there are the equivalents of many species in these realms, Dora used the term "fairies" to refer generally to a variety of nature spirits. Her choice of title may have been inspired by a children's book entitled *The Book of Real Fairies*, written by Fritz's sister, Alma Kunz Gulick, and published in 1918 by the Theosophical Publishing House in India. It depicts anthropomorphic garden fairies that teach a child about moral behavior. Dora's approach, however, was to present anecdotal evidence of a variety of fairies from many parts of the world.

Dora's book, though written during the depths of the Depression, is happy, charming, and engaging. It combines modern science with an otherworldly perspective on nature and human beings. She described her role with fairy informants much as the anthropologist Margaret Mead described her research role as "participant observer." Without spoiling the sense of mystery, Dora brought readers closer to comprehending the mysteries of nature and the tremendous dynamism in the world.

The Real World of Fairies begins with a foreword by Claude Bragdon, a progressive architect of the Prairie School. He supported the style and philosophy of the architect Louis H. Sullivan, and Bragdon's own work would in turn influence R. Buckminster Fuller's architectural design. Bragdon began as a graphic designer, a stage designer in theater, and a writer of fiction and nonfiction books. Born in 1866, in his twenties Bragdon started a regular meditation practice, and, according to Dora, "he had a keen interest in Theosophy and he even wrote a little booklet on the Theosophical Society."[1] Indeed, he wrote two books and several articles for *The Theosophist*. Like Dora and Fritz, he had been introduced to Theosophical ideas as a child. His father introduced him to the Transcendentalists, and he was particularly inspired by Emerson. He also studied Eastern philosophies and brought those perspectives to his architecture.

Bragdon derived inspiration for his forms, not from previous great periods in history, but from a universal order, apparent in mathematical and geometrical proportions, as the basis for his architectural design. Bragdon's influence on Dora as an independent thinker can be seen in her reluctance to impose her own character or religion on her work. Another sign of his influence is that she rarely referred to previous systems of thought in her lectures or attributed ideas to other scholars.

Bragdon's foreword to *The Real World of Fairies* brought relevant concepts from modern physics to bear on the reader's understanding of clairvoyance. Bragdon wrote about the principle of "necessary uniformity" and about Werner Heisenberg's principle of uncertainty. He counters Dora's lighthearted storytelling style with his own mature awareness of the complicated world of human beings. He explains that all phenomena are of the nature of consciousness with an underlying "unity of life, the dominance of love, and that 'all is well with us all' despite every kind of evil seeming."[2] (This introduction, after all, was written during the years leading up to the Second World War.)

Bragdon may also have been the primary force behind Dora's narratives about fairies, because as early as 1929, he devoted an entire chapter in his fifth book to her and to fairies and angels. *Merely Players*, published by Alfred A. Knopf, included a chapter entitled "Faery Lore (Dora van Gelder)."[3]

The chapter begins with a description of the similarities between Dora and fairies. Along with Bragdon's foreword to *The Real World of Fairies*, it unwittingly promulgated the belief that Dora's birth as a human being was a "crossover" from the angelic kingdom. Early Theosophical literature posits that angels and human beings have parallel evolutionary lines and that "crossovers" occur according to karma and favored conditions for realizations.

Bragdon wrote, "Preposterous as such an idea may seem to the conventional thinker, it is the only one, to my mind, which at all explains Dora. . . . Not that she lacks human sympathy and understanding: these she has, but one feels that it was just for the acquirement of them that she assumed a fleshly garment in this harsh world of stained dreams."[4] When presented with the hypothesis that Dora was a crossover from the angelic kingdom, her son, John Kunz, emphatically replied, "Nonsense!"[5]

Even when Dora was in her mid-nineties, the myth that she was an angel lingered. One man who had been a colleague of Fritz's and had known Dora for fifty years believed that there was something to the idea. The best evidence for Dora's true identity as a deva, he said in a lowered voice, was that she was "basically asexual." (Literature on fairies often suggests that they are asexual; Dora herself writes that they are neither male nor female and do not reproduce through sex but are created by angels.) The elderly scholar went on to concede that if she was not asexual, she certainly suppressed her feminine sexuality. Presumably her inattention to fashion, her clumsy application of makeup—when she wore it at all—and her ignorance of sexual or flirtatious humor had not escaped his notice. Her vast knowledge of fairies and angels seemed to support his hypothesis. Never mind that Dora was a generation older than the elderly scholar, had known him since he was a little boy, and in any case did her best not to be cast into the role of sex object.

On the other hand, Beatrice Wood's poetry in the previous chapter comes closest to describing Dora's sexual nature as a woman in her twenties. She was also described by those who knew her during her last decades of life as womanly "in a motherly way." Since sexuality, at its best, is associated with love, Dora's own familiarity with love is best expressed in *The Real World of Fairies*, when she describes the love of a devoted sylph for the angel it served. The sylph is concerned, not with physical attraction, but with joyous service to a greater being.

> The ambition of the sylph is to become an angel. They are almost that, and with a little more they individualize and rank as angels when they next take form. They try to achieve this goal by staying close to angels and by being of as much service as possible to the angels around them and even to humanity.

It is through service and an understanding of the work of the angels that they attain the higher level. What usually happens is that they become the assistants of some angel and learn to be of special service to him. They perform certain specific tasks which he assigns to them and also act as his messengers or personal aides. Thus many angels have several of the sylphs attached to them. In this way the fairy gains in experience and also in affection, and the latter is important. The angel tries to bring out all the latent love in his companions. The relation is one of delicate tenderness, for the fairy is exceedingly happy in the angel's service, and is often proud of his post. Indeed he is, in the purest and truest sense of the words, "in love" with his angelic chief, and the relation is one of such delicacy as to be almost indescribable to human beings in whom this emotion has always some residuum of physical attraction. He is, furthermore, permanently in love—another great difference![6]

Nevertheless, Dora did not denounce rumors that she belonged more to the world of devas than the world of human beings. To have contradicted such notions would inadvertently have fueled them. In the introduction to *The Real World of Fairies*, Dora emphasizes her own pragmatic approach when she describes some of what can be learned through clairvoyant investigation of fairies and angels.

I have never been discouraged in my observations of fairies, because there are many people there [in Asia] who do see— and very many more who believe in—fairies. For this and other reasons, the not uncommon power among children to see them has, in me, persisted. Then, I have had the good fortune to fall, in this life, among family and friends that included several who could also see; and travel has enlarged the list. Therefore, what I have here set down is not the imagination of an isolated child. It is information gathered from many contacts and conversations with fairies all over the world in circumstances perfectly natural, however unusual. One can communicate with these beings in just as definite a manner as we human beings talk to one another—more so, for though the method . . . is slightly different, it is more rapid than speech, and, in some ways at least, it is a more accurate exchange.

It is important to mention these things, for if once we see the world from the fairy point of view, we get a glimpse of a new universe. So many things that matter very much to us do not seem to matter at all to them. Life and death, for instance, are things that they know all about; to them there is no uncertainty and no tragedy involved. Mankind so often shrinks from life and fears death. Fairies actually see the flow of life through all things. We live in a world of form without understanding the life force beneath the forms. To us the loss of the form means the end of the life, but fairies are never deceived in this way. They have a penetrating and powerful lesson for us. . . .

Furthermore we must remember that the whole business of seeing fairies is a delicate operation at best: the power to see requires conditions of quiet and peace; and then, fairies are themselves quite as shy as wild creatures and have to be tamed and attracted.[7]

She goes on to write, "People who live close to nature, such as peasants and farmers the world over, know of fairies." Love of nature is cultivated by living closely with it. Even if one only visits an urban garden occasionally, Dora describes how imagining the presence of fairies attracts them and attunes one to them.

How can fairies be attracted to a garden? Admiration of flowers and plants pleases and attracts them. Silently asking fairies in the area, when one is out in nature, to help a person who lives nearby can also attract them. Certain kinds of fairies are similar to children who like to help, and they playfully cultivate beauty and harmony. Children, especially small children, have special advantages in attracting fairies and getting to know them.[8]

During World War II, both the fairy manuscript and the research that would later become *The Personal Aura* were set aside. Dora entered what may be considered her silent years. On a practical level, she may have sensed that the world was too embroiled in war to care about fairies and auras. Dora did not tell stories about how she and Fritz and John survived the Great Depression. She never uttered a word about friends who worked for the resistance in Europe or about wartime rationing in the United States. Instead she talked about the bold cooperative effort they initiated with an entire community of people in the autumn of 1936, when a small group of Theosophists purchased an old farmhouse and the surrounding land in the Hudson River valley in upstate New York. The site was chosen for its location. It was close to Theosophical lodges and study groups in Schenectady; Hartford; Boston; Springfield, Massachusetts; and New York City. The farm was intended not to produce crops, but to grow into a community and to realize the Theosophical ideal of brotherhood. Discussion, meditation, and study there were also meant to encourage a depth of self-knowledge that realizes underlying oneness and the immense potential for transformation in each being.

Pumpkin Hollow Farm, as it was called, would become, not a center for permanent residents, but an ever-changing community of people who stayed for days or weeks, for a single year, or for several years. Many students returned briefly each year for decades and brought their spouses and children with them throughout the years. For Dora, Pumpkin Hollow Farm was not a "retreat center"; it was a "spiritual center."

Dora's own words from a 1997 letter about Pumpkin Hollow Farm, written when she was ninety-three, offer insight into its importance. The letter is handwritten, five and a half pages in length, and is addressed to Loren Wheeler, the Pumpkin Hollow camp manager. It emphasizes the people involved, the waterfall, garden, and community, the discussion of concepts, the helpfulness of volunteers, and the new methods of helping people that were born there. She states, "John, Emily, Fritz, and I helped to find and start Pumpkin Hollow with the ideas that we would like to start a spiritual center in the Eastern part of the country like we had [on] Orcas [Island] in the West. We hoped that the old house and the ancient barn and the rocky waterfall would be an ideal place to develop a community to encourage the unity of Nature and man."[9] She continues the letter, seemingly as people and events enter her mind, rather than by chronology. She seems more interested in the individuals involved rather than in the usual list of accomplishments. Her letter communicates gratitude and affection for the few people she mentions and the many hundreds who helped create the center.

Margot Wilkie, interviewed when she was over ninety years old, said that her mother, Katherine Loines, was familiar with real estate acquisition and was part of the search committee. The group traveled backcountry roads in New York and New England and searched for many weekends. One day, after they had already seen several properties, they reached a particular site. John Sellon was driving a sedan, with Mrs. Loines in the front seat and Emily, Fritz, Dora, and John Kunz all in the back seat. They parked the car by the road. Emily got out of the car and looked at the massive beams of the huge old barn. From a distance they could see the abandoned farmhouse and the outbuildings. It was a gray after-noon in early winter. As Emily later recalled, "When we first came to Pumpkin Hollow it was just getting dark. I felt very strongly that this was the property."[10] Dora and John Kunz followed the sound of the brook and located the waterfall. John Sellon remembered that Dora and John Kunz rushed back to the car; Dora said trium-phantly, "This is it. The angel agrees."[11] Emily remarked, "All of us had a feeling about it despite the gloom of that wintry afternoon." Then the five adults and young John Kunz packed back into the sedan for the hour-long trip back to Port Chester. According to Emily, "In January the place was born." The year was 1937.

The property, in the Taconic mountains near the Berkshires, had no electricity, running water, or indoor plumbing. The drafty floors in the house were uneven, and the stairs were steep. The house was heated by a cookstove in the kitchen and a fireplace in the living room. Dora, Emily, and others were soon up to their elbows in warm soapy water. Some of the first work Dora did in the house was to peel wallpaper and paint.

The name "Pumpkin Hollow" was chosen for a nearby area of the countryside, and "Farm" reflected continuity with the property's past rather than an intention to till the soil. Though a fertile area near the brook continues to be cultivated for vegetables, there were no livestock and most of the fields were not mown. The neighbor-ing farmers must have wondered at the sight of twenty or thirty people sitting around the orchard discussing ideas while poplars and alders slowly overtook the fields.

From the stories about the early days of Pumpkin Hollow Farm, there were hardly two nickels to rub together and not a farmer among the group. But they were a sturdy lot, with a variety of skills, and they managed to patch the place together. Over many years, cabins were built by various families, and trenches were dug to bring water to the far end of the field to create plumbed cabins. Downed limbs were cut; wood was split, hauled, and stacked. The cookstove was tended and the wood boxes kept filled. Ashes were lugged and scattered in the garden and in the compost heap.

Fritz always seemed to have his shirtsleeves rolled up when photos were taken. He did carpentry and repaired plumbing. Just as he had built their three-room cabin at Indralaya, with the help of friends he built a one-room cabin at Pumpkin Hollow. Their cabin was next to the Sellon cabin at the far end of the upper road. Another "Kunz cabin" was built after a massive steel bridge was constructed across the gorge. Fritz and Dora camped during the weeks they were at Pumpkin Hollow Farm at the remote cabin about a quarter mile up the hill.

Emily and Dora worked together—with many hundreds of others—to create and support Pumpkin Hollow Farm from the first snowy day when the property was found to the first camp in 1937 and throughout the years. The two of them were both strong, fiercely independent personalities, but each had realized some degree of nonattachment to ego that allowed for a healthy give-and-take. More than one person mentioned that Emily and Dora could disagree in loud voices with each other and then, within a few minutes, be perfectly agreeable and calm with one another. Emily and John, like Fritz, had the ability to help keep Dora down to earth. Dora listened to opinions that differed from her own ideas and learned to say "I stand corrected" or agreed to disagree.

The Sellons and Kunzes shared common worldviews and a sense of altruism. The quartet was affable and was not given to pettiness. Along with the many others who created and maintained Pumpkin Hollow over the years, they had a considerable task. The physical plant was a rundown farmhouse and outbuildings, and the community came from various parts of New York, New England, and Canada. After the first decades of restoration and building, visitors from all over the world came to teach and study. There were many immigrants who lived in cities along the East Coast, so there was a sense that people were exploring the spiritual dimensions according to their own religious culture and spiritual aspirations. The mission of the Theosophical Society and the experiment in Theosophical living brought the participants together. During Fritz's life, the summer gatherings coalesced around his presentations and discussion groups. After World War II, there was renewed strength and conviction that peace must start with each individual and cultivated in small communities in order to influence the larger world.

If the decade after Fritz and Dora married was one of innovative research and writing, the war years were creative in a different way. Dora had come of age during World War I. Her realizations during World War II were tempered by maturity and by new responsibilities.

Chapter Six

The War and Postwar Years (1939–1953)

Dora was thirty-five years old when Germany invaded Poland in 1939. Her previous war efforts and her greater maturity allowed her to persevere through those difficult years for the world and her family. The fact that she played a small part in relief efforts helped her withstand the deaths of many family members in Holland. She responded to the war and to the deaths in a way that remained consistent during her long life. She avoided overly emotional and what she termed "personal" involvement. She was not uncaring, nor was she immune to anguish during the war. She accepted death and change as constants; as she said, "Death is *part* of life." Life does not end at death. Though Dora did not view death as a cessation of all levels of consciousness, she nevertheless experienced separation and feelings of loss. The Nazi regime's calculated, methodical genocide, the violent deaths, starvation, and other forms of suffering associated with World War II were tragic. That sense colored the war and postwar years.

When Dora was asked about the occult background of the Nazis, she did not attempt to explain their arcane theories; she responded pragmatically, "Of course from our point of view, they were evil. There was such tremendous violence all over the world. We were trying to meditate and all that. So many people died in terrible ways; isn't that so? So [as Theosophists], we discussed that and did a lot of meditation and helped people. I resumed all that work that I did during the First World War—for myself—therefore, not so much for CWL. So my father's relatives in Holland were badly hurt and damaged."[1]

Here, in her shorthand manner, Dora reveals that she indeed worked in the astral field to help "the deaders" again during World War II, even though on other occasions she spoke proudly of her ability at age twenty-one to leave that difficult work behind. In counseling some of the recently deceased, she mirrored millions of others who found ways to contribute to the war effort. Certainly her manner of helping was somewhat unique: not many volunteers were capable of entering the rabbit hole, so to speak, and make sense of the astral field. But Dora could mentally communicate with people whose physical existence had ended. To others, they were dead; to Dora, they continued to need counsel, and their family members often sought reassurance.

Most surprising from Dora's brief recollection of the war is that, almost as an afterthought, she adds that her father's family was "badly hurt." This understatement does little to reveal the crucial information—that they were Jews and that many of them were imprisoned in concentration camps and killed.

Major events contributed to Dora's entry into what she later characterized as a period of silence. She was silent, for example, about her European family's Judaism. The reason for Dora's determination to maintain privacy about the real threats to her family in Holland are unknown. But she was so silent about her father's Judaism that even her own extended family members in the United States were unaware that Karel's family were among those who suffered and died because they were Jewish.

Dora was silent about her interests in clairvoyant investigation and healing because if Fritz's new endeavor—to significantly influence education—was to be successful, her clairvoyance and very different time-space perception could not distract or bring disdain. Fritz started *Main Currents in Modern Thought* to serve as the journal of the Foundation of Integrative Education, an organization he founded with others in 1940. Though neither endeavor was affiliated with the Theosophical Society, Fritz viewed the work as an extension of his Theosophical endeavors.

Dora laughed in retrospect at the decades in which she felt "like two people." She did not describe feeling stifled; her silence was accompanied by resolute perseverance and patience. Because of the changes in science, there was the probability of greater acceptance of the paranormal, of different ways of perceiving and varying modes of knowing. There were no certainties that she would be able to break out of the silence and be respected for her otherness. There was no certainty that the world could know peace and avoid anything as tragic as World War II.

Dora was by no means mute in all settings. With Emily and Dr. Bengtsson, and certainly at Indralaya, Pumpkin Hollow, and the lodges, she was well known for her clairvoyance.

Two of Dora's brothers enlisted, Harry in the Royal Dutch army and Arthur in the Netherlands East Indies army. The Dutch forces were no match for the Japanese, and Java fell within a short time. In March 1942 Arthur was taken prisoner at Bandung by the Japanese army. He survived three and a half years of internment, which ended with liberation of the POW camps by Allied forces at the end of the war. Somehow Dora's parents had received a report that he had been captured. Nonetheless, the long years of uncertainty and the lack of communication with him heightened Dora's awareness of war's effects on the family members of combatants.

Harry van Gelder was working in India when the war started, but because Holland had been occupied by the German army in May 1940, he went by steamer to London to enlist. He reported to the Dutch government-in-exile and enlisted in the Princess Irene Brigade. He trained in England for the invasion of France. While there, Harry met Mary Wright from Morecambe, Lancashire, and the two were married in London in January 1944. Five months later his role in the European theater began in earnest with the invasion at Normandy. During his years in England and Europe, he wrote frequently to his parents and even managed to mail several letters during the campaign. Many of Harry's letters from those years included gruesome details and expressed anger toward the enemy soldiers he called "the Huns." By autumn of 1944 the southern part of the Netherlands was liberated after four and a half years of Nazi occupation. Dora's uncle, Dirk van Hinloopen Labberton, who had immigrated to California, also joined the war effort and translated Japanese documents for the Federal Bureau of Investigation.

During a talk forty years after the war, Dora spoke forcefully about two prevalent misunderstandings about karma. First, she rejected what she considered a simplistic understanding of it as reward and punishment. Second, she said that it is counter-productive to speculate "why a person has these misfortunes. I don't think we should ever say, 'What has he done in the past to deserve it?' I think that's a terrible thing. I really feel that, because then we are sitting in judgment. Am I making that clear? We don't know; do we? By sitting in judgment, we may block ourselves from helping somebody else."[2]

When she began to speak to non-Theosophists about karma, she presented her views pragmatically and in unsentimental language: hatred toward those who torture and kill is negative karma and binds one to the object of hatred.

During these years, occultism, the science of very hidden phenomena, became associated with the Nazis' lust for power. Concerns that clairvoyance in turn would be associated with occultism contributed to Dora's silence during the war and in the postwar period. Public perception mattered a lot to Dora. To prevent misperceptions, "occultism" was dropped from the lexicon. Dora temporarily set aside her research in clairvoyant investigation to work alongside Fritz.

Beginning in 1940 with the launch of *Main Currents in Modern Thought*, the magazine that Dora described as "very highbrow," she accepted her role in Fritz's two-person career.[3] Fritz had been developing his thoughts about curricula in universities and colleges. All the subjects were compartmentalized, as if there were no common ground between them. He wanted them taught as interrelated inquiries into nature and existence that would stimulate a realization of human mutuality. To that end, he shifted his focus from public speaking with a lecture bureau to speaking at universities. He enlisted the support of major scientists and philosophers such as Henry Margenau, F. C. S. Northrop, Benjamin Whorf, Kirtley F. Mather, Donald Hatch Andrews, and other luminaries. This led to the Foundation for Integrative Education.

Some of those dialogues incorporated Theosophical principles, and many members of the Society subscribed to the journal, *Main Currents in Modern Thought*. Fritz's friendliness and intellect set the tone and helped create a sense of shared search for truth and mutuality among people across diverse disciplines and geographical borders.

As Fritz wrote in an early edition of *Main Currents*, participants at the first meeting discussed "requirements for a planned, sustained and concerted effort to knit together the whole domain of knowledge and experience, to translate such concepts in to educational method and content, and to give currency to such wholes in the institutions of society."[4]

Fritz and Dora, along with Emily and John Sellon, were busy with *Main Currents* and the Foundation for Integrative Education. Dora took the train into the city and spent one day a week in the stacks of the New York Public Library. She searched for new scientific research and articles and books by bright new authors from various sciences. John Sellon served as the financial adviser for the journal. Emily contributed her secretarial skills and soon discovered her aptitude for editing. She scoured journals in search of a unitive field theory that would validate the principle of Oneness proposed by Blavatsky. She became Fritz's senior student and gained confidence in her own abilities as a public speaker on complex and abstract topics, and she honed her skills as an editor. Fritz served as editor of *Main Currents*, with Emily as the associate editor.

In addition, the four of them continued to serve as officers in various capacities for the New York Theosophical Society, the Northeast Federation of the TS, and Pumpkin Hollow Farm. Dora was immersed in many of the discussions at Pumpkin Hollow Farm, Indralaya, and the New York lodge. She was, for the most part, quiet during Fritz's sessions. She would occasionally say, "Fritzy, they don't know what you're talking about." He would laugh and take it in stride. Dora implied that her interruptions were based on her astute observations, not only of body language, but of personal auras. Perhaps she saw when yellow, the color she associated with intellectual functioning, was less predominant in the students' auras. Maybe she saw thought-forms associated with irritability and noticed that participants were becoming restless. She was attentive to the group, so she would interrupt and suggest a break to allow those who were restless to leave. In those ways, she acted the role of the good wife in much the same way that her own mother did during gatherings in which Karel led the discussions in Krebet or Sydney. Dora also cooked meals, played with the children, worked in the garden, read auras, and greeted new arrivals. This was true at Indralaya on Orcas Island as well.

John Kunz accompanied Fritz and Dora back and forth across the country each year, and pencil marks to indicate his height are still found on the porch of their cabin at Indralaya, where they maintained the simple tradition of marking his growth year after year. The work at Pumpkin Hollow Farm and Indralaya was creative when so much of the world seemed bent on destruction. There were large gatherings of children, teenagers, and adults during the weeks of the Theosophical Camp at Pumpkin Hollow each summer. There were group discussions in the morning, on some afternoons, and around the campfire in the evening. The brook, with its roaring, splashing waterfalls, was invigorating, and being close to nature and away from the city and the suburbs helped keep things in perspective. Just as the Great Depression had prevented people from going to Indralaya and Pumpkin Hollow, there were two or three years that Dora and Fritz were unable to make the cross-country trip to Indralaya. Those were the years when too many of the men were at war, too many of the women managed alone, and gas rationing did not permit extravagant travel.

After the war ended, Dora heard from Harry, who suggested how she could help those in Europe. He was stationed in Holland at the end of the war, and during leave he located two of their cousins in Amsterdam who were safe and staying with their aunt. Harry learned about the fate of their uncle Max: "One day in 1942 Max was sitting at a sidewalk café in Amsterdam drinking coffee with a friend. The Gestapo and some members of the NSB[5] drove up, hauled him into the car, and sent him to the transit camp at

Westerbork." From there, according to Max's great-nephew, he "was packed into a train to Sobibór, where on June 4, 1943 he was gassed to death."[6] Max's wife was also taken by the Nazis and killed in the death camp in Sobibór, Poland, that same year. Karel's brother, Abraham, died of unknown causes in 1940; his wife, Sofia, was killed in Sobibór. Though Dora's Uncle Abraham and Aunt Sofia died, their son and his wife both survived. Someone had procured false documents for the young van Gelder.

During leave in postwar Holland, Harry also visited Tante Bet and her companion, Coos, in Oosterbeek. He wrote to Karel and Melanie, "The house had all the windows smashed, holes in the roof and walls . . . & everything was stolen out of it, clothing, food, coal, piano, furniture, beds, etc. But they all need clothing & sheets & blankets. If you can send Bet a few shirts, a pair of trousers or a pullover & cotton or other material it would be very good. . . . Send dried fruit, flour in tins (not packages) as food to the people—& sugar, coffee & tea, besides clothing and shoes."[7]

Dora's brother Lucius and his family stayed in India during the war and lived close to Karel and Melanie. Lucius and Karel both worked in the sugar industry, and it was fortunate that they had sought work outside of Java. By immigrating to India they had escaped internment by the Japanese and the post-war violence during the revolution. Many of their friends and relatives were not so fortunate.

In 1945, Dora's beloved grandmother, Theodora van Motman Schiff, died in India at the age of ninety-five. The war in Europe officially ended in May, but months passed before Dora and her family heard from her youngest brother, Arthur, who was interned in Java. The war in the Pacific and other parts of the world continued until August. When the internment camp in Java was liberated at the end of the war, Arthur was described as being "in terrible shape.

He had beriberi caused by vitamin B deficiency and general malnutrition and had lost 49 pounds."[8] The Netherlands East Indies army required him to continue in war-related efforts. Instead of being discharged, he was sent to Singapore in September 1945. None of Dora's family members returned again to Java.

In Singapore Arthur served for several months as a laboratory technician, where he helped triage the men, women, and children who had survived internment. While there, he wrote to his parents in India to request necessities such as clothes and, most of all, food.[9] By December he was discharged and was permitted to travel to India. In a talk to lodge members there, Arthur communicated a key to psychological health: refuse to passively accept difficulties as one's karma. View them as challenges to be overcome. An article in the Adyar *Theosophist* entitled "Starvation in Java" revealed that starvation was used as a weapon of war and mentioned many of the families Dora and her family knew from Java. The article communicated not anger and defiance, but efforts to turn misery into motivation in order to help relieve the suffering of others.

Back in India, Arthur recuperated for several months in Srinagar with his parents, where they rented a houseboat. He then spent some time in the beautiful hills of Kashmir before returning to Rampur, where he lived with his parents and worked in the sugar industry.

Arthur's determination to help others after the war prompted him to rescue a small boy from the streets of India who was dehydrated and starving. He did for that child what he had not been able to do for those who starved during internment: he fed him a teaspoonful of milk mixed with beaten egg and bourbon four times an hour throughout the night until the boy regained consciousness. The boy, who is now a grandfather, helps tackle the social problem of health care for the elderly in his adopted country—the United States.[10]

Dora was also determined to help, and she was offered a perfect opportunity. She and the other members of the New York Theosophical Society did what they could to relieve starvation for at least a handful of people. They participated for several years in the European Parcel Project of the Theosophical Society. Its purpose was to relieve shortages of food, clothing, and household items for those who lived in regions that had been devastated by battles, rationing, and loss of lives.[11]

Dora's efforts as president of the NYTS were much like her first efforts as president of the Young Theosophists in Sydney during World War I. She organized volunteer efforts and donations. She ensured that the weekly aid packages were mailed to the ten or so families in the Netherlands to which they had been assigned. Dora's literacy in Dutch allowed her to maintain correspondence without having to employ translators, since she was also responsible for follow-up; confirmation from aid recipients ensured that packages had not been intercepted and diverted by black marketeers. She also corresponded on a regular basis with the coordinator of the project, Ann Wylie, at the Theosophical Society headquarters in Wheaton.

Many of the larger Theosophical lodges around the United States also participated in this effort. Each one was assigned to a different country and given a list of names and addresses. Most of the recipients were members of the Society who had been identified as lacking sufficient sources of immediate aid.

One of Dora's practical suggestions helped prevent cumbersome translation problems. She recommended to the national coordinator that the Spanish lodge of the NYTS assume responsibility for aid packages to the general secretary of the Spanish Section. The change, made for the duration of the program, is a good example of one of Dora's traits. If she saw a problem, she spoke up to solve it. Some people welcomed her suggestions, though those with rigid administrative styles would likely have found her meddlesome.

During the Parcel Project, efforts were made to ensure that the maximum weight allowed would be shipped on a weekly basis so that families could distribute excess to others in need. Some of the letters suggested that shoes and clothes be mailed even if the correct size had not been determined, and to make adjustments for safe storage of food by mailing tins rather than paper packages. One of the lodges in Hawaii regularly mailed ten pounds of sugar to each of the individuals on Dora's list. This was very helpful, since sugar was still being rationed in the mainland United States.

In addition to the European Parcel Project, Dora and her parents assumed responsibility for helping Karel's remaining family in Holland, the Westermans in The Hague, and Tante Bet and Coos in Oosterbeek. Dora later taught students what she had learned from this process about psychological health. Too much attachment and identification with the victims, and she would be unable to be of service. Too little regard for the suffering, and she could become self-absorbed and ineffectual.

When speaking of the efforts of the NYTS during the war, Dora also mentioned the Wednesday meditation group that was held from September through May. Leading groups had the secondary effect of inspiring her to be a calm center for others. To be still within and to resonate with a level of consciousness focused at the area of the heart was expansive and comforting. These meditations also contributed to the harmony of the group, something Dora continued to emphasize throughout her life. Healing meditations could not replace food for those who were hungry, but as a clairvoyant who could intuit at a distance, she maintained that meditation did help the victims. She also said that it also helped the meditators, particularly those who were sensitive, because they were participating in something calming and positive in a supportive group setting. Dora recommended the practice of healing meditation for sensitive people, if for no other reason than to give them something to do; it was, she said, much better to project calm, stable thoughts and emotions than anxiety and grief.

Several months before Indian independence in 1947, Dora's parents moved to the United States. They purchased a house in Port Chester close to her and Fritz. John Kunz, who was then attending Harvard, said that the three years that his grandparents were in Port Chester were wonderful for the family. With John away at college, Dora had time to help her parents adjust to the new country. Neither Dora nor her parents drove a car, so when they went into the city, Fritz, Emily, or John drove them to the train station. Both Dora's parents were actively involved in the Theosophical lodge in Manhattan and attended the weekly members' meetings and the camp at Pumpkin Hollow during the summertime. They also enjoyed concerts and other events in the city.

Though she did not lecture publicly, Melanie continued to write and had published a third booklet shortly before leaving India on the purpose of yoga from a Theosophical perspective. She often led meditation groups in her home and shared her psychic insights with others. Melanie made friends easily wherever she lived and was loved for her warmth, kindness, and generosity. In an interview Dora said, "For a woman who never in her whole life had to do one single [domestic] thing, when she left India she had to learn how to do housekeeping. Really, I take off my hat to her; she learned to do all those things. And my father had to do it; that's very hard for somebody."[12]

Dora introduced a new concept when she spoke of her mother's "emotional friendliness." She compared her with Fritz, who was also friendly but not, she said, "that type of person. He was emotional, but not in that way. [He was] like his parents, like his sisters."[13] She said that Fritz and her mother got along, but their interests varied widely. On the other hand, Fritz and her father got along very well.

Dora was becoming more drawn to the logical processes in medicine and patient care through her work with Dr. Bengtsson; she was also immersed in Fritz's work and had to read a lot of scientific articles.

During these years, while Dora researched spiritual healing, she continued to travel with Fritz to what she later referred to as "endless conferences" associated with the foundation. Fritz was clearly in the spotlight, and she was in the wings. She described her role at the conferences as Fritz's helpmate. Their lives were full, and Dora's synthesis of the healing studies occurred in between many other commitments and family concerns. Dora considered her growing interest in healing as her "separate life."

> When I went to all the conferences we had with Fritz, I did a lot of hard work. I met very many brilliant scientists etc. and so I didn't mind my separate life. . . . I helped him in every way I possibly could, finally. And he helped me in his way, not by participating, but by chauffeuring me around and that sort of thing. And that seemed fair, didn't it? I think we tried to cooperate with one another.
>
> He hadn't the slightest interest in disease or any of those things. . . . Fritz never met my doctors. They never knew one another. He took me to the train; he went to meet me. He never came to any of them; he never went to anything of mine, nothing, never. He never went to Wainwright House. He went and picked me up, and brought me there but he never went.

Fritz's absence was not due to any conflict about Dora's interest in healing. "That was my life and he helped in every way he could," she later recalled." But he never went to anything and that was fine. Medicine is a very dull thing if you're not interested in that sort of thing."[14] Fritz was immersed in a world of ideas, especially philosophical thought and how to bring new perspectives to education. As Dora said once, "Fritz lived in his own world."

When asked during her last years of life whether she had been interested in introducing a new philosophy of education, she said that it was *Main Currents* that held her interest. She then added, "You learn to appreciate chemistry, physics, philosophy, etc. And it's a world of ideas, isn't it? Through that I met some brilliant people and I made friends with a lot of them."[15]

Chapter Seven

Wainwright House and the Spiritual Healing Seminars

Wainwright House, described on its Web site as "the oldest non-profit, non-sectarian holistic learning center in the United States," is a large private house in Rye, New York, near Long Island Sound. In 1951 its owner, Fonrose Wainwright, donated it for the work of the Laymen's Movement for a Christian World, an organization set up to help realize Christian ideals in public life. Wainwright House serves as a center where, according to an early brochure, "people from all backgrounds and all beliefs and even no beliefs at all could aspire for a greater understanding of the creative force of life we call God." The center's emphasis on the study of human potential drew support from prominent business leaders, including John D. Rockefeller and E. F. Hutton.

Elaine Peterson, whose mother-in-law, Lucille Kahn, participated in the center's early healing seminars, observed, "In the 50's and 60's Wainwright House was 'THE' (perhaps only) place in NYC that was available for workshops in the alternative healing fields, which included parapsychology. The circle of alternative healing was small at the time."[1]

As Dora said, Wainwright House was located "just around the corner" from her home in Port Chester. In 1954, Dr. Bengtsson introduced her to the seminars, which explored spiritual healing as an expression of both expanded human potential and religious faith.

She used her maiden name, Dora van Gelder, at the seminars, because she wanted to avoid controversy among conservative members of the Foundation for Integrative Education. Dora sought to protect Fritz's reputation and confirmed that she led what she called a "double life":

> Part of my life has been with very famous, very conservative people; they knew nothing about Theosophy, and they never knew anything about my clairvoyance or anything. Then I worked for the Theosophical Society and I had medical people. They knew nothing about my other work. I had two separate parts of my life, which is funny. And the two never met except once by accident.[2]

> Kirtley Mather—I knew him very, very well. He was once invited to speak at Wainwright house and I, just by accident, stood in the door. I met him at the tail end of one of my healing conferences. He said, "Hey, I'm so surprised to see you. What are you doing here?" He was very surprised to see me. "Oh," he hugged me and said, "I am so glad to see you. . . . I felt so strange. You are the only person I know." That was funny. Fritz's professors never knew anything about me so I had a double life all that time.[3]

Kirtley Mather had gained recognition in the 1920s as one of the witnesses for the defense in the famous Scopes Monkey Trial, named after the schoolteacher who, against state law, presented the theory of evolution in a public school in Tennessee. Mather, a respected Harvard geologist, presented scientific support for the theory of evolution. He had long been interested in the interface between science and religion but, according to Dora, did not know that she was interested in healing and had clairvoyant and other related abilities.

John Kunz mentioned another example of Dora's silence involving the Duke University psychologist J. B. Rhine, who, along with his wife and other researchers, pioneered research in the early 1930s in what they called "extra-sensory perception." Rhine's work included clairvoyance, clairaudience, telepathy, and precognition. John said, "[During] one of the meetings that my father was doing for his educational work, she and my father and Rhine were together. She knew Rhine from that [and] from a few [other] occasions. But the context was not my mother's clairvoyant ability at all; it was an irrelevancy which she was not about to go into with any of these people." The famous medium Eileen Garrett, whom Dora knew, had been a research subject for Rhine's studies. Had Dora offered any hints of her own sensitivities or offered to assist him in research? "No, very definitely not," said John, "because I can remember her telling me very plainly that she carefully didn't and was amused at it."[4] She kept her work and Fritz's separate.

Dr. Bengtsson had attended the first of the Wainwright House Spiritual Healing Seminars. Dora joined her for the second, third, and fourth seminars in March and October 1954 and June 1955. These initial seminars amounted to just nine days over the course of two years, but they were pivotal for Dr. Bengtsson and Dora. They were organized by Dr. Robert W. Laidlaw, who was a member of the board of the American Society for Psychical Research as well as chairman of the department of psychiatry at the Rockefeller University Hospital. A wide variety of medical professionals, clinicians interested in healing, scholars of religion, members of the clergy, and lay practitioners attended. Some of the participants were intellectually intrigued by reports or personal experiences of healing, while others were devoted to helping their parishioners.

Dr. Bengtsson proved to be a wonderful navigator in the new waters. She and Dora were both newcomers, as were most of the participants, and like the others, they were altruistic and shared an attitude of open-minded exploration. Dolores Krieger, who later became instrumental in the introduction of the concept of healing to the health care professions, recalled that Dr. Bengtsson "was particularly helpful. Dora and she were collaborating very closely. She was what you hope every doctor would be: a compassionate, very knowledgeable person who would go to any ends to help somebody. She had a delightful sense of humor, a wonderful laugh."[5]

Spiritual healing was a new area of enquiry for Dora; it implied a holistic perspective that was as potentially transformative in health care as Fritz's integrative curricula were to education. Prior to the Spiritual Healing Seminars, Dora had served as a lay consultant to Dr. Bengtsson's patients, she explained, "not for healing, but for counseling. I saw them [clairvoyantly] and [assessed] what was wrong with the patients. I got interested in medicine and then this psychiatrist, [Dr. Robert Laidlaw] got me to join his group—the first group in the United States for psychiatrists and [other] doctors. That's the first time I ever thought about healing."[6]

Dora's earlier visits to the New York offices of the American Society for Psychical Research had familiarized her with researchers who studied paranormal phenomena and healing. She had not, however, explored spiritual healing in a setting where she could clairvoyantly observe the healing phenomena while healers provided treatments. Nor had she had an opportunity to discuss healing and a wide range of related topics with well-educated clergy, physicians, and healers.

During the first seminar that she attended, Dora said little. She had not yet overcome her shyness and was considered as a case study during one of the sessions. Dr. Bengtsson presented the phenomena of Dora's clairvoyant investigations to the group, and then Dora answered questions from participants regarding her process and perceptions, both clairvoyant and telepathic. Dora told the group:

> I don't feel that I have anything to contribute. I was born with a very peculiar gift which I have used to a certain extent, and that is, I seem to be able to perceive—I think that is just as good a word as any—where a person is ill, even in the endocrine glands and various parts of their body. I can see what a person has emotionally wrong with him. I have been for several years working with Dr. Bengtsson who is a medical doctor, and also working with other doctors. We have been working, not on the healing process, but much more on diagnosis. I am interested to see—what is the relationship between emotions and how [do] they affect bodily function? That is really our interest. . . . That is all I have to say, and there is absolutely no religious background to this of any sort. So I really feel I shouldn't say any more."[7]

This first presentation was so short that Dr. Bengtsson spoke immediately afterward.

> Dora is to my mind one of the most innately religious people I have ever met, but she does not belong to any church. I work in allergy, but I am tremendously interested in what gives a person peace of soul so the body can get a chance to heal when doctors do something. And I must say from the bottom of my heart that I am in accord with what Dr. Sladen of Detroit

said about wanting to get some kind of a hookup between medicine and religion. With that I don't mean phony medicine and I don't mean phony religion. And I am terribly, terribly interested in the matter of psychosomatic medicine on a basis which will make man's body, mind and emotion at one with his soul, and the person from whom I have gotten [by] far the biggest help is Dora van Gelder.[8]

Bengtsson told the participants how she had arranged for Dora to see one of her patients, a twenty-two-year-old woman who suffered from infantile paralysis due to polio and had partial paralysis in one leg as well as severe asthma. She said, "We arranged to have her come in and sit down so that Dora couldn't see that she was crippled. Dora looked at her and made the diagnosis [of the paralysis]."[9] Bengtsson said that the patient interview interested her for another reason: Dora clairvoyantly observed an area in the center of the patient's aura that appeared grayish and flecked with small red lines. The colors and pattern usually indicated anger, but their location in the aura was unusual.

Bengtsson realized the significance of the red-flecked area, because she knew that the patient had self-administered an injection of adrenalin to manage asthma exacerbated by stress from being late to their appointment. One side effect of adrenalin can be anger. "Of course, Dora knew nothing about the [use of] adrenalin in those days. I never told her anything about the people [beforehand] because I wanted to use what she gave as evidence [of correlation or contradiction with the medical findings]. When a person is very angry there is a secretion of adrenalin which naturally affects the aura. Here was a perfectly wonderful picture of the effects of adrenalin in the emotional aura that gave a spot of the same color. In other words, there was a slight bad effect in the emotions of taking adrenalin physically—just as we know from Cannon's work on bodily changes that in hunger and rage adrenalin is secreted."[10]

Bengtsson shared another anecdote to communicate Dora's discernment of a predominant emotional habit pattern in the aura of a patient. Bengtsson was consulted by an anxious woman who she described as "almost hysterical over her aches and pains. I thought I would relieve the situation by asking her what she did. She said, 'I teach school. I hate the kids; I hate my job; I hate everything connected with it.' She was screaming away. I was racking my brain—how to get her interested in something that would give her relief? I thought of Dora."[11] Dr. Bengtsson then arranged for the woman to attend a meeting where Dora shared the "aura pictures" that they had produced during the 1930s.

While describing a particular habit pattern, Dora indicated someone from the audience. Dr. Bengtsson said, "I realized the one she pointed to was my unhappy friend. I asked Dora about it. She said, 'You see that in the aura of the person who dislikes their work.'"[12] Dora was aware, not only of the woman's strong feelings, but of the object of her hatred—her work. Moreover, Dora made this assessment while delivering a presentation rather than during a formal patient interview. Because she could clairvoyantly and intuitively perceive particular emotional issues among members of her audience, she often addressed a specific concern of one member in a way that maintained the person's anonymity. The effect was psychologically powerful and affirming for the person she tried to help. Often, however, other audience members who did not understand Dora's approach viewed her presentations as tangential or scattered.

To the participants at Wainwright House, Dora had been identified, along with Eileen Garrett and Ambrose Worrall, as a "spiritual healer," but she drew an immediate distinction between her clairvoyant assessment and spiritual healing. She did not view her assessment and counseling as spiritual acts. During her early work with Dr. Bengtsson, her goal was to determine a person's habit patterns associated with health problems and to motivate him or her to adopt new perspectives and patterns.

Dora described at length how she made clairvoyant assessments as well as the ways in which that can potentially contribute to effective counseling. Until those seminars, Dora had primarily counseled patients. She emphasized that a person can be clairvoyant and intuitive without necessarily using those abilities to help others as a healer:

> The work I am doing has not anything to do with healing. I don't claim to be able to do any healing, and I really don't think there is any religious significance to what I am doing. I am going to describe this instance which Mr. Huckabee [the chairman] brought to your attention. All we knew was the man's name, and we knew that he had something wrong in the line of allergies.
>
> The way I work is this: I have been born with a peculiar capacity. When someone, like the man in this case, is brought before me, I get *en rapport* with him, and I am able to see the area from the physical point of view where that person is ill. I perceive this, but not with my eyes. I think telepathy is what really describes it. When people come before me, I have immediately a sense of where they feel pain or discomfort. I never diagnose disease, because I do not pretend to be a doctor.
>
> When I looked at this man, the thing which struck me was that he was exhausted. He was very below par in his energy. I saw that he had a very low thyroid; that his basic metabolism was way down. When I look at the endocrine glands of a

person I can perceive whether they are plus or minus, and I can perceive where the seat of sickness is. I saw in this case that while all of the man's bodily functions were not organically exactly wrong, the whole body, particularly the liver, was sluggish. He digested only a very small bit of what he ate and the rest, I should think, would turn into poison. And I didn't feel a proper functioning of the two parts of the thyroid.

Then I can see the structure, you might say, in the patterns of a person's emotions. I can see and sense the emotional habits which might lead to the physical disability which the person has. The first thing I noticed when I looked at this man was that he seemed to be suffering from a sense of terrible shock. His emotional state was that of a person who had gone through a shock. Also, he suffered continually from a sense of inadequacy. I think he was always struggling with it. And another thing I could see was that he bifurcated his life. He hated the work he did and he put it in one compartment, as it were. He thought it was horrible, and that is the way he went on in his daily life. So he was separating. When a person thinks that what he does to earn a living is wrong, that puts him in a constant state of conflict. We talked about these things.

I look where I think a person is ill and I try to correlate this observation with what I sense are his emotional disorders. I am telling you in three minutes about something which takes at least an hour. Even the physical correlations, if I did a good job, would take a long time. And if you try to delve into a person's emotions, it takes longer. I can trace to some extent how far these emotions or shocks go back—ten, fifteen, twenty years, sometimes more. In the case of this particular man, I think some of his difficulties developed when he was extremely young. Sometimes there are constitutional difficulties, psychic constitutional difficulties, which may develop as a baby, or as a young person. He had something like this against him from a time when he was very young. Afterwards, . . . this man told us that he was an alcoholic. . . .

I have given just a rough outline of what I do when I work with Dr. Bengtsson. Most of these people I see again; sometimes I never see them again. There is really no spiritual healing involved in this. I try to help each person to the best of my ability.[13]

The pastor of an Episcopal church in Pittsburgh then asked about her frame of mind while she made her assessments. Dora responded pragmatically: "Focusing my attention upon something. I think that is probably the best way to describe it. I carefully try not to look at the actual person. It makes them uncomfortable if you gaze at them."

A man who conducted healing services at a Methodist church in Baltimore asked, "Could you describe what clues you find in the aura that help you to identify the disease?"

Dora answered, "There are colors; there are also patterns. There are many habit patterns into which a person falls. People often are in conflict and in difficulty because they are not consciously aware of these habit patterns. When I look at a person I never consider whether he is good or evil. I see only that some people have difficult habit patterns, and they are imprisoned by these habit patterns. What I see isn't only something in emotions, in feeling. I can see it as in a dynamic rhythm. Am I making that clear? I look at the habit patterns, definite things which to me are almost material. Then I search for the emotions."

A female internist from Manhattan asked, "Could you describe the aura of a person harboring great resentment or anger or joy?"

Dora replied, "Resentment has a pattern which cuts off the person from other people. It has an isolating pattern. A person who is resentful is caught. Sick people suffering from resentment often would like to go out, but they are caught in a negative pattern, and the energy rebounds and hits them."

The leader of the Baltimore healing group asked another question: "How do you distinguish between your telepathy and your aura? Do you get the idea first and then does it become objectified for you in pictures, imagery, colors, movement—or do you see the color and movement first and deduce from that what may be the difficulty?"

Dora responded, "These things seldom come one after another. Perception and telepathy are things which happen instantaneously. You can't see exact boundary lines. It is one thing, not two or three things."

A psychologist from Virginia Beach said, "You use the term 'habit pattern.' I wondered whether you actually meant a pattern of action of the individual."

Dora replied, "Yes, I mean habit patterns that most people have, sometimes from childhood. A person, say, would like to be nice or loving to somebody. But instead of saying something nice, something sharp sometimes comes out—unconsciously. This is energy misdirected by a habit pattern. To me any emotion is an energy. That is how I see it."

The same man asked, "Do you see it as a color?" and Dora said, "Yes."

A lay member of the group asked, "If a person is predominantly mental he gives off a certain design and a certain color, doesn't he? And if he is emotional he gives off another design and another color?"

Dora replied, "Yes, but I don't like to separate people. I think we are a whole, a total personality. . . . I can see, of course, these

155

differences quite easily. But I never see the separation between the emotion and the physical mechanism."

The female internist asked another question. "Couldn't you isolate, for instance, the sluggish liver? How did that appear to you? Did it come from that spot? If it is dull gray, then it is sluggish; is that the idea?"

Dora answered, "No. The liver has to do with the process of elimination and toxins. The first thing I saw in this case was that the man was in a very toxic condition. When a person is toxic in his liver, it influences not only the liver, but also the elimination all over the body. It isn't only in one spot. A single organ affects a lot of different parts in our body. I saw this toxic condition all over him; I saw again the same thing in his liver."

A psychologist from Howard University in Washington, DC, asked about a person's aura, "Does largeness and brightness signify anything of positive character as you have observed people?"

Dora answered, "Well, surely, some people have larger auras than others, but I am lucky in this way: I can turn this capacity on and off completely. And I never, never look at the person's emotions, except with permission, because it isn't my business. I have no curiosity in my makeup whatever. What people are, they are. If I don't have to delve in them I don't."

A psychologist from Chevy Chase, Maryland, asked a series of questions. "Did you mean by 'pattern' the kind of thing which we think of as visible? In other words, is resentment a lot of jagged lines and red in color, or is it more or less wavy and dark blue? Does that describe the pattern?"

Dora replied, "With anger and resentment always you visualize the color in shades of red. But the patterns differ, because no two people feel resentment about the same thing. The color will be the same, but not the pattern."

The internist from Manhattan asked, "What are the darkest emotions, the darkest colors of the aura with certain emotions? I mean the real black, brown, gray, purplish things. What is the deadliest emotion that shows up in auras?"

Dora answered, "Well, I suppose complete and absolute cruelty and selfishness. I don't see that very often. I try never, never to judge anybody who is in front of me."

A woman whose affiliations were not identified in the transcript asked, "Would you tell us about the origins or the beginnings of this gift of yours?"

Dora said, "I was born with it. I was born in the Orient. When I was a little girl I saw these things. I always got impressions. I suppose there are thousands of people in the world who have this impression of seeing a color around a person. One friend of mine says that when he goes to a lecture he occasionally can see these colors."

The chairman of the seminar then said, "A question is asked here, how many here in the room have seen auras, or think they have—a show of hands? Seven." Dora recalled that there were at least twenty people in attendance, so that a large percentage of people at that presentation claimed to have seen auras.

A female psychiatrist from the University of Pittsburgh School of Medicine asked Dora, "I just wondered whether you would explain further your idea of how habit patterns are changed. Habit patterns are very tricky things to change."

Dora replied, "I think a person has to be first aware of the habit pattern. That is the first requisite. If you don't know you have it you can't alter it. Many people don't wish to change, and until they realize that, they can't change. Most of the people I see are pretty sick. People who are very sick sometimes are willing to try to change. That is the beginning of everything. Some people don't want to change, and there is nothing I can do about it. A desperate state of mind sometimes is the beginning of really wanting to change. Then I can persuade them to see what these habit patterns are. But it is very hard for a person really to make themselves over. Only the total man can do that."

A psychiatrist asked, "After you have discovered this resentment, where do the people go to get rid of it? I wish to know whether just simply talking about it gets rid of it."

Dora said, "In some cases it is possible to help a person by talking. If a person is very sick, I suggest that they go to psychiatrists or to a minister." Dr. Bengtsson again interjected on Dora's behalf:

> I wonder if I could just say something because I am afraid there is a little misunderstanding here. I think some of you have gotten the idea when Dora says that she is not a healer, that some of these things are on an irreligious basis. I think that Dora is so sincerely religious in the finest sense of the word that she doesn't want people to fool themselves by stereotyped phraseology and the kind of thing that is so easy to say, and then put it off in one place.
>
> Religion to Dora is, if she will excuse me for saying so, an every minute, every day consecration of her life. I do know Dora, and I can say that I have met very few people who have even a fraction of her consecration to her idea of the highest, and her love and sincere desire never to criticize or judge a person, but to help him or her to see what is the failure in the structure of their personality, so that they can live their life happily and creatively.
>
> St. Paul says that the fruits of the spirit are love and joy. If you worked with Dora even for half an hour you would never

doubt her love. And anybody that I have ever brought to see her has gone away a happier individual. Dora is so anxious to be honest about not being a healer, about not claiming powers for that kind of thing, that she has unconsciously misled you. She is anxious to show you what the personality can do to block the life of the Spirit that she really believes in.[14]

Dora met several other people during the seminars. One of them was Hugh Lynn Cayce, who represented the Association for Research and Enlightenment in Virginia Beach, Virginia, founded by his father, the famous "sleeping prophet" Edgar Cayce. Dora said that she had met Edgar Cayce only briefly and so did not know him well. "But," she added, "I've been to the Cayce Foundation quite often. And one of my best friends and patients really—I have done a lot for her—is on the Cayce Board. They have very fine people, and they have a big following. They go in for healing but they are so pious that I didn't feel comfortable. I don't like piousness [sic] very much, and that's bad of me."[15]

At Wainwright House, Dora met Ambrose and Olga Worrall, two devoutly Christian healers. Otis Rice, the chairman of that session of the healing seminar, described Ambrose Worrall as "a business man, and not a clergyman or a psychiatrist or a doctor, but he is a healer."[16]

Worrall was educated as an engineer, and as a businessman was responsible for negotiating and managing contracts for a firm in Baltimore. Dora recalled, "Ambrose Worrall and I really became friends. He was a Scotsman. He was a man like my own [father] and didn't exaggerate. So I used to come with him—he didn't ask me to—while he did the healing; I sat next to him and watched him. I think he had a tremendous intuition. I don't think he said that he had clairvoyance."[17]

Though Worrall was a deeply religious man, his ability to analyze and then clearly describe his healing approach without reference to Christianity was instructive to Dora. He discussed many aspects of healing in a methodical manner, including the steps or phases of his treatment process. His terminology differed from hers and from those of other healers, but there were similarities. Dora understood the complexity of the human being as a system of energies, while Worrall referred to them as "dimensions"; for example, he spoke of the sleep state as another "dimension." His term "Mind" correlated with what Dora referred to as "mental and emotional fields and beyond." His term the "spiritual body"—a duplicate of the physical body that includes the various senses—corresponded with Dora's use of the terms "etheric field" or "vital body."

Worrall's term "Spirit" corresponded closely with Dora's use of the term "Higher Self," or "buddhi and beyond." Dora often used the term "soul" when speaking of the Higher Self with Jews or Christians, but she avoided religious terms as much as possible. She did not describe the state of consciousness associated with the Higher Self except to say that it is unitive and associated with peace. At its deepest levels, it is considered beyond words and cognitive constructs—ineffable. Worrall stated that it is "the most exalted. It is in perfect attunement with the Divine Essence, the Omniscient, the Omnipresent, the Omnipotent. It is probably a part of God. If permitted, it will illuminate the mind with knowledge."[18]

Where Worrall spoke of "illumination of the mind with knowledge," Dora spoke of "higher levels of intuition." He associated "the Spirit" with awareness that is capable of recognizing truth that is 'beyond' conceptual cognition. Moreover, he said, "The reason that better results are not obtained from our spiritual efforts today is that the Spirit is looked upon as something afar off, either a vague, powerful ruler more to be feared perhaps than loved, an invention to satisfy the masses, or something entirely beyond our comprehension. . . . It would be better if we realized that our needs are already known, that guidance is already available, and that, with the help of the instructions received from the Spirit during silence, we can with diligence and effort solve our problems or reach our goal. I believe that all spiritual healing is achieved by the power of the Spirit operating through diverse channels upon the minds of the healer and his patient."[19]

Worrall acknowledged the role of multiple factors in extrasensory perception on the grounds that physical vision alone cannot explain perception-at-a-distance. During the seminars, participants learned that there are various types of extended perception, some of which do not depend upon the five senses. Dora's perception of the aura required the use of her eyes, but her perception of the other levels of consciousness depended more upon telepathy and intuition.

After Worrall explained his treatment approach, he practiced what he called "attunement" with the patient. As he described it, "the one thing that makes attunement possible is the fact that the Spirit in the patient and the Spirit in myself are in perfect harmony. This must be so because they are one."[20] That view was consistent with Dora's view of the Higher Self, which she later called the inner self, and with her view of human beings as localizations of interpenetrating fields of energy.

Worrall said with humility that after thirty-five years of treating patients, "healing works in mysterious ways. I don't know how it works. I do whatever I am impressed to do." He was a man of such faith that when asked to speak to the religious element in his work, he said, "I am not qualified to talk on religion, being a layman. But I have people who come to me and expect that I am going to say a prayer over them. . . . Why should I pray and ask for something to be done from a source that already knows what to do and is willing to do it, providing you allow it to work, providing the conditions are correct?"

Worrall continued with more details of the way his approach varied from some of the other healers who had spoken.

> I focus my attention. I am a receiving unit. I am listening as for a telephone call. I am expecting a knock on the door. The Presence is there. It knows what to do. And if the conditions are right, it can heal. I would not want to impose any of my own thoughts on the subject, because the Power, which is going to do the work, already knows all things. I wouldn't want to be so presumptuous as to feel that I could add anything to it. I believe that you should have a religious type of mind, that you should live always in that condition in which you are trying to do the greatest good for the greatest number. And if you live continuously in that particular frequency or wave length, after a time you no longer feel the necessity to tune out the things on these other wave lengths. It is a matter of tuning in continuously to the source of the divine Power. And that tuning in continuously makes you sure that it exists, which may be the adding of knowledge to faith.[21]

Worrall spoke about healing and the importance of being without desire for reward. To people who offered him money or gifts, he would say, "'If you want to give some money just give it to charity.' Something inside of me just wouldn't let me take it." He went on:

> The more you give the more you receive. The vessel must be empty before it can be refilled. As you empty the vessel the channel becomes wider, over the years, until the force can flow

> through with tremendous power. As for remuneration, I have
> been in positions many times where remuneration would have
> been very acceptable. . . . I was offered a house one time.
> I didn't own a house. In fact, at that time it was a little difficult
> to pay the rent. But I didn't take the house.[22]

Dora also followed a similar practice in her life. She did not encourage remuneration of any kind and flatly refused payments. On one occasion she said to a patient who insisted on giving that the money should be donated to a charitable organization, and she suggested a worthy group. Even that was a rare occurrence.

Dr. Bengtsson had a similar practice when her patients offered gifts. She once accepted a bowl of chicken soup when she made a house call to a family in Ossining. Although she was a vegetarian, she made an exception to her diet because she realized the hardship the family had assumed to offer her the food.[23]

Worrall told the group at Wainwright House that it was important for either the patient or someone interested in the patient to *ask* for his help. He viewed the request as though a door were being opened. Similarly, Dora told participants at Wainwright House that she did not observe or assess out of curiosity. She waited for people to request help.

The guidelines Worrall presented to the group during that Third Spiritual Healing Seminar served Dora and her associates in their later healing work. Worrall said that he would not do any of the following: "1) practice hypnosis, 2) pry into personal affairs, 3) make inquiries as to religious affiliations, 4) discourage the patient from seeking medical help, 5) tell the patient he must have faith and believe in my theory, or 6) take remuneration for my services."[24]

In treating patients at a distance, Worrall said that he gained greater attunement with a patient by looking at a photograph or holding jewelry or something else that belonged to the person. "Knowledge of the things that are wrong comes to me sometimes when the patient is hundreds of miles away, patients I have never seen," Worrall said. "And it comes as an inspiration; it is just knowledge, there is no question about it, and it is done by simply directing the attention to the location where the patient may be, and sometimes not even that, because sometimes I don't know where the patient is located. It is difficult to explain. It is knowledge without experience, approaching the instinctive perhaps."[25] Dora very occasionally employed psychometry—seeing or holding an object that belonged to the person in order to gain sensitivity and an intuitive link with the person. But like Worrall, she did not require an image or object to attune to a patient.

One example of the way Dora helped illustrates that she could be *en rapport* with a patient who was a hundred or more miles away. The anecdote is unrelated to the Spiritual Healing Seminars but illustrates how her perception-at-a-distance and timely counseling benefited a troubled teenager. Dora helped a teenage girl over the course of several years following the start of the girl's disturbing memories of early childhood sexual abuse by an uncle. The girl's mother, a nurse, arranged for her daughter to meet with Dora. For several years afterward, Dora phoned and often, with urgency, asked to speak to the girl. Her sensitivity to the girl's intermittent acute anxiety—from a distance of over a hundred miles—contributed to the healing process. Dora timed many of her supportive phone calls to particularly stressful days during the girl's recovery.[26]

During the fifth healing seminar at Wainwright House, a kindergarten teacher named Miss Adams shared anecdotal evidence of the powerful role of intention in healing and how she learned from mistakes in her early attempts to help. On two occasions she had prayed fervently, not only that she could heal, but that she could take the patients' suffering onto herself. She said that she did indeed assume some of the patients' symptoms and became so ill that in both cases she required medical care.[27]

A physician in the group, Dr. Michael Ash, responded to her claim and said, "This business of taking upon yourself these things, I think, is a reality. We did discuss this morning that we, in our professional work, deliberately 'mirror' upon ourselves certain things, but we *only* mirror them. We can see it objectively and not get so tied up in it."[28] Olga Worrall added that she and her husband counseled the young woman about the importance of avoiding martyrdom and warned against asking that illnesses come into one's body. In later decades Dora preferred to teach health care professionals who had already established professional boundaries with those they attempted to help.

Over the course of the Fourth Spiritual Healing Seminar, June 24–26, 1955, Dora distinguished between the various types of phenomena introduced by the seminar chairman, Dr. Cyril C. Richardson of Union Theological Seminary. It was her job to clairvoyantly describe the differences between Eileen Garrett's demonstration of trance mediumship and Ambrose Worrall's demonstration of spiritual healing. Worrall's perspectives and healing approach described above differed markedly from those of Eileen Garrett.

At the end of the session that day, July 25, 1955, the group observed Dr. Laidlaw interview Eileen Garrett while she was in a trance. When the participants reconvened at eight o'clock that evening, Dora spoke about her clairvoyant observations of Garrett during the afternoon session. *Trance medium* is the term for a person who self-induces an altered state of consciousness and allows a disincarnate person to take possession of his or her physical body. There are many differences among mediums, who range from the

amateur to the highly skilled; Dora considered Eileen Garrett
an exceptionally skilled medium. Mrs. Garrett had been invited to
the United States by the American Society for Psychical Research,
was very wealthy, and founded her own research group, the
Parapsychology Foundation, in New York City.

Dora began by describing Eileen Garrett's aura as unusually
weblike:

> It looks like a very fine, natural web of lace. In most of us
> who are not mediumistic, this aura is much more solidly put
> together. . . . Mrs. Garrett, I think, has that to a very remarkable
> degree, and from my limited experience with mediums it
> often goes with a watery constitution. . . . And the whole
> organization of such a person's body is definitely different
> than for most people in this room. When Mrs. Garrett goes in
> trance, it appears to me that she begins to let go her own
> personality; that her own personality is laid aside and another
> person takes possession.
>
> I shall use two terms and I shall explain them. Etheric is this
> invisible part of the aura which really inter-penetrates the
> physical body, which is a body of energy, if you like, and then
> [there is] the body of the emotions which inter-penetrates this
> vital body or etheric body. When Mrs. Garrett went into a
> trance, I could see why it would be an uncomfortable process.
> There is the pressure there of this other person coming in
> from above and her personality going out. The holes for a
> moment are stretched. Even if she is already webby by
> constitution, it probably is uncomfortable to have this feeling
> of stretching taking place, and I think part of the discomfort
> (which I think a great many mediums do go through) is that
> for a moment this webby stuff comes open, as it were.

Also, there is emotional pressure. The possessing entity comes in from the world of the emotions. The link has to be made from that emotional world to this world of etheric. Mrs. Garrett is speaking, but this controlling person is using her vocal cords. Certain connections are made for the time being between this new person and this lacy web. . . . They would be hooked together in the solar plexus. The etheric is hooked together with her physical body.

The personality of Mrs. Garrett withdraws, stands aside, and the controlling person steps in. Of course, the controlling person is only temporarily superimposed upon Mrs. Garrett. . . . It is just hooked to the surface. The difference between the person as we think of ourselves and the superimposing person coming and entering Mrs. Garrett's emotional and visible body is this: We are inside ourselves and this other person is only a little bit within Mrs. Garrett's body, and mostly outside. . . . For the time being his aura is different from Mrs. Garrett's. Mrs. Garrett's aura fundamentally is still there. But it is displaced. Yours and my auras may not be able to be pushed so, but hers has the ability to be pushed aside. They aren't together completely. They are only partially mixed. It is not integration of the two in any way. It is a definite superimposition of the other personality, and then it is as if this other personality assumes a form. You can see the personality. You are asking if he assumes a recognizable form . . . and surely he does.

This particular person is of oriental cast, but light. I think he would be essentially very refined. Some Orientals have typically refined faces. . . . And there is a feel or an expression of a very positive personality, but of his time. . . . He has a sense of humor and a sense of wisdom combined, and I have a feeling of great refinement.[29]

The chairman then asked Dora to discuss what she called the "hookup" between the auras of the medium and the disincarnate person. Dora noted that the mind of the medium, though not absent, is passive and not under the control of the medium.

> The solar plexus is one of the main organs. I was interested in it because some people talked today about the subject of possessions, didn't they? I think the solar plexus is one of the links where some of these beings come in. It may not be something evil; it may be something good. Through control of this center, which has a powerful effect upon the physical body and our nervous control, a person who is evil-possessed can do all sorts of unpleasant things to a person's body. . . . I have seen a few people who have unpleasant entities attached to them in that way and I have always noticed it came through the solar plexus.[30]

In a keynote address for the Theosophical Society in 1980, Dora described the effect of mediumistic activities on the health of the medium. She observed similar physical factors among mediums that she called a "watery nature" and noted a tendency toward fluid retention and kidney disease. She said that mediumship "doesn't mean that you're attracting unpleasant entities but you have to have 'a build.' I've known quite a few of them [including] Eileen Garrett who probably was the most well-known medium today. She was a medium and I'm not. I use myself and I never lose consciousness. I don't let other people come into me or give me messages. I'm in complete control of myself."[31]

On another occasion, when asked if she could function as a medium, Dora said, "No, I'm not [mediumistic] by temperament and do not wish [it]." She added, "I'm in complete control at all times. If you are a medium, you're seldom in complete control. And I'm in complete control of my intellectual faculties too."[32]

As early as 1955 the seeds were planted for Dora's future efforts in teaching others to heal. In response to the proposition that healing could be learned and developed, Olga Worrall said that she herself had "the gift of healing," but that her husband, Ambrose, instructed her in "how to use it intelligently without emotion and to keep it under control."[33] Olga Worrall provided anecdotal evidence to Dora that education specifically designed for healers was beneficial. She claimed that most of the healers she met at Wainwright House and later in California rejected the view that healing can be taught; they believed that it was a gift from God.

Wainwright House provided a unique supportive environment in which Dora could share her rationale for her frequent use of incorrect grammar and occasional mispronunciation of select words when speaking to patients and when teaching. She said that she did so in order to actively engage the listener in the learning process. "If I see these emotional patterns, I talk to the person about them. *I am very careful not to use words people are too accustomed to.* You might think that is a bad thing for me to do, but if they think they understand, they are lost. *It is much better at first for the person to work a little harder with me so that it is a working together, you see.*"[34]

A physician from Manhattan asked whether Dora had clairvoyantly observed a person going to sleep. "Does a psyche, etheric double, or something seem to leave them in sleep?"

Dora responded, "Part of the person, yes, does go out. When a person is normally asleep, I don't think as much of him goes as when Mrs. Garrett is in psychic trance. When we go to sleep nice and comfortably it isn't a painful process. We don't suffer from going to sleep. Nobody, I hope, takes possession of us. Mrs. Garrett's trance is not exactly the same thing as going to sleep. I really don't think it is an identical process. When a person goes to sleep, the vital body, [etheric body], I think, stays close to the body. I don't think too much happens to it. But part of us, the emotional part, does leave."

The chairman, Dr. Earl Loomis, then asked Dora to explain how she helped physicians and patients through what he called "her healing gifts." She replied:

What I do is this. I look. . . . When I say "look" in this case, I personally do not feel that I can distinguish between telepathy and clairvoyance. In my case, at least, the two work together. You get the impression and then you proceed. The thing is one to me. Before I start, I am quiet for a moment. In this work, I do feel completely and absolutely impersonal. It has nothing to do with me. Whether somebody believes or whether somebody listens to me is unimportant. I feel that very strongly.

Then I get some focusing. I think "focusing" is a good word because in a kaleidoscope you really turn the thing, isn't that so, and you see. It feels almost like focusing. And when I have achieved the sense of quiet, I feel this sense of perception. It is not in my eyes, because I don't really use my eyes. The center of perception, if you like, is located somewhere in between my eyes here. That I can say.

When I see a person, the usual procedure that I go through is this: From my point of view I have to talk about different levels, I am sad to say, and it is not simple. The first level I describe as the etheric body. It is part of something which is invisible to most people, which inter-penetrates our physical body. When I focus my eyes, I can see where there is a blockage in the person, whether it is the stomach, heart, lungs, spine—whatever a person is sick from. When I first look at it, I always look at the person quickly, as it were, to see from my point of view if there is something which is out of rhythm. Rhythm has something to do with it, if there is something out of order. It appears to me like a grey spot, a dark spot, but it is out of harmony, out of link. Going from the person's solar plexus [or] the person's heart, I quickly trace where there is something wrong. Many people who are very nervous, for instance, have what I call spasms in their stomach. It gives them all sorts of symptoms. I can see the intestines, and I can see, as it were, a blockage in a person's intestines. Each organ has what I call its own rhythm.

Like Mr. Worrall, I never studied books on anatomy in my life. I get a flash that appears before me. That is how I see. I never give a name to a sickness. I deliberately don't do that, even if I get a hunch about it. It is for the doctors to say. It is much better for me to say where I think the person is sick than for me to call it cancer or any other known disease. If I see a person who has something wrong with his kidneys, I describe what I think is wrong with the person's kidneys. Whatever I think, I don't give it a name. Sometimes a person, for instance, may have sinus trouble. Very often I can see that the sinuses are filled but that that isn't the primary cause of infection. Very often that has nothing to do with the primary source of whatever is making the person sick. I try to trace it. That is the first thing.

And I am very interested in this: I am able to perceive the endocrine glands in a person. . . . They have a powerful effect on the rhythm, the balance of the whole system. They affect different parts, and I can see like a minus or plus that shows up in the rhythm. . . .

Now, the second part, and it is again like the changing of the focus that I do, I look at a person's emotions. Now, how do I do that? First of all, we are all constantly breathing, and by our feelings colors are produced, but I am not particularly interested in that, although it gives me some clue. Most of the people I see are sick and they, therefore, have developed a pattern, a habit pattern, which I can perceive. I have a feeling of being *en rapport* with the person who is in front of me. . . .

If you have felt something for ten or fifteen years, [as in] some of this mental illness, it is as if they built a pattern image. The moment they begin to feel something, they don't really feel what is spontaneous for them at the moment. The moment they come into that area, they are not themselves. They fall [instead] in that habit pattern, and almost always the aura, the energy falls in that habit pattern of isolation, of feeling hostile, or any of these things which a person feels.

Dora then explained a significant aspect of her counseling method. She attempted, she said, to lead the person who is sick to recognize or discover something about himself.

Now, if the person is very sick, when you pick a sore spot they are going to back out of it. They are going to say, "That isn't so." Nobody wants to be hit on the "sore spot" right away. I walk around it, and it makes them break loose. It is not a one-way talking. The sick person does a great deal of the talking. We walk around it until they have said in their own words, and they have agreed with me. . . . It is really amusing because the first time they say "No, it isn't so." Then we tackle it again in such a way that the person has said exactly and identically the same thing. I have experienced it and then they have experienced it.

[Initially] they don't know they agree with my words. They don't know what I am talking about. If a person sees what I am talking about and they say the same thing they have said "no" to, then it becomes a real experience to them, doesn't it? Then, if they can see it for themselves, whatever it is, I can make suggestions about how they can proceed if they wish to help themselves to cure it. That, I think, is roughly how I work.

Dr. Loomis summarized, "You would say that the three stages were the perception of what tissues or organs or parts of the body are having trouble; the second step would be what the emotional difficulties are; and the third step would be helping them to recognize their own emotional troubles and somehow, to use the social worker term, 'work through them' and come around to direct contact with themselves, and in that process they get better. Is that the way?"

Dora replied, "I can feel what a person is feeling, so I describe to him what he does from the moment he gets up until three hours after he quits work. I can show him the relationship between his disease and what he has agreed to about his feelings. That pulls him up. If a person can visualize what he does and what he would do if he wishes to get well, that, of course, is the big thing. That will always pull him up."

Dr. Bengtsson added her own observation about Dora's patient interactions. "They always get salted down with a great deal of laughter. I have never in my life seen what is supposed to be a research clinic where there is so much laughter, and it is all spontaneous. And I think when they laugh like that they soak in a lot of Dora's wisdom and it works very well." Dora continued:

We have [a] good time. Of course, they all think it is very queer, so that is why I never look at the person. When I see a person for the first time, I don't know but what he sometimes really dislikes seeing me. He thinks I am terrible. So when he enters the room, I don't look at him. I don't look at him with eyes open and gaze at him. I make a practice of looking the other way until we get together, and then I look at him, and he forgets I am looking at him physically. People think I am going to uncover their dreadful secrets. They sometimes come in shaky. But within five minutes I am able to make them feel completely at home, and then I am not very serious, and people do laugh. I think it is good for people to laugh.

Dr. Bengtsson added that she and Dora occasionally provided dietary advice to patients who were not absorbing nutrients well. Dora then turned the conversation toward an enduring interest of hers: the "sensitive child." Here, however, she was not talking about children who were admonished for seeing fairies, but about those who suffer more than less sensitive children when two parents quarrel repeatedly.

Some people have no protection. I think children are in that category. I am awfully concerned. I have seen a lot of disturbed children. They worry me the most. You and I, let's say, we are perfectly healthy. We are all mixed up together in this room, so in our aura structures, we take in and we throw off. When we are healthy we take in one another's emotions and we throw off a good part of them because we are able to. But when a person is sick, other people's emotions begin to affect him. Don't you think that is true, Mr. Worrall?

Worrall responded, "I think you can take on the other person's condition if you are not aware of the condition. It is possible."

Dora then made a distinction between basically healthy people who are highly sensitive to the emotions of others and those who are mentally or emotionally disturbed and have a psychic ability.

> I mean, if people begin to get sick, that they are [then] affected more by other people, or don't you think that is true? Some people have constitutions in which they have very little protection and so when they are in the hospital, or if they are in with a lot of people, they become affected by other people's emotions. They don't put it [in words] that way, but it keeps them in a state of nervousness, and I think particularly, the children. They are powerfully affected by their parents' emotions. It is almost like waves which go through them. They have no words, no explanations for them.
>
> Some people who are disturbed do have a psychic ability. Now, the psychic ability is, let's say, one-third correct but the other two-thirds are distorted by their emotion. They do have perception. They are bright, they are able, but they are not aware of the distortion. They do not discriminate the two-thirds distortion from the one time when their insight is true. So very often they build a lot of their lives on what you might say is genuine intuition, but they fall down the times they do not perceive truly. Do you think that is true, Dr. Laidlaw?

Dr. Laidlaw responded, "I think patients with emotional ills— I speak more from experience with the psychoneurotic and psychotic whom I have more chance to study—I think they are often extremely sensitive, but their sensitivity is out of focus and distorted by their emotional illness."

Dora was asked if sensitive people are protected by prayers or thoughts directed toward them. She responded:

> If *you* think of prayer and praying for somebody to heal, I consider that "sending energy towards the person." I think you can help other people very much and protect them in that way. It can either be new color or a new energy. Certainly, it is a new energy which enters into that person. If a person needs protection, for instance, the ends of such a person's aura look sort of caged-in or droopy. New energy helps him to stick out the ends of the aura and protect himself. It releases a certain energy in that person so that for the time being he can develop his own protective mechanism.

When Dora was asked about different colors and rhythms in the aura, she distinguished between colors associated with emotions and those associated with what she considered spiritual qualities. She also shared observations that she later published in *The Personal Aura*. In that book the artist's illustrations depict Dora's observation that emotional difficulties tend to sink to the bottom of the aura and give it a "muddy" appearance, while emotions such as unselfish love, altruism, and intellectual yearning for truth appear as striations of light, subtle colors at the top of the aura.

> When I perceive a person I see a color and . . . most of the people have muddy colors. All the difficulties are more or less in muddy colors at the bottom. When it comes to rhythms, everybody has a different rhythm. The aura in most cases lights up in its colors in the different strata. Every person is unique, so I don't suppose there are any two auras alike. If a person is upset, if he feels love, if he feels hostility—all these

things come out in different colors. Above the emotional there is again a different rhythm. If you like, there are the person's spiritual qualities. By spiritual qualities I also mean that the colors are much lighter. They aren't so solid. They aren't so dense.

Red always stands for anger and rose stands for love, and if you see a great deal of grey and red in a person's aura in different patterns, it stands for depression and anger.[35]

The final day of the 1955 seminar began with a prayer and silent meditation and was chaired by an Episcopal priest. There was discussion of the writings of Carl von Reichenbach, a German chemist from the mid-nineteenth century. He used the term "odic force," which the presenter correlated with the etheric field. The presenter also described ways she had experimented with that force through the use of magnets and crystals.

Dr. Bengtsson was then asked to share a summary of the ways in which she and Dora worked together. She gave a condensed presentation of how she met Dora beginning with the first meditation class she attended:

Dora has an amazing gift in working with people. She helps them to understand themselves. I had known her for a little over a year before I had the slightest intimation that she had any unusual faculty at all. I happened to just walk in, as I might come in now to this group and found she was reading auras in a small class of people who were interested in developing the practice of meditation. She happened to be reading the auras of people whom I knew she didn't know. I was amazed at the accuracy with which she told them their particular strength and their particular weakness. Most of the time she doesn't bother with your strengths because they take care of themselves, but she tells you the little things that inhibit the thing that you really want to accomplish.

So she had never seen me when my main weaknesses were most evident because I was then in a group where I just kept still because I was so interested in things. I asked her if she would read my aura. She hit upon the things that make me lose my energy, and I knew she couldn't have found it out from anyone else. I said to her very naively, "You have an amazing gift. Would you be willing to work with doctors?" having no idea what a hard shell the medical profession would be to crack. She said, "You know, I should, but I think you will find this is premature."

Anyway, in order to get the material I began bringing cases to her. She knew my field but I deliberately took people who had a number of other things the matter with them that would never be considered related to allergy. Time and time again I was amazed with what she saw. . . . I have brought her people, for instance, from the clinic who didn't have too high a mentality, for it isn't only just the physical thing I want. I generally bring her people who are physically ill but who also are sort of lost for something to be interested in.

Dora has an amazing faculty of making everything light. I mean before the session is over, everybody is having a good time. She is absolutely impersonal as far as she, herself, is concerned, but she is personal as far as the person is concerned. Her interest in getting them to go one step higher always gives them a sense of new life. She can meet with anybody just exactly where he or she is.

She made diagnoses on people whom other people sent her, patients I didn't know, and she would say to me, "You should have a basal metabolism [blood test] done on this person because I think that is the crux of the matter," and when it would be done, it would be as Dora said. Over and over again when she got into the emotional level she would see the hookup between the block in the etheric double and certain habit patterns, and she would tell them some simple things to do. . . . She would enable the person to get hold of himself or herself so that they could do things. Sometimes she would say, "This person needs regular visits to a psychiatrist because he can't pull himself up alone." And she would then suggest somebody, or have me suggest somebody. Sometimes she would suggest further medical treatment, but always she gives the person something that gives him a sense of light.

This was an outgrowth, as I said, of her interest in meditation. In addition to doing this work, she conducts a class in meditation. She has people feel harmony. Then she has them feel love for somebody that they really love. And as she watches the group aura she can tell whether we are united, whether there is harmony or disharmony. All that lower control of the personality is the preparation for meditation.

In addition to seeing auras, she has the faculty of seeing spiritual personalities of the great religions. We know there are angelic forces, forces that work on a different kind of evolution but also doing the will of life, if you want to put it in that term. She tells us that there is a whole section of angels who work close to human beings in doing healing and that they use our human love; it gives them a link so that they can use that in connection with the healing of the patient.

I must say—whether it is due to my imagination I don't know, but I don't think so, because the others feel the same thing—that when we do that group meditation you can actually feel a cleansing energy. There is a force in group meditation for healing which she can watch clairvoyantly step by step, and it does work.

Dora never puts in a claim for healing, she is so afraid of misleading people. You can see for yourselves that she is a most beautiful, unselfish character; but along with that she is a person of great wisdom, and she really, from her observation of many cases, has a true scientific understanding of the way these things work, the way blocks originate.

There was an old lady, a most delightful character, but very, very rigid in her ideas of everything. She read a great deal of oriental literature, and instead of meditating on God, she meditated on Brahma. She had made a little image of her Brahma which was so strong in her aura that Dora said she completely prevented anything coming in that had to do with Brahma or a higher nature because it was her own little god that she had made which actually hindered the very energy of Brahma from coming in.[36]

Dr. Laidlaw challenged participants who believed that religious faith was the primary characteristic in healers:

Any plans for a further study of healing would be diametrically different if we were thinking in terms of a rare gift or in terms of a universal phenomenon. It is obvious that we all, actually, are not healers. Now what is the difference? What makes the healer? What differentiates him from the well-wishing person who nevertheless cannot be a healer?

I am not sure that I have anything near the answer to that, but I should just like very briefly to indicate some psychological factors which may be important in such a differential. The average person in approaching this subject of healing, well-wishing though he may be, tends to trip over his own ego. The examples that we have had of people preeminent in the art of healing—Mr. Worrall, Eileen Garrett, and Dora—all have as a common denominator a selflessness, an ability to lose self, to set aside the critical faculty which we all in our educational system have had drummed into us through our formative periods.

The ability to merge with the universe, as it were, to lose the personal "I," apparently is a very fundamental thing in this healing process. And, if that is true, it is something which we with our egos sticking out all over us can, with sufficient zeal and determination and application, alter considerably in ourselves.

Another indispensable factor which delineates the healer from the well-wisher is the characteristic of faith. Here, again, I think the average person may always be sort of looking over his shoulder at himself while engaged in a healing attempt, and one millimeter of doubt can upset the whole applecart oftentimes. Certainly, I think this is in line with the teachings of Jesus who indicates that with faith—faith full and overflowing—our abilities are limitless. With faith you can remove mountains.

Those of us who have been brought up in a scientific background tend to trip over our own doubts just as we trip over our own egos. So, I should feel that for the average person to thoughtfully attempt to encourage and develop his own innate healing abilities, he should concentrate upon the effacing of the ego and the increasing and deepening of the personal faith. I am not talking about doctrine; I am

not talking about faith from the standpoint of what the
Christian believes the relationship of God and man to be. I am
talking about faith in the ability to heal.[37]

Dora continued to attend meetings at Wainwright House for
many years, though not the spiritual healing seminars. She got to
know Laurens van der Post, Aldous Huxley, Shunryu Suzuki, and
many other people who influenced her. She regarded the initial
healing seminars as seminal in her development of her own abilities
as a healer, and they clearly influenced the way she taught others
about healing.

Astonishingly, during the years the seminars were held, Dora did
not realize the significance they had in her life. She later said,
"I never would have thought this was predestined; I was bored very
often, if you wish to know the truth. I really learned a very great
deal. I don't know that I ever would have gotten interested in healing if I hadn't gone."

At age ninety-three Dora said that karma played a part in
her participation in the Wainwright House healing seminars.
"I think some things which are important—they change our life—
are fordained. ["Fordained" was Dora's word for "preordained."]
I suppose my going to Wainwright House was fordained.
I think certain things are absolutely set but how you work [them]
out—that is free. . . . My going to Wainwright House really has
opened a completely new world and a lot of people are affected
because I taught them Therapeutic Touch. So I think that was
predestined."

Going into a little more detail about karma, she added, "And I
suppose the person you marry is 'fordained.' But then how you
work out that relationship, there is free will. [Some] people have
[sufficient] money; I suppose that's predestined too. . . . I think

particularly if it's a violent death, that I think, is all "fordained" because you're working out your [negative] karma. But I mean, how you react to all sorts of things and people you meet isn't in your karma. You have karma, but how you work it out in a relationship is up to you."[38]

Chapter Eight

Dora's Turning Point

Dora had no immediate opportunities to apply what she learned about healing. She had a busy life with Fritz's work. John Kunz mentioned the stimulating intellectual environment they created. "My father was one of the most knowledgeable people I have met in more subjects than you can imagine. And the Integrative Education movement my father started had them in contact with some of the leading scholars in all sorts of fields in the country." Despite the effect of the McCarthy era on the intellectual environment, the 1950s and '60s were an exciting time. The economy was improving, and new ideas were being shared worldwide through telephones, television, and improvements in travel. According to John, "In her education . . . it was what she read and the people she associated with; she read a vast amount."[1]

Dolores Krieger, who would later work with Dora to create Therapeutic Touch, described her as brilliant: "She was extremely well read. Dora used to bring home literally armloads of books every single week from the Port Chester Library. They became an excellent library because of the fact that Dora and Fritz would be requesting these books. She would not only read it, she would understand it. In a way she's a self-made woman because she never went to an official school—never in her life—so that whatever she's learned, she's learned in a different way. I have never once seen a person of unusual caliber—an academician, a scientist or whatever—who has not been enthralled by the depth of her insight in whatever field they're talking about. I've never seen her at a loss for words, never once."[2]

Dora met her match in brilliance with Shafica Karagulla, a neuropsychiatrist who had immigrated to New York from Canada. Dora learned more about her own sensitivity through her participation as a research subject for Karagulla. Up to that point, she had refused requests from the Society for Psychical Research to participate as a research subject.

Their first meeting occurred at Dora and Fritz's house in Port Chester in 1956.[3] Karagulla had been in medicine for sixteen years when they met. She had become a member of the Royal College of Physicians in Edinburgh, where she conducted research in electrical shock therapy. Following that, she worked in association with Wilder Penfield, the respected neurosurgeon at McGill University. He studied the effect of electrical stimulation to the brain of conscious patients. She had been particularly interested in patients' reports of hallucinations when particular areas of their brains were electrically stimulated. Were altered states of consciousness—whether through electrical stimulation of the brain, disease, or drugs—the results of disorder in brain function? Were all visions the result of illusion or delusion? Karagulla's research interest in neuropsychiatry broadened, and she moved to the United States to pursue areas of interest in greater depth.

She continued to practice as a psychiatrist and was assistant professor at the State University of New York in the department of psychiatry. She attributed her research interests to Edgar Cayce, who allowed his sessions to be recorded. A tremendous amount of the data that he provided could not be explained through the functions of the brain and neurological system alone. Following her review of some of the material at Cayce's research center in Virginia Beach, she wrote, "What struck me most out of all the evidence was Cayce's ability in certain states of consciousness to describe accurately what he 'saw' at distances of hundreds of miles. What he saw was confirmed over and over again as clear and accurate information."[4]

Karagulla was unable to attribute Cayce's perceptions to hallucination and insanity. Challenged by the anomaly that Cayce represented, she was not deterred by the lack of technology necessary to identify and quantify similar capacities in other people.

The recording of Karagulla's first meeting with Dora was surprisingly devoid of small talk. Emily Sellon, John Kunz, and Dolores Krieger interjected occasionally, and at one point Emily served tea. Both Karagulla and Dora displayed a sense of humor; Dora's laugh is apparent, but Karagulla expressed the serious intent of a busy professional. She was assessing Dora as a potential research subject.

Perhaps mirroring Dora's preference for short sentences, Karagulla led the assessment, and almost the entire meeting consisted of dialogue such as the following:

Karagulla: Now what else? Have you ever seen people who are acromegalic?

Dora: Is that too much pituitary?

Karagulla: Yes.

Dora: No.

Karagulla: You haven't. Have you seen anybody in whom the pituitary has been completely destroyed

and removed? These are the things that interest me greatly to know what changes occur in
these–

Dora: I've seen people with operations on part of the
thyroid but I don't think I have seen anybody
with complete removal of either the thyroid or
the pituitary.

Karagulla: You haven't seen any of them?

Dora: Not with total removal. With just some operations, you know what I mean, but not totally
removed.

Karagulla: You haven't seen any patients in whom the
pineal gland has been removed? [At that time,
the pineal was still considered a vestigial
artifact that, like the tonsils, was no longer
necessary for modern humans. Further
research showed that it produces a chemical–
melatonin–essential for regulating sleep.]

Dora: Pineal gland? No.

Karagulla: That's supposed to be the "center of the soul."
(Dolores Krieger laughs.)

Karagulla: I'd be very much interested to know what
changes occur in those instances.

Dora: I've looked at mice (laughing).

Karagulla: I'm not interested in mice.

Dora: I'm looking at little mice and all the changes in
cancer (laughing).

Karagulla:	Yes, what are you seeing in them? (Dora is laughing.) Are you seeing anything in them?
Dora:	Yes, certainly mice have things like we have; they have some of these chakras and they have all that sort of—the pituitary. They are so minute but I've been watching some of them. They're so minute; they're just like little dots of everything.
Karagulla:	Can you magnify them at will?
Dora:	Yes, to some extent.

Karagulla's question about Dora's ability to magnify what she saw in the mice is important, because magnification is regarded as a type of higher sense perception. It is considerably rarer than clairvoyance of the emotional or etheric fields. The ability to magnify is associated with Leadbeater's research for *Occult Chemistry*, a book he wrote in collaboration with Mrs. Besant that will be mentioned later. Dora said that magnification of an object requires intense concentration for long hours. Leadbeater's research for *Occult Chemistry* also required knowledge of chemistry and physics. Dora lacked the requisite education in chemistry to attempt to replicate the research, and she said that she decided at an early age not to do that kind of research.

Karagulla's questions for Dora continued at a rapid pace, and Dora responded quickly and succinctly. Her assessment of human development associated with the crown chakra was significant to Karagulla's study of higher sense perception. Dora communicated that she could clairvoyantly assess the degree and type of higher sense perception in a person.

Karagulla:	Now if we take the top chakra, how well-developed is it in the average human being? You don't see it?
Dora:	Yes, but it isn't very well developed.
Karagulla:	Now do you see any coloring in it?
Dora:	It depends upon the person. If there's a lot of color [in the crown chakra], that would mean high development. And if there isn't much color in it—and that's in most cases—not so much.[5]

Karagulla not only accepted Dora as a subject, she asked to work with her for twelve hours a week. Karagulla was exacting, and had she not been gentle and what Dora called "cosmopolitan," she might be described as unrelenting in her focused attention to detail. Dora was not her only subject. Karagulla compared one sensitive's assessment to that of another. She compared an assessment of Dora to an earlier assessment of her and observed environmental conditions that affected the sensitivity of the subjects. She catalogued the various types of sensitivities and attempted to determine whether the act of perceiving could be broken down into a series of steps.

Dora contributed to Karagulla's research over a period of several years. Dora later said, "All clairvoyants are unique and they all draw on their own experiences to express their clairvoyance. You look at it from your point of view. Everybody in the world puts his own point of view in; that applies to clairvoyants too. I don't think that two people practically ever see the same thing. Your individual background affects your interpretation; that seems reasonable."[6]

The research was painstaking, requiring, in Dora's words, "a lot of concentration, focusing and concentration." Karagulla noted that "sensitives" were unable to work for more than two to three hours at a time and still maintain accuracy. Clairvoyant investigation of the etheric, according to Dora, required more concentration than clairvoyant observation of the aura.

Through the work with Dr. Karagulla, Dora continued to acquire knowledge that proved helpful to her in healing. She met other sensitives and had the opportunity to learn something of their approaches. On two or three occasions, Karagulla conducted joint sessions with Dora and Olga Worrall, whom Dora had known from Wainwright House.[7]

In her book *Breakthrough to Creativity*, published in 1967, Karagulla used the pseudonym "Diane" for Dora in the book. She wrote, "I found in Diane a woman of very exceptional ability with unshakable integrity and a willingness to work on my scientific experiments with untiring dedication. She has the most exceptional ability of any person I have so far tested. She has become a friend as well as a subject of scientific research."[8]

Elsewhere in the book, Karagulla wrote about "Diane's" observation regarding the challenges of working in group settings rather than with individual patients. "When a sensitive is dealing with one person alone he finds it easy to tune in on the things which concern that one person. Where a number of people are sitting close together in a group or meeting it is not so easy. He may be getting flashes of impressions and pictures which are associated with different people. In such a case it may be difficult to sort out the individual person to whom a picture or impression belongs."[9]

In 1965 Dora met Colonel Oskar Estebany at Wainwright House. He lived in Montreal with his family and had been a research subject for Sister Justa Smith, a biochemist, and Dr. Bernard Grad, a neurologist and researcher from Canada, both of whom did pioneering research on energetic healing. Grad was on the advisory council of the Commission for Spiritual Healing, and it was through him that Estebany gave presentations at Wainwright House in August 1965 and again in late November and early December.

Estebany and his family had emigrated from Europe following the failed Hungarian revolution in late October 1956, after which a repressive regime composed of supporters of the Soviet Union took power. During that period nearly a quarter million Hungarians became refugees. Dora said, in her characteristically blunt way, that Estebany had been "thrown out of his own country." He and his family resettled in Canada.

Dora made one of her most insightful commentaries about Estebany when she spoke with a colleague about change and rootedness. Regarding his refugee status, she said, "He never felt disgraced by that but went into the healing practice and had very little money. I think he found his place at another more profound and deeper level. He always had a deep sense of responsibility in everything he did. This may have been a carry-over from his days in the Army. He never lost his rootedness and had a place within himself. He was willing to scrub the floors for his wife with devotion and did not feel degraded by it. He retained the ethics of the Hungarian Army life; that rooted him to some degree. His spiritual values helped him to become rooted and to have a place within himself that was a strong foundation even when his life situation was devastating." Regarding rootedness and its role in personal development, particularly spiritual development, Dora said, "Mr. Estebany achieved that; as an example, he had the altruism and the caring."

Dora also understood that other factors were involved in dramatic and lasting healing, as she acknowledged when telling how Estebany discovered his ability to heal. "Mr. Estebany was a colonel in the Army and he liked it. He had an experience of healing a horse which had to do with synchronicity and karma. He deeply felt the results of his ability and had a deep trust in being able to do healing. His character was changed from being a very rigid army officer and he discovered his healing ability."[10]

A decade earlier, at the Wainwright healing seminars, Ambrose Worrall told a story similar to Estebany's. He realized that he could heal several weeks after his sister fell and hit her chin on a table. As a result of her injury, she suffered from paralysis of the muscles that hold the head erect. As though he were being drawn to the area of infirmity, Worrall placed his hands on his sister's neck and recalled that "in one minute her neck was no longer paralyzed. That was how it started."[11]

Dora and Dr. Bengtsson selected Pumpkin Hollow Farm as a quiet residential setting to assess healing phenomena and the potential to learn to heal. They did not write grants or create a special planning committee. Estebany came from Canada for several weeks each summer for four or five years. He provided treatments to patients, some of whom were members of the New York Theosophical Society or known to Dora or Dr. Bengtsson. Dolores Krieger was present as a research assistant and monitored vital signs and made assessments. Dora and Dolores both commented on Estebany's "deep sense of commitment."

Estebany's general approach to healing was similar to Ambrose Worrall's, although Estebany did not incorporate spinal adjustments or dietary recommendations, as Worrall did. Neither of them used hypnosis or practiced mediumship, and both had great Christian faith. Several factors, including the restrictions of the research methodology and the language barrier, kept Estebany from providing explanations and from trying to be selective about which of the patients he agreed to treat. Both Dora and Dolores said that he often treated a series of patients throughout the day and had to be encouraged to rest.

An approach similar to the Wainwright House Spiritual Healing Seminars was employed at Pumpkin Hollow Farm. Analytical enquiry facilitated by quiet observation of a healing session was followed by group discussion of the case and related topics. Records include patients' statements about changes they perceived as well as physical assessment such as blood pressure and pulse. Based on what she had learned, particularly from Worrall, Dora discerned that strong religious faith or strong faith in the healing or the healer was not absolutely critical, but that a fair degree of open-mindedness was necessary. During the early research at Pumpkin Hollow Farm, Dora and Dr. Bengtsson asked people to participate as research subjects, requiring them to be willing to be treated at least once a day over a period of seven to fourteen days.

Dolores Krieger continued to serve as research assistant for the four or five years Estebany participated in the research. Dora's interest in family dynamics was evident in her observation of a supportive wife who negatively affected a healer during treatments. During the two years that Estebany's wife accompanied him, Dora discovered that he was more effective in healing if his wife was not present; her habit of interrupting him inhibited his ability to help patients. Dora was confident enough in her observations of this impediment that she contacted the researcher, Sister Justa Smith. Laboratory research was to begin and Col. Estebany had agreed to "heal" beakers of barley seed. Though dubious, Sister Justa ensured that Estebany's wife would not accompany him during the research sessions.[12]

Over the course of this research project, Dora gained confidence in her own abilities not only to assess patients but to provide energetic treatments as well. Dolores Krieger recalled the beginnings at Pumpkin Hollow Farm of what would become "Dora's healing group" at the NYTS. Dolores herself is credited with providing the name Therapeutic Touch (TT), cofounding the healing technique with Dora, and spearheading support and research within the nursing profession.

Following one of Estebany's early visits to Pumpkin Hollow Farm in the late 1960s, Dora selected members of the NYTS to meet on alternate Saturdays to learn and practice an approach to healing that gradually became a technique called Therapeutic Touch. Ed Abdill, later vice-president of the TSA, was a member of that first group at the NYTS. He later recalled:

> I was fortunate enough to be among those members. Dora would bring in a patient that only she knew. We were first asked to place our hands a few inches from the patient's forehead and gradually move our hands down to the feet. We were asked to make a mental note of any sensations we might feel in our hands. Each of about a dozen participants did this without any comment from Dora. When all had a chance to do the experiment Dora asked each person what, if anything, they had felt. I said I felt something around her eyes but was certain it must have been my imagination. The patient had glaucoma.
>
> When we began to experiment with the healing treatment Dora would blindfold the patient to avoid any preconceived

idea about who might be good [at healing or helping] and who might not. Then Dora would point to two people and direct that one work on the front of the patient and the other on the back. While working on one patient I noticed a draw of energy at a particular spot on her back. When all had a chance, Dora had the blindfold removed and she asked the patient what, if anything, she had felt. The woman I worked on pointed to the exact spot on her back where I felt the energy and said that she had felt it there. Those two experiences convinced me in the reality of TT and that I could do it.[13]

During those years, Dora accompanied Karagulla and another researcher, Violet Petit Neal, on several occasions to healing sessions in the Los Angeles area. She attended sessions that had thousands of participants in the audience. Some of the audiences for Kathryn Kuhlman, the well-known evangelist and faith healer, numbered over ten thousand. "We went to three or four famous healers; I've seen a lot of healers, the famous ones. Kathryn Kuhlman I watched, and how she helped somebody I really don't know. There were so many thousands of people in the building. Until this day, I've never been to anywhere else where I had [seen] so many people. She had the biggest audience."[14]

Dora acknowledged religious faith as a primary factor that enabled healers to effect significant changes. She saw that ability in Kathryn Kuhlman to a remarkable degree and to a lesser degree in Estebany. Regarding Kuhlman, Dora said, "The force is like an avalanche, whereas to Mr. Estebany, the force is more like a little tree, that is, the quality of energy that flows through. . . . Mr. Estebany never quite got into totally letting himself go in that way. This is part of the tremendous religious feeling [of Kathryn Kuhlman]. Most of us still feel personally responsible to some extent. She did not feel that at all. She is a channel of the tremendous healing energy. She has a total belief system about not being Kathryn." Kuhlman's religious faith contributed to her trust in God's will above all else. Dora stated, "Very few have that sense of openness with a belief system which knows you can completely flood the other person with this healing energy. Most people are not secure inside themselves. [However,] outside of the healing service, she was always worried that the Holy Ghost would leave her. There was only one Kathryn Kuhlman, and when she left, there was no one like her to replace her. There are small healers but none like her with the same powers."[15]

Dora also attributed the profound and lasting healings that occurred during Kuhlman's huge healing services to "the tremendous help from the audience." Music, singing, and spontaneous utterances of faith were encouraged. Dora could not possibly replicate Kuhlman's religious faith, nor for that matter the music and singing. Dora's work was very modest; she sought to adapt healing so that it could be offered in nonreligious environments such as hospitals and spiritual centers such as Pumpkin Hollow Farm and Indralaya. For Christians and Buddhists alike, Dora knew she could turn to the tremendous potential of what she called "the healing forces in nature." Where Dora lacked choir and pipe organ, the sound of the brook at Pumpkin Hollow Farm and the sight of towering spruce trees at Indralaya provided potentiating music. Even with scanty resources, reverence for life can be expressed.

Though Estebany, like many others, thought that healing could not be taught, Dora applied her analytical abilities to the matter. She concentrated on what was necessary to help altruistic people who worked in secular settings to cultivate the ethics and knowledge needed to heal. She studied and read; she observed many healers; and she quietly led the NYTS healing group. But before she began to teach others to heal in earnest, she and Fritz spent his last decade of life traveling and teaching in the United States, Europe, Sri Lanka, and India. Competing demands intervened to produce another period of incubation for Dora's creative contributions to healing.

Chapter Nine
Healing and Therapeutic Touch (1972–1975)

D ora really came into her own in 1972 when her "double life" ended with the death of her husband. Because he was recognized as a brilliant speaker and educator, Dora and Fritz traveled all over the world. They met with educators, dignitaries, philosophers, scientists, and religious leaders. It was not until his final two years of life that Fritz slowed down. In the late '60s, Fritz had surgery for prostate cancer, but opted out of radiation and chemotherapy. He believed that he would die before the cancer recurred. Dora later said that they didn't know that "it would be so bad." Within a few years, the cancer metastasized, and bone pain caused severe and then excruciating pain. Two years before his death, he was forced to curtail his activities. At the end, his pain became so severe that he spent the last days of his life in the hospital for pain management.

During the last year of Fritz's life, Dora still visited her parents. Her father, Karel, was ninety-six, very frail, nearly deaf, and virtually blind. He died the same year as Fritz. While Dora undoubtedly grieved, she understood death in a very profound way from her religious studies and her personal experience through clairvoyance. For both Fritz and Karel, death was a relief from the suffering of old age and infirmity.

Dora was exhausted after caring for Fritz during his last months. According to Dolores Krieger, who had been a student of Fritz's and stayed at his bedside during his death, Dora was in a poor state of health for about two weeks afterward. But she knew how to draw on energies in nature to restore her balance and health. She had several trusted friends and relied on them, though they too grieved. Her son, John, and his family lived right next door, and John and Emily Sellon were right across the little woods. Letters of support poured in from those who knew Fritz and Karel. After a short period of rest, Dora got on with her life.

She had never regarded herself as an unequal partner, but Fritz's world almost completely revolved around physics, philosophy, and academic research. Dora was now free to engage herself entirely in her own work, to focus on healing and Theosophy with little reference to family obligations. She had developed a unique combination of psychological, clairvoyant, and intuitive insight during her years with Dr. Bengtsson, Dr. Karagulla, and Dr. Laidlaw and had gradually applied that to healing. In addition, she had incorporated elements of style from three lay Christian healers: Ambrose Worrall, Oskar Estebany, and Kathryn Kuhlman.

Following her clairvoyant observation in 1970 of Kathryn Kuhlman, Dora and Karagulla observed her a second time in 1974. Dora was particularly interested in Kuhlman and spoke of her with great admiration many times throughout her life. Karagulla and Dora's research was compiled and published in 1989 in a book entitled *The Chakras and the Human Energy Fields*. Publication had not been without obstacles, the greatest of which was Karagulla's sudden death from a heart attack. Nevertheless, Emily Sellon's skill and tenacity as an editor resulted in the compilation and analysis of a vast amount of data. "The chakra book," as Dora preferred to call it, describes Karagulla's research and related efforts in detail; Dora is identified as "DVK." Its investigation of the vital (etheric) field and its association with the chakras and endocrine system was groundbreaking. The book also describes some of the remarkable results of Kuhlman's healing based on Karagulla's follow-up research with those who reported spontaneous and sustained healing.

In *The Chakras and the Human Energy Field*, Dora and Karagulla write:

> In the case of healers, the appearance of the etheric field varies. The majority of those who use their hands during healing are to some degree using part of their own etheric field to help the patient, though energies from the universal field also come into play. As a result, their etheric fields seem to have more elasticity than the average, thus enabling them to transmit energy to the patient. An exception to this was the case of the well-known healer, Katherine [*sic*] Kuhlman, who transmitted a type of energy which was not directly related to her own etheric field. She acted somewhat like a lightning rod, in that she was the agency through which etheric and/or astral energies in the general field were activated and transmitted. In the case of exceptional healers, such as Miss Kuhlman, there are other factors which come into play. . . .
>
> We attended two of Kathryn Kuhlman's healing services in May, 1970 and January, 1974 . . . We arrived an hour early so that DVK could observe Miss Kuhlman both before and during the healing service. At both of these services there was organ music and a choir of over two hundred voices which sang hymns. DVK's opinion was that the rhythm and vigor of the music played an important part in preparing for the

healing, by building a tremendous thought-form which enveloped the whole auditorium and united the energies of the thousands of people present.

Observing the healer's chakras, DVK noticed that the solar plexus, the brow and the crown chakras were the most powerful, and that there was a state of almost perfect harmony between the etheric and astral centers. There were no blocks. When Miss Kuhlman prayed, she tuned into the tremendous spiritual power which she called God, and she became for the time its focus and channel.

As the service progressed, the concerted force of the prayers and singing focused and consolidated a link with the healing forces. The unity of the immense audience enabled Miss Kuhlman to draw on some of its etheric energy in order to help her build up a condition of enormous power. This energy was both etheric and astral. As she began to talk about the Holy Spirit, she became tremendously charged with energy, and all her vehicles (that is, her aura) began to stretch and expand. She became like a great electrical dynamo, or a lightning rod which attracted this higher force. When she started to speak with deep conviction her face became pale, and DVK believed she was not fully conscious of what was happening, although she was aware she was being used as a channel by a force beyond herself. She constantly repeated that she herself was not the healer but rather the Holy Spirit, of which she was the instrument. . . .

At the moment of the healing, the patients felt a tremendous stream of energy passing through them, which many described as "a bolt of lightning," coming from a deep spiritual level right through the emotional and etheric fields. The solar plexus and crown chakras were the two most affected.

The "bolt of lightning" sensation came when these two and then all the other chakras were speeded up.

According to DVK, it was this sudden speeding up of the chakra system that checked the disease process. Those who were healed were told to throw away their braces and crutches and walk up to the platform in order to test what had happened. . . .

There was a question in DVK's mind, however, as to whether the experience of being healed would change a person in the long run, and whether it might make one more sensitive to the needs of others. She had an opportunity to observe a patient with rheumatoid arthritis who had been healed by Kuhlman the year before, and noticed that a tiny link had been made between the person's higher or spiritual level and the emotions. It was as though the healing energy had penetrated the astral body, and this had effected a real and enduring change in the person.[1]

Just a few months after Fritz died, Dora held what she called the Invitational Healers' Workshop at Pumpkin Hollow Farm. The response from those who attended the first Healers' Workshop was positive, and from then on, the workshop was offered annually at Pumpkin Hollow. Within a few years Dora offered an annual Invitational Healers' Workshop at Indralaya as well, and both events often had waiting lists for applicants. Dr. Susan Wager, who went on to write *A Doctor's Guide to Therapeutic Touch*, and Dr. Michael McGannon, an emergency room physician, were among the physicians who helped with the Healers' Workshops on Orcas Island. For many years at Pumpkin Hollow, Dr. Bengtsson attended as camp physician; other physicians, including Kathi Kemper, also assisted. Dora was careful and said that she preferred to have one of "her doctors" present during healing sessions. Emily Sellon and

Dr. Renee Weber attended as often as possible. As advanced meditators, they supported the group meditations that preceded each session and contributed to the harmony of the group. Renee was at that time a philosophy professor at Rutgers University. She had been a student of Krishnamurti's for many years and had known Fritz, Dora, Emily, and John (and many of their colleagues) since she was a young graduate student.

Erik Peper was a young psychologist when he began to study Therapeutic Touch and Dora's unorthodox counseling approach at Pumpkin Hollow Farm during the early 1970s. Not only was he Dutch and dear to Dora's heart, he had wit and intellectual curiosity. He was particularly helpful to Dora because he brought family therapy perspectives as well as his own clinical specialties to bear during Therapeutic Touch clinical practice sessions. He could formulate questions quickly and well, and he was also able to push Dora's lines of enquiry through successive questions. Most presenters find it challenging to respond to new questions, but Dora seemed to enjoy his logical approach.

Though Erik Peper was outnumbered by nurses at the workshops, he learned to laugh heartily at the occasional ribbing. He had studied many other healers and read as voraciously as Dora. Both Dolores Krieger and Dora were subjects in pilot studies he did with his biofeedback equipment, which provided helpful insights about the effectiveness of Therapeutic Touch in producing a relaxation response. Erik was one of many young, well-educated health care professionals who volunteered year after year to supervise clinical practice sessions and lead discussion groups at the annual Invitational Healers' Workshops. He and other professionals attended the workshops for over twenty-five years. These were unique in that each year a number of sick patients attended.

Though in some cases very weak, the patients helped participants develop compassion; they also contributed to the immediacy of the case study approach and increased the motivation to learn.

Dolores Krieger attended almost every one of the Healers' Workshops at both Pumpkin Hollow Farm and Indralaya during Dora's life and then continued for another decade after her death. Though Dolores initially attended the Healers' Workshops as one of the students, within a short time she helped Dora and Dr. Bengtsson screen patient and student applications and teach. Whereas Bengtsson, Emily Sellon, and Renee Weber preferred to remain quietly in the background, Dolores Krieger's outgoing and positive temperament allowed her to act as facilitator alongside Dora. She was able to "translate" Dora's clairvoyant and telepathic abilities to health care professionals and to model a sense of humor and perseverance. As mentioned, she and several of the other health care professionals, as well as Dora, each supervised a clinical session. Dolores Krieger held afternoon discussions on related topics of research, concept exploration, or the integration of Therapeutic Touch into academic curricula and clinical settings.

When Dolores gave the name *Therapeutic Touch* to an aspect of the healing approach that Dora taught, she effectively launched this healing modality into the nursing profession and into the world. Dolores Krieger became the "face" of Therapeutic Touch among health care professionals. She became identified as the cofounder of Therapeutic Touch, and in 1977 she started Nurse Healers–Professional Associates. Both independently and together with Dora, Dolores lectured and demonstrated Therapeutic Touch in medical centers, universities, continuing education departments, and integrative education centers. She traveled internationally to teach Therapeutic Touch and to present research to support its effectiveness in clinical settings. She promoted the potential of TT to reduce pain and anxiety, facilitate healing, and decrease "burnout" rates among those who practice it.

Dolores Krieger recalled the first steps taken to help health care professionals understand their own potential as healers.

> The paradigm at the time—if healing occurred, it would occur within a religious framework and nowhere else; you had to be in a particular religion. . . . After all that time observing, she really felt that you didn't have to be a special person [that is, someone with religious authority] to be a healer. She had this idea—that it could be taught; that it did not have to be within a religious context. . . . What I suggested was that we have a workshop, and since I was on faculty at the university I had access to loads of people. We had this workshop [with] about fifty people from the health professions: psychologists, nurses, doctors. That was the first one—in 1972—and I was one of the students. From her point of view, she could see that people had the propensity for it. . . . Out of the realization that it was a natural potential, that's when Therapeutic Touch really blossomed.[2]

Dolores was a professor in the New York University Division of Nursing, and by 1973 she had begun teaching Therapeutic Touch to graduate students. The NYU nursing curriculum is based on the work of the innovative nursing theorist Martha E. Rogers, who developed what she called the *science of unitary human beings*. She postulated that human beings are energy fields that are interdependent with the environment. Drawing upon modern science, she introduced the concept of *integrality* to refer to the interdependence of human beings and the environment. Her term *helicy* speaks to the pattern of energies as continuous: fields exist as continuums, are not consistent with determinism, and are increasingly diverse. Her third principle, *resonance*, acknowledged the continuous alteration in energy fields from lower to higher frequencies.[3]

Like Dora's model for healing, Rogers's model was based on field theory and postulated a human field and environmental field that were interrelated and dynamic. Renee Weber's "healing hypothesis" relied largely on field theory as it applies to human beings and included the "universal healing field" as a matrix field of order and compassion.

According to Rogers's human field theory, a human being is an open energetic system. Unlike a machine, which is a closed system, human beings can change and optimize their potential because they are open systems. Health therefore is determined by the fulfillment of one's potential as well as by physiological indices. According to Rogers, "Health is a rhythmic patterning of energy that is mutually enhancing and expresses full life potential."

Because Dolores had earned her doctorate at NYU, she was conversant with Rogers's model. In 1973 she introduced the course "Frontiers in Nursing," which incorporated Therapeutic Touch, and by 1979 Therapeutic Touch was incorporated into Rogers's theory of the science of unitary human beings.

Students applied to the undergraduate and graduate nursing programs at NYU specifically to explore the implications of Therapeutic Touch. Janet Macrae, one of the early healers to provide Therapeutic Touch in private practice, completed her doctorate and began a continuing education program at NYU to teach Therapeutic Touch and explore related modalities and topics. In addition to Dolores and Janet Macrae, many other nurses completed their doctorates in nursing at NYU, and nearly twenty doctoral dissertations were related to Therapeutic Touch. Many of the nurses and other health care professionals who attended the Healers' Workshops began to teach Therapeutic Touch in academic and other settings. Within a decade thousands of health care professionals, mostly in the United States and Canada but in other areas of the world as well, identified themselves as Therapeutic Touch practitioners or nurse healers.

In 1974 Dora and Dolores Krieger were invited to participate in one of the early Council Grove Conferences associated with the Menninger Institute. At that time there were few other groups in the United States offering week-long conferences on healing that included healers from various disciplines. Edgar Cayce's organization in Virginia Beach, the Association for Research and Enlightenment, was also studying healing and offered conferences, but it limited its studies to Cayce's work. Council Grove, like Wainwright House twenty years earlier, was on the forefront of research methodologies for advancing the understanding of healing phenomena. Gay Luce was one of the psychologists who coordinated the Council Grove Conference the year that Dora and Dolores attended. She said, "What's now taken for granted— what's now 'alternative medicine'—was then completely unknown; . . . biofeedback was in its infancy." Even within Dora's lifetime, significant progress had been made in terms of the acceptance of complementary and alternative health care modalities. Even rural hospitals in the U.S. offer patients alternative therapies; urban medical centers often have complementary medicine clinics, particularly for people with cancer.

According to Gay Luce, the participants at the Council Grove Conference that Dora and Dolores attended were interested in the ability of sensitive individuals to assess patients' health. During the conference, Dora and Dolores as a team, along with several other healers, were asked to assess patients. Ken Wilber, the chairman of the conference, was the only person who knew the etiology of the patients' health conditions. The healers were allowed to ask the patients questions if necessary and then tell the group about their condition. Gay Luce recalled one patient in particular. "I remember Dora and Dee [Dolores Krieger] coming very close in their diagnosis. They knew that it was neurological, and they knew that the whole nervous system had been in shock. The man had been electrocuted on the job. But I was impressed that the 'diagnosis' of Dora and Dee was so close."[4]

Therapeutic Touch continued to gain interest and was practiced, mostly by nurses, in a variety of clinical settings. Dora and Karagulla continued along new lines of research. Together they made a systematic study of the etheric, i.e. vital, energy related to the chakras. Dora clairvoyantly observed a number of patients while Karagulla asked her a series of questions. The data from her observations were then compared with medical findings. Pushed and challenged by Karagulla, Dora had the tenacity to make detailed and sometimes tedious clairvoyant observations. Several cases mentioned in "the chakra book" document Dora's ability to observe pathologies before they were clinically diagnosed. Because of that ability, Dora became well known among friends and colleagues, prior to the advent of CT scans and MRI, for her skillful clairvoyant assessment. She refrained from diagnosing, but would instead indicate whether it was necessary to seek medical care immediately or if "watchful waiting" was an option. She sometimes suggested medical follow-up with lab work or other diagnostics. Other times she recommended consultation with specialists in fields such as psychiatry, psychology, osteopathy, chiropractic, and nutrition. She was consulted by friends of friends, even from outside the country. For those she knew, she was often willing to provide a distance assessment and provide suggestions for care over the phone.

From clairvoyant observation, Dora was able to determine when a person sought help as an expression of self-absorption or just out of intellectual curiosity. On more than one occasion when a person had been erroneously labeled a hypochondriac, Dora's assessment indicated an incipient condition that had been disregarded by the medical community or could not yet be detected with the available technologies.

Phantom limb pain experienced by some people following amputation was a field effect that Dora and Karagulla explored in "the chakra book." Dora clairvoyantly observed patients who had been diagnosed with chronic fatigue syndrome and fibromyalgia—conditions that are still not fully understood by the medical community. During the last few years of her life, she began an informal comparative study of patients who had been diagnosed with fibromyalgia.

In the case of the well-known journalist Dorothy Thompson, Dora described her observations in a section of *The Chakras and the Human Energy Fields* entitled "Diseases Related to the Solar Plexus Chakra." Dora observed, "It has ten petals, and under normal conditions it is multicolored with light red and green predominating. . . . In the life of the ordinary person, the solar plexus center is probably the most important and active of all the chakras, since it is very much involved in the emotional life. It is active in a person with strong desires, and plays an important role in the projection of personal energy."[5]

In this case, the etheric energy associated with the subject's adrenal glands was "droopy," and Dora described irregularities in her general etheric energies. Other observations contributed to a timely medical intervention.

> DVK noted that there were color changes around the abdomen, above average luminosity, and dysrhythmia in that the rate of

motion varied from fast to slow. . . . Looking at the abdomen and the internal organs, DVK described a blockage in the left upper region of the abdomen (near the splenic flexure), which she identified by pointing to the area. The subject had not complained of any gastrointestinal symptoms nor indicated any malady, and as mentioned above, she had not been medically evaluated. . . .

After her evaluation, DVK recommended that the patient consult her physician and undergo an X-ray examination. The result of these tests showed a blockage of the colon exactly at the point DVK had indicated. Three days later, cancer of the descending colon was diagnosed and removed surgically.

As a follow-up, the patient was seen again a few weeks after surgery. DVK observed that the general etheric was less droopy but had not returned to normalcy. The blockage was gone, but the adrenals were still under stress. In this case, the correlation between the clairvoyant observation and the medical findings was exact, but the observation preceded the diagnosis.

Dorothy Thompson was one of the first female journalists to broadcast on the radio and was also the first woman to lead a significant foreign news bureau. Dora would have been well aware of the patient's career and of the fact that her husband had died very recently. Dora observed the following:

> The color of the petals of the solar plexus chakra was a pinkish-yellow, and from this DVK deduced that the patient was a person with very strong emotions, which she controlled and checked with her mind and will. She at times inhibited her personal feelings if she felt this was the right thing to do.

This placed her adrenals under constant stress, and in addition she continually pushed herself to work at a pace which was really beyond her physical capacity.[6]

Like her father, Dora was achievement-oriented, but she also renounced motivation associated with status, wealth, or power. Later in her life, when she became president of the Theosophical Society in America, she pushed herself, like Thompson, to work beyond her physical capacity for many years. That may have been a contributing factor to the development of Dora's mild digestive disturbance and the serious cardiac dysrhythmia she developed at around eighty-nine years of age.

Dora was kind and she laughed a lot, but she was as demanding of her students as Karagulla had been when Dora worked with her on the research for *The Chakras and the Human Energy Fields*. Not everyone had the perseverance and confidence to remain Dora's student. As a rough estimate, for every hundred students that tried to learn from Dora, there were eighty who walked away. Erik Peper said that there were some healers, such as Lawrence LeShan, who were better than Dora in teaching healing. Others, such as Kathryn Kuhlman, effected more dramatic and frequent reversals of serious disease processes. Nevertheless, according to Peper, Dora's powers of observation were remarkable. So was her ability to analyze and synthesize disparate and detailed information based on her observations and then to apply that knowledge.

Dora's disciplined approach to clairvoyant investigation found expression in healing. She observed the past, the present, and the probabilities that influenced the future. She also perceived psychological obstacles as well as the person's willingness and ability to overcome difficulties. Dora could visualize patients as they had appeared to her when she first treated them a year—or twenty years—earlier. Dora believed that this ability had more to do with a warp in the time-space continuum than with memory. Her memory was remarkable until she was around ninety, when her short-term memory became less acute. She often substituted telepathic abilities for memory to good effect.

Through healing, Dora balanced her intellectual curiosity with her lifelong interest in helping others. She did not pretend to have all the answers or to be the voice of spiritual authority. She insisted that neither Therapeutic Touch nor her own healing were functions of the Theosophical Society. Although she applied her understanding of Theosophy to develop her ability to heal, the curricula for teaching Therapeutic Touch was not developed by the education department of the TSA. Certainly the NYTS, Seattle lodge, Pumpkin Hollow Farm, and Indralaya supported healing with many workshops and lectures. Dora recognized that "her nurses" and "her doctors" were instrumental in those efforts. Dora indicated her own independent temperament when she said that she did not seek formal recognition or funding from the Theosophical Society to develop her healing or Therapeutic Touch.

It was not until Dora was over sixty years old that she really came into her own. Leading a group of intelligent, capable professionals in meditation and then supervising as they treated patients at Pumpkin Hollow Farm and at Indralaya, she was really in her element. Initially she wanted to know if healing could be taught. She knew that Ambrose Worrall had successfully taught his wife to heal, but Olga Worrall was very religious as well as clairvoyant. Could those who had little or no religious education learn to heal? Could students with strong religious beliefs change their language and enlarge their views in order to practice in secular institutions without imposing their own religions on others? For example, could healing be practiced in nonreligious settings without reference to the Holy Spirit or other religious terminology?

At Pumpkin Hollow Farm, most of the treatments and discussions took place outdoors in the orchard near the brook. A patient sat on a bench as Dora demonstrated. Because the patient's localized energy field extends beyond the physical body, Dora encouraged students and practitioners to gently move their hands and keep them four to six inches away from the patient's body. She started at the top of the head and moved her hands over the patient's head, neck, shoulders, all the way to the patient's feet. That was repeated while she stood in front of the patient, again starting at the top of the head and moving down to the feet. Dora wanted people to become aware of subtle energies. She often kneaded a patient's shoulders and upper back with her strong hands or put the palms of her hands on her patient as she worked. However, she encouraged others to keep their hands away from the patient's body in order to become more sensitive to subtle variations in the energy field. Dora observed the students and modified her approach accordingly.

Dora introduced city people to nature at Pumpkin Hollow Farm or Indralaya workshops while seated on a large canvas tarp, plastic chairs, or the grass in an old orchard. She did not present outlines or flow charts, glossaries, or other handouts. She told stories about healers. She was a master of understatement, so only those who could get in sync with her could make sense of the stories and follow their logic. For those who expected a logical progression that required little more than rote learning, she was frustrating. Without attuning to her through listening to the brook or participating in her meditation or respecting her for her fearlessness, her presentations came across poorly.

Dora was invaluable to those interested in clairvoyant validation of their experiences of subtle consciousness and the appropriateness of their meditation practice. Dolores Krieger shared an example of the way Dora validated Dolores's awareness of a devic consciousness. The experience occurred while the two of them were walking through birch woods after picking wild blueberries. Dolores had a sudden perception of beauty and unity. Though she was awestruck by it, Dora merely agreed, matter-of-factly, that the woods were beautiful. However, several weeks later Dora spoke to a group in California about the beautiful birch woods near Pumpkin Hollow Farm and the deva associated with it. Only then did she validate Dolores's exhilarating experience. Listening to a tape recording of Dora's presentation, Dolores understood that she had experienced more than the physical beauty in nature: she had perceived a deva's consciousness.

> She's done that time and time again and—even though people would think she's abrupt—she won't give it away. She won't throw it away, her world, by talking about what she's seeing. Very guarded; it's as though she has a treasure and she realizes how silly most of us are with that kind of information. If you get the right question and if you, yourself, have the insight or the wisdom or the understanding about something, it's a whole other story. And then you find her to be completely different, a whole other person than you think she is . . . not because she wants to withhold it but she realizes that it's more important for you to find out; it's more important for you to perceive it.[7]

Dora was not a philosopher. She gave simple teachings, and she acknowledged students' insights and validated their realizations. Her attentiveness to individuals' development reinforced one of her fundamental teachings: "We can change." Human beings have the potential to change profoundly; they are not closed systems like machines. The transformation process encompasses vastly more than a single lifetime. There is a continuity of consciousness far more subtle than that associated with sensory awareness of three-dimensional space and linear time. Dora encouraged those she called "potential healers" to gain familiarity with the inner self and with expanded, subtle states of consciousness.

Cookie Jurgens was a nursing professor. She met Dora for the first time during the first Invitational Healers' Workshop held at Indralaya in 1976, having met Dolores Krieger six months earlier. The night before the workshop started, Cookie and her husband received a phone call. Their friend Jim had been shot and killed in Berkeley, California. He and Cookie's husband had been roommates in college, and she had also been friends with him at that time. She recalls that the morning after her arrival at the workshop,

> We did our meditation and we were starting to break down in groups and Erik Peper was the leader of our group. Lavaune [another participant] and I were put in the same group. There were just five or six of us and Dora just wanted us to start beginning to assess one another. Well, I can't quite remember how I got in the chair first; we didn't have patients at Camp then. Anyway, within a very short time, I was just hysterical—really, really.
>
> Lavaune told me later that she saw Dora running across the field towards us and she just shooed them all away and she said, "Get away; get away; you're just making it worse." She had them sit down around me and be quiet and she came behind me and took a hold of me with her hands over my heart and I could immediately just feel—the most incredible thing I've

ever experienced. I began to just breathe deep and she talked to me a little bit and patted me.

Then she came around—and I'm sitting in a chair and she's standing—and she's not much taller than me; she's a small woman. She took me by the shoulders and she shook me and she said to me, "You stop it and you stop it right now." She said, "You are not helping him one bit. You are pulling on him like a toothache. You go to your cabin and meditate." She said, "You send him love and you let him go. You tell him you're okay and you let him go."

I got up and I went to the cabin and I did what she said and I fell asleep for a little while. And Lavaune came and I said, "Lavaune, did you talk to Dora?" And she said, "Cookie, I haven't said a word to anybody." She said, "This is your story and I haven't told anybody." So nobody in Camp even knew what had happened [to Jim] except Lavaune and me.

When asked if she accepted Dora's radical approach to death and dying, that is, to help the person who has died rather than overly mourning, Cookie replied, "Obviously I took it to heart because that afternoon I went to the phone and called my husband and told him what had occurred. So he started to meditate—to let him go—and talked to Jim's mother about letting him go."[8]

The anecdote expresses the way Dora transformed "preachments" about those who mourn into timely interventions.

Dolores's championing of Dora and Therapeutic Touch was crucial, though she conceded, "Dora really was the leader—because she had these capabilities." Dora assessed patients much as nurses and other clinicians use observation of gait, balance, skin tones, respiratory rate, and other indications. Those physical assessments were combined with clairvoyance and an assessment across the past, present, and future. She could see pathologies in the vital (etheric) field as well as habit patterns in the emotional field. To some degree, she determined the likelihood for change—for better or worse—by being attentive to each patient's unique temperament. She provided counseling, but her approach involved much more, since she also worked on energetic levels. She attempted to resonate with the patient's inner self, that is, the more subtle levels of consciousness associated with wholeness. By using her hands to focus healing energy, she helped patients experience calmness and meditative quietude. From that level of awareness, it was possible to catalyze the healing process and restore their integration with the matrix of wholeness.

Renee Weber conducted an interview with Dora that appears in Dora's third book, a compilation of articles entitled *Spiritual Healing* (published initially in 1985 as *Spiritual Aspects of the Healing Arts*). Weber entitled the article "Compassion, Rootedness, and Detachment," and in it, she introduced those concepts relevant to healing. Weber was direct: "The healing force and its energies somehow speed up the innate tendencies toward order in the body. Now what is the specific role of the healer in this?" Dora replied, "The role of the healer is just to be an instrument; by his compassion and by his focusing to allow this healing force to flow through him to the patient. [The healer] is not necessary if the person himself has the strength to open himself up to the healing power, and is willing, at the same time, to become aware of his emotional and thought patterns which help to keep him in the state of illness, and to change them."[9]

The book *The Chakras and the Human Energy Fields* cites a case in which a woman with a poor prognosis avoided surgery and meditated for several years to consciously change her habit patterns. She was successful, but Dora said that self-healing is rare, often occurring when a patient is very close to death. As a result, Dora very rarely indicated that a patient dispense with orthodox health care. In the interview mentioned above, Renee Weber described self-healing as "the direct harmonization of the ill person with the healing power." She postulated that self-healing, without the intervention of a healer, is possible and Dora responded:

> Yes, but it requires one's awareness of his disordered patterns and a willingness and ability to let go of them. It is very difficult. I have worked with a great many people who are ill and they often feel that they *are* their patterns so that it's more comfortable not to make an effort to change them. A person's self-image—what he (often unconsciously) thinks of himself— is a very important factor in healing. [10]

Dora offered a specific example of a person who "thinks of himself as constantly failing and rarely able to achieve his goals fully— this makes for a negative self-image which is very difficult to change. We may feel patterns of depression recur without connecting them to the lack of self-confidence in ourselves that we repeatedly are building up within us." Once the person is aware of the negative patterns, changing them, she said, "is a very tedious process."

> One has to become aware of how one develops the beginning of this self-doubt every day and say to oneself: "I have enough desire to be willing to stop it the moment it starts and at that first moment of awareness to open myself to the positive energy which I can draw upon, which is also *me* because I am part of the universe and thus part of this healing power." By becoming aware of the pattern the moment it begins,

we nip it in the bud and change it by drawing up the will. That *de-energizes* the disturbed pattern and allows a new energy to enter in that may attenuate it. Self-image and health are connected because the different levels of consciousness are interconnected at all times.

Part of Dora's approach as a healer was to help the individual become aware of negative habit patterns. She skillfully conveyed what she perceived in language that the patient would not reject. Unlike psychotherapists, she did not have weekly visits with patients for a period of years. She may have developed her habit of bluntness from her attempts to help a patient gain insights and motivation to change, even though she often had only a single session with the patient.

In the dialogue between Renee Weber and Dora, Dr. Weber asks about the role of the healer when a person is unable to change a negative habit pattern. Dora responds:

Dora: The role of the healer is to focus on the person's potential for wholeness, which I feel is present in every individual. From my point of view, there is a point of consciousness within everyone which has the seed of wholeness. By wholeness I mean the potential to realize integration within oneself, and to actively *direct* the forces of one's life, not to *react* only to the problems or the negative parts of one's self. In each person's make-up there may be many negative patterns but there is also strength, creativity and insight; a person need only be willing to draw on them, and these forces I consider the potential for wholeness.

Weber: Most human beings therefore scarcely tap the great reservoir of strength and potential creativity which you are calling wholeness. Do you actually perceive these to be part of our makeup, as you observe the fields in your diagnostic work with patients?

Dora: It is part of our human constitution. People who are born with great handicaps in life surmount them through something within themselves and reach that other level. Practically every person, if he can move through a crisis in his life and surmount it, feels at that moment a sense of inner calmness, a sense of direction.

Weber: Why don't most of us draw more on that calmness and strength in daily life? Why does it seem to be latent and passive instead of active in most people?

Dora: Our whole attention in daily life is given to the minute details of living, particularly in our present society where we seem to depend on entertainment and stimulation from outside. We really are not aware of our own potential. Most people are involved with what catches their immediate interest or with the search for pleasure, not with the search for creativity and self-renewal.

Weber: Do people who become aware of these potentialities in themselves—people who are interested in healing—do they at the same time strengthen that side of themselves?

Dora: I think they strengthen that side of themselves, but of course that does not mean that they turn into perfect human beings. They may still feel distraught and distracted by periods of lack of self-confidence or by other problems. It is hard for us to realize that everything is in flux, and most people have moments of feeling down, moments of lowered energy; but if they accept this period of fallowness as temporary they will regain the sense of being active.

Weber: To function in that outgoing way renews one's energy, whereas to be self-absorbed and always revolving around the self [i.e., personality] drains one. Have the great healers that you've known been centered?

Dora: Centered and altruistic. I have worked with many different healers and what is remarkable is that during the healing process, the healers can continue without a loss of energy because all their attention is focused on an outward movement—helping others, and during this process they forget completely about themselves. In teaching Therapeutic Touch we stress how essential it is for the potential healer to know something about centering. Centering is a practice which must be done daily. If one is a nurse, for instance, this form of meditation is not only practiced in solitude at home but right in the emergencies which come up during a busy hospital day.

Centering is a focusing within. It is helpful to focus one's energies in the heart region. The first step is to be aware of any anxiety we might feel at the time and to try to dissociate from it for the moment. Shifting the focus to this center of quiet within is important in the healing process. Most healers experience it in one form or another, though often it is second nature to them and they can shift into it without much effort, without prodding from the conscious mind. When we train nurses, however, we teach them to do centering consciously. There are many modalities of healing but Therapeutic Touch is one that seems eminently suitable for nurses. Therapeutic Touch entails that the nurse or healer, after centering, visualizes himself as an instrument for healing. The use of the hands makes it more effective, but it is not essential. The energy fields of the healer are focused through his hands and reach the energy fields of the patient and this helps speed up the innate healing power within the patient himself.[11]

In the interview conducted by Renee Weber, Dora also mentions qualities a healer must have:

From my observation, there are several common denominators which seem essential. First, the healer has to have a conviction or faith that there is a power which is greater than himself, on which he can draw. Secondly, he of course must have a genuine compassion and the desire to help others. Thirdly, to be truly effective, he has to leave his own ego or sense of self-importance out of the healing process.

Dora spoke about the importance of nonattachment:

Dora: Between the healer and the sick person there often develops a close, empathic relationship. If the healer feels that he is personally involved in the patient's pain, he will feel anxiety, and anxiety, at whatever subtle level, is an energy that will be conveyed to the patient along with the healing energy. This will

interfere and in some cases I have even observed
that people who identify with other people's disease
process may feel the pain in their own body. This is
really not good for the healer, because it weakens
his own energy.

Weber: You said that the healer has to have faith in a healing power, can that power be described in any way?

Dora: To me, this healing power exists and is real. I feel
it has three characteristics: order, wholeness, and
compassion. It's part of nature and it's universal.
Therefore, it does not matter who calls upon it nor
by what name. It is not for any race nor any particular religion.

Compassion was to become the touchstone in Dora's efforts to
help students develop the quality of humaneness. Compassion is
the fuel that drives the transformation from "concern for others"
into "altruistic action to avoid suffering and its causes." According
to Dora, compassion, altruism, and nonattachment can transform
the actions of nurses and doctors into actual healing.

In general, Therapeutic Touch is not recommended for people
with severe mental illness, particularly those with hallucinations or
extreme delusions. But in a discussion with Erik Peper, Renee
Weber, and John Kunz, Dora said,

I do know lots of people who have made changes. Mentally ill
people actually change. Maybe that has to do with synchronicity
in some ways. Such people suddenly may feel that they could
change and they do. This also has to do with basic survival or
their sense of it. [Also] out of pure affection, people have
changed.[12]

One woman who had worked for a number of years in psychotherapy asked Dora to meet her psychiatrist. The woman said later Dora surprised her: instead of attributing her tremendous progress to the good doctor's skilled efforts, Dora gave full credit to the woman's two dogs. It was love and affection for the dogs, she insisted, that had effected healing.

Dora claimed that first steps, literally and metaphorically, are the most difficult. In one case, she was helping a woman with multiple sclerosis who attended the Healers' Workshop at Pumpkin Hollow Farm. The ground in the meadow was uneven, so the woman was assisted in walking by a nurse on either side of her. After half a dozen steps, the patient was helped to sit again, and Dora congratulated her as though she had walked fifty yards. Dora then explained that when there are neurological problems, the first steps are the most difficult and require concentration. Not only did she encourage mental focus on the part of the patient, she helped her experience a sense of achievement. Dora employed common sense; it was not necessary to push beyond the point of fatigue into frustration. She made the process fun and never once directly addressed the woman's fear of falling. She introduced objects of concentration, the feeling of confidence and upright posture, when she encouraged the patients' first steps after her treatment. Then the object of focus was shifted to "rhythmic walking." Here the accomplishment was not in distance, but in steady, rhythmic walking. Dora worked skillfully and often employed what appeared to be basic common sense. But as she quipped, "common sense is the rarest faculty of all."

Without Dolores's pioneering efforts to establish Therapeutic Touch firmly within an academic environment and the nursing profession, Dora's innovative contributions in healing would not likely have received much recognition outside her circle of associates. Therapeutic Touch reflected Dolores's contributions as much as Dora's insights; Dolores introduced a research-based approach and brought the nursing process to Dora's healing. Dolores helped codify the workshop content and present it in a didactic way. She introduced the concept of the "renaissance nurse" and gave demoralized nurses a new perspective. Therapeutic Touch has the imprimatur of nursing, and "the TT nurses," as she called the practitioners, helped to advance the nursing profession.

Dora credited Dolores Krieger with bringing nursing professionals to the Invitational Healers' Workshops. Dolores championed the healing method on radio and television, in journal articles and newspaper interviews, in nursing and multidisciplinary conferences, and in academic courses. She lectured and demonstrated Therapeutic Touch in many academic settings, medical centers, and other settings across the United States and abroad. She advocated for the role of nurse-healers and for the relevance of Therapeutic Touch in health care institutions and community settings.

Both Dora and Dolores were interviewed by anchorwoman Barbara Walters, and similar segments on Therapeutic Touch have been done by many nursing organizations and news groups. Although Dora did not accept pay for her treatments, workshops, or lectures, Dolores and other Therapeutic Touch practitioners accepted pay commensurate with their education and experience. Those who charged a fee for TT treatments reasoned that the requisite studies and office rental and other expenses warranted remuneration. Dolores understood that it had to be cost-effective for institutions to include TT as an aspect of the professional care that was offered. Those settings required written policy and procedures similar to those for other nursing interventions. Documentation of the treatment and the patient's observed or stated response to it was required as an aspect of quality assurance.

Nursing professionals developed ongoing education and support. At NYU, Renee Weber brought her philosophical views to bear on a continuing education conference in nursing entitled "The Spiritual Aspects of Touch."

Dolores published a number of books, beginning with *Therapeutic Touch: How to Use Your Hands to Help or to Heal*. Many publications by Dolores and others followed, including an early compilation of articles entitled *Therapeutic Touch*. It was edited by two nurses and included Renee Weber's article on the "healing hypothesis." Chapters on TT were included in *The Many Facets of Touch* and *Foundations for Holistic Health Nursing Practices: The Renaissance Nurse*. Dora was surprised by the response to TT by professionals. Initially she had thought that a few people might benefit from Therapeutic Touch, and she had not expected it to become a worldwide phenomenon.

Those who learned Therapeutic Touch introduced it quickly into their various clinical settings. Janet Macrae realized that patients' responses to Therapeutic Touch were variable. Her clinical observations are included in her first book, *Therapeutic Touch: A Practical Guide*:

> As is the case with any method of treatment, people respond in their own way to Therapeutic Touch. This is true even among those with the same type of problem. One evening, for instance, I treated three school-age boys who were admitted to the hospital with acute asthmatic attacks. The first boy stopped wheezing immediately afterwards; the second boy's condition did not improve at all; and while the third boy continued to wheeze, his breathing became much easier and he fell asleep. Sometimes a person with several ailments will find that each one responds differently to Therapeutic Touch. One man, after

his first treatment, said that his asthmatic condition was unchanged but that a rash which had been bothering him for weeks had disappeared almost immediately.[13]

Dolores's approach had been to reframe healing as a discrete technique with a set of identifiable steps that could be replicated. That allowed policy and procedure guidelines to be developed for approval by nursing departments in facilities. Curricula for beginning, intermediate, and advanced practitioners were developed, and the minimum education required for practice in nursing settings was determined.

Janet Macrae wrote the article "Therapeutic Touch as Meditation," which was later published in the book compiled by Dora that is now entitled *Spiritual Healing*. Macrae wrote about the meaning and purpose in life that was introduced through the practice of TT:

> This sense of participating with the whole of oneself in a universal process brings with it a feeling of meaning or inner purpose. . . . this experience of meaningful participation in the healing process is particularly important for health professionals in our modern, technologically oriented health-care system. As lack of meaning and purpose, boredom and frustration are symptoms of "burnout," health professionals could benefit by learning to care for patients in a meditative manner.[14]

Aside from nursing scholars, educators, and clinicians, support for Therapeutic Touch came from physicians who were intellectually intrigued and welcomed efforts to help patients. There was particular interest in the consistent reduction in anxiety experienced by those who received TT treatments. Dora remained chary; she understood that there can be harsh consequences when good relations with members of the health care community are not cultivated. Dora sought the support of physicians in particular. She did not try to convince those she perceived to be "dated" or "narrow-minded," but when she met physicians and researchers who were open-minded and altruistic, she endeared herself to them. According to her own temperament and the knowledge gained from "Fritz's scientists," Dora avoided exaggerated claims for Therapeutic Touch. Her goal was to find ways to benefit suffering humanity. A physician with the power to usher TT into a major medical center deserved all the recognition Dora bestowed. She developed Therapeutic Touch with awareness of the uniquely difficult and demanding role of nurses in the health care system. One well-intentioned physician, she learned, could help a thousand nurses by opening the doors to innovative approaches like Therapeutic Touch. Each nurse, in turn, could benefit hundreds of patients. In order to help healers develop their expertise as respected members of society, and ultimately to help those in need, Dora learned to be respectful of the power of the medical establishment.

Dora took imbalances in power in society for granted. The focus of her interest was to help people overcome their own *inner* imbalances in power. The dominant personal ego has no place in healing. The attempt to resonate with—and reach toward—wholeness in others activates the tremendous power of the subtle levels of consciousness within that patient. In order to be effective in that process, the personality, the ego, has to be integrated in subservience to the "inner self." As Fritz put it, people have to "get out of the way of their own light." Dora said by "centering" one's efforts to help in deeper levels of consciousness than the personality and reaching towards that deeper level in patients, it helps patients realize wholeness. It has the potential to bring spiritual aspects into daily life.

The desire to learn, to grow, to transcend our limitations, is basic in all of us. . . . Beyond this, many of us aspire to become more caring and more altruistic—to rid ourselves of narrow attitudes and selfish motives. Having become convinced that there is a spiritual reality that is deeper, more enduring, more joyful, more compassionate, more unitive than anything else we can experience in life, we want to align ourselves with that reality. To do so, we know instinctively that we must try to escape the bondage of the personal ego.[15]

Dora recognized the busy lives of her students and advised "her nurses" to pause and evoke—even for a moment—the image of the tree as a symbol of wholeness. She reminded patients and busy professionals that each person is part of a larger wholeness, part of nature, and that tremendous benefits can arise from cultivating that awareness. Without using the term "faith," she made it possible for spirituality to be developed among health care professionals. What Fritz Kunz and his colleagues considered a "matrix field," others associated with Allah, the Divine, Brahman, God, the Spirit, the Buddha nature, the Beauty Way. Dora affirmed the sacred and the potential for wholeness in every human being.

While doing Therapeutic Touch, practitioners perceived that the most gentle affection and love radiates from the hearts of physically "imperfect" patients, such as the child with Down's syndrome or the infant suffering drug withdrawal from maternal cocaine abuse. Wholeness in the field was apparent in the infant born with underdeveloped arms from thalidomide exposure and the man who had limbs amputated from war injuries. The most sublime, subtle consciousness interpenetrates the denser energies of the vital field and the physical body. Dora encouraged students to see the person and not just the pathology. She encouraged patients to identify with the inner self rather than with the disease. To nurses and doctors, she suggested that a patient be described as having asthma rather than as an asthmatic.

As Dolores Krieger recognized, even learning to center one's awareness in the subtle aspects of the Self was transformative. As a preliminary practice to Therapeutic Touch, it was essential. Dolores spoke about her early studies with Dora in the decade after World War II.

> One of the things that she taught us was the power of a small group like that to be able to influence for the good, a larger community. There we were in New York City and it would seem silly because people were killing each other right and left. If anything, aggression was the keynote [in the world at that time]. However in doing meditation, not only on peace itself, but on *sending* peace—which is a little different because first you have to get yourself there—it changes you. I have [realized] the effect of it because obviously I've changed my life and it has become something quite different—many times over—from what it started out. . . . I really was ready for it, I suppose. For me, it worked. It was a lot of hard work but it worked. . . . My life was dramatically changed.[16]

In 1975 Dolores published an article entitled "Therapeutic Touch: The Imprimatur of Nursing" in the *American Journal of Nursing*. She suggested that Therapeutic Touch can facilitate healing through an exchange of *prana*, a Sanskrit term that means "life force" and is associated with the breath. She postulated that since human beings are open systems, there is an exchange of energy from the healer to the patient.

In 1979 Renee Weber published a landmark article of special interest to those who studied and taught Therapeutic Touch.[17] In "Philosophical Foundations and Frameworks for Healing" she introduced the view that there is a universal healing field and presented a "healing hypothesis." By suggesting that healers draw upon a universal field characterized by order and compassion, she distinguished the "healing field" from prana. She suggested that there is potentially vastly more to healing than the mere transfer of etheric energy from healer to patient. She implied that reverence for life and upliftment to the greater force of the universal healing field are determining factors in spiritual healing.

Dr. Weber posited "the existence of energy and consciousness in various states, qualitatively differentiated, with supremacy over gross physical matter; . . . the relativity of time in various dimensions of space and its absence from the n-dimensional space of pure spiritual energy where the healing power originates; . . . the increasing physicality and density of this energy as it enters the space-time sphere of organisms, a process in which the healer acts as a conduit." She goes on to say:

> The healing hypothesis further involves the power of intentionality of unbounded living systems such as ourselves, ceaselessly interpenetrating one another, rather than being restricted to the discernible boundaries of our bodies and personalities; and the resultant interchange of qualitatively charged energies among all organisms in the universe, resulting in either creative or destructive consequences for the cosmic ecology, spreading order or disorder depending on the wholeness or fragmentation of those energies. Finally it may be stated that this universal healing energy is not neutral nor value free, but is an energy of order, intelligence and compassion.[18]

For several reasons Dora considered herself different from the other healers she observed. "I've worked with the medical profession a very long time, and to work with them you've got to be precise, not exaggerate, and not always think you're going to be right and that God spoke through you. That's what the others think. All of them call on this healing field, but they are set on certain religious principles so it works for them."

Dora based her approach to healing on the view that people from all parts the world and from differing religions and cultures can draw on the healing field. "It doesn't matter if you're a Catholic, or God knows, or nothing." Dora did not perceive the fact that she had, as she said, "no religious upbringing in the ordinary sense" as a particular advantage or a disadvantage. She said, "It doesn't matter either way. It depends upon your temperament. Some of the healers are very religious and so that's how they draw it and that's right for them. Most of the healers in the United States belong to some religious sect or other."[19] Dora, as an immigrant, had experienced vastly different cultures with a variety of religions and languages. This background contributed to her view that healing is not the sole domain of one group of people or one religion. That set her apart from the Christian healers she knew in the United States.

At one point Dora started to say that it does not make any difference whether a healer has strong religious faith, but she corrected herself and said, "I think it helps."[20] She also observed:

> I think I can heal and there's one thing, as a result of my work, there are thousands of people who do some healing. . . . I'm very unemotional about it; I have been very careful about my language so that it would be accepted by science, and it has affected people all over the world. By being very careful, never exaggerating and not saying that you have to believe in Jesus

or anything [specific to a single religion]. I say that there's a "universal healing field" and that's a scientific term that even surgeons will accept. I'm very fortunate. . . . I've been indoctrinated by science all those years I worked with Fritz with those utmost scientists. And also I've been working with the medical profession but not sentimentally. I don't say I'm a Buddhist or a Hindu or anything. I take all of those things in, whatever I'm using. I believe in this universal healing force, field, and I think if you meditate and give out, you can draw upon it.

Being a Theosophist I've been brought up with respect for all religions, and from childhood I've contacted Hinduism, Buddhism, Islam. Very few people have had a background like me.

But perhaps the biggest distinction between Dora and other healers in the early '70s was that she taught others to heal. "I have broken all the rules because all the healers disapproved of my teaching Therapeutic Touch—most of them. They thought God gave them [*sic*]. I broke with them by teaching when all the famous healers I talked [to] about it didn't believe that was the right thing to do. They were very doubtful about it."[21]

In her characteristically blunt way Dora implied that just intellectually accepting a universal healing field does not make a person a healer. "They have to learn certain things and I taught them. There are some people who are just no damned good whatever [at healing]." When asked what she thought of those who advertise on the Internet to teach healing, she said, "There are many people from religious backgrounds [and] nonreligious backgrounds. A whole lot of people make quite a lot of money on it. I've never taken one cent for myself; that's my particular desire."

Dora also suggested that she had helped people from all walks of life. "The thing is, I see the bad and the good in people. Of all these [famous healers], who [among them] have been in as many prisons as I have—with all religions and with all different people?"

When she was asked during an interview what she concluded from having observed people of great diversity, she responded, "Some people can be helped and lots of people can't be helped. And some people are very set in their ways—I'm different in that way!"

If Dora observed that some people who wanted her help were set in their ways, she would have to "crack her brain," as she put it, to find ways to loosen their rigidity of thinking and emotional patterns. Prejudice is a mind-set, and the mind can be trained and cultivated. In her life and her teaching, she held to the motto she created for herself as a leader of the Young Theosophist movement: "Laugh a lot." To that she added a new aphorism: "We can change."

Dora helped through counseling in much the way elders have served communities for centuries. As Erik Peper noted, some of Dora's counseling was based on "extended logic" that did not require clairvoyance or intuition. Some of her interventions with patients expressed plain common sense.

Nelda Samarel, a professor of nursing, met Dora in 1980. She shared some of the practical ways Dora and the community of potential healers supported her and her family. Nelda said that when her son was nineteen, she missed the Invitation Healers' Workshop, although she had attended for five previous years. At the time Nelda was staying with her son, Adam, on the Adolescent Unit at Mount Sinai Hospital in Manhattan, where he was undergoing surgery. Dora and the participants included Nelda and her son in the morning meditation. At the time they meditated, Nelda sat in the waiting room during her son's surgery. She said that she experienced a sudden feeling of calmness "as though . . . sunlight had come through that little window—but nothing was there, just the building next door. The 'distance healing,' I don't know if it works, but I could feel it."[22]

Several days after Adam's surgery, Nelda said that she planned to spend a few days at Pumpkin Hollow Farm to rest before his discharge from the hospital. The Healers' Workshop had ended, and it was quiet there. Nelda had been caring for him in the hospital and was feeling exhausted. She described how the day after she arrived, Dora intuitively intervened when Adam's medical team had not been able to inform Nelda of an alarming change in his condition.

> I was meditating at the falls and I started to sob; it wasn't tears of release; it was heavy-duty sobbing. So I went to find Dora; she looked at me and she said, "You will go to your cabin and pack and get everything into your car and then you will have lunch. You won't leave until you have lunch. You are undernourished and you need to eat and then you will go back to your son in New York."
>
> I said, "But Dora, I'm not supposed to leave until tomorrow morning."
>
> "No, your place is with your son. You will leave now, as soon as you have lunch." She never told me why, but you don't argue. Dora throws you out of Pumpkin Hollow, so you leave. And I'm driving to New York and as I'm getting really close, I had this real urgency to get there quickly and I'm speeding and I'm driving like a New York taxi driver.
>
> I walk into his room and I see a team of doctors around his bed. He looks at me, "Mommy, I'm so glad you're here." There was a complication and they were rushing him into emergency surgery just then. I got there just in time.

> [Dora] knew this because . . . somebody who had been at
> Camp told me that as soon as I left, they rang the [dinner] bell
> and Dora summoned everybody who was at the Camp—
> fifteen people or so—to have a healing meditation for Adam
> and me. She said Adam was very sick and would need our
> help. So she knew this but she didn't tell me when she sent me
> back. . . . Isn't that amazing?"[23]

Adam recovered very well after that postoperative setback. In situations such as this one, Dora sometimes had flashes of intuition, as though she were seeing another person's experience in the past or future. Other times she said that she had a sense of urgency, much like the urgency Nelda felt as she reached Manhattan.

Dora learned a lot from the health care professionals with whom she worked. She also counseled health care practitioners about some of their patients. Sometimes she met with the patient and clinician together in the way she worked for many years with Dr. Bengtsson's patients. Other times a clinician would phone her or meet with her, and Dora could intuitively assess the condition and offer suggestions. On one occasion, a hospice nurse mentioned a patient and identified the primary problem as pain management. Without pausing, Dora responded that the man was also suicidal, and indeed that proved to be a complicating factor in his care.

Nelda provided Therapeutic Touch over a five-year period for a very ill child who died at age seven. Over the years the nurse had often sought Dora's advice about how to help the child, so she asked Dora how the girl was doing several months after her death. She said that Dora described Claire on the astral plane. The nurse said that Dora had been a guest in her house and was awake a lot during the night, and the nurse thought that Dora's assessment of Claire was done while she was awake.

I said, "Dora, do you know how little Claire is doing?" And she said, "I don't know but if you want, I'll find out tonight." . . . So I called her the next day and she said, "There's an older woman—maybe in her thirties—taking care of her." She described what the woman looked like in detail and said, "She's taking loving care of her. Claire is so happy and she has a full head of hair." She was bald when she died. "And she's jumping with a smile on her face just enjoying this pain-free body like a child should."

So I said, "Thank you so much. Do I have your permission to share this with Jennifer?"—who was Claire's mom. And she said, "If you think it would be helpful; I'll leave that to your judgment."

Later that day I called Jennifer to see if I should say anything. She said, "Nelda, before we go any further, I have to tell you something remarkable. I had a dream about Claire last night and I saw her with a full head of hair jumping and enjoying her body." She described what Dora had said to me. . . .

I told her what Dora told me and I described the woman to her and she said, "Oh, my gosh. My sister never met Claire; she died just before Claire was born." That description was of Jennifer's sister who Dora never knew existed. And it gave Jennifer so much comfort.[24]

Nelda's husband, Jack, was more interested in sports and finance than in Therapeutic Touch until one evening during one of Dora's meditation workshops at Pumpkin Hollow Farm. At the campfire in the grove Dora asked Jack to sit next to her during her evening talk. She usually started with a meditation of fifteen or twenty minutes. During the deepest part of the meditation Jack said that he felt as though he had been "shot in the forehead."

Nelda calls the affected area "the third eye": another name for the brow chakra. Dora's "Chakra Book" describes it as "the chakra which is mainly concerned with the integration of ideas and experience with the capacity for organization. . . . It is the organ of visualization and the center of perception, which may be directed upward toward higher things or downward to the mundane world; it thus reflects the twofold nature of the mind."[25]

The experience was powerful and unexpected, and there was no continuing discomfort. On the contrary, Nelda said that their midlife marital tensions and disagreements were resolved after Jack's experience. What was going on here? Perhaps as a skilled meditation teacher, Dora was aware that Jack was "ripe" for spiritual realization. She may have sensed that he was also sensitive to energies and that with the meditation workshop as a catalyst, he might have the karma to make a leap in his inner growth. She perceived a person's potentials as well as a person's openness to change. Perhaps Dora asked Jack to sit next to her so that he would not be frightened by what is sometimes called the "opening of the third eye." Unfortunately Dora was not interviewed about this experience, so this interpretation is speculative. But it is noteworthy as another possible case in which Dora intuited an event before it occurred.

Dora was able to be helpful in so many situations partly because she was not attached to outcomes. If people benefited from Therapeutic Touch, learning the method or just being part of the groups, she did not overreact. Similarly, if people did not benefit or rejected her approach to healing, she did not plunge into the doldrums. She saw the world as being much more complex than a series of successes and failures. She accepted the fact that some people are more set in their ways than others and that healing is not for everyone. As she said many times, "The results are not in our hands." The same was true of the acceptance of Therapeutic

Touch into the health care system. She and others tried skillfully and knowledgeably to create a healing technique that could be used in a variety of settings with diverse patients. Whether it was accepted or not was not in her hands.

Today in the United States the federal government continues to support the integration of complementary and allopathic approaches to health care. In 1991 the National Institutes of Health (NIH) developed the Office of Alternative Medicine, which in 1998 was the National Center for Complementary and Alternative Medicine. The center is intended to support research, career development, outreach, and other forms of education. It also tries to integrate scientifically supported complementary therapies into medical practice and into the curricula of medical, dental, and nursing schools. Therapeutic Touch, along with Reiki, qigong, and electromagnetic therapy, are included in a broad category called "energy therapies." There are other broad categories such as "whole medical systems," which includes naturopathy and homeopathy. "Mind-body medicine" includes prayer, meditation, and art and dance therapies.

Nelda Samarel was one of the experts who served on a committee called Research Infrastructure: Institutions and Investigators. Its general purpose was to research alternative and complementary health care as well as to address some of the unique issues in researching alternative modalities. Nelda's research on the effect of coaching in cancer support groups had earned her recognition and grant support. She was the recipient of a National Cancer Institute award for her studies of breast cancer support groups and was also among a group of researchers who received an NIH grant to replicate and expand that research. She had studied with Dora for many years and represented Therapeutic Touch as much as she represented the expanded role of the nurse. For many years she kept Dora informed of the progress of the National Center for Complementary and Alternative Medicine.

As Dora recognized, people cannot passively expect government or professional mandates for healing. Small groups of people contributed a lot, and with tremendous perseverance Dora provided leadership, as did many others in differing ways. Emily Sellon, Dr. Bengtsson, Renee Weber, and Dolores Krieger were all leaders who helped develop and support Therapeutic Touch. Emily Sellon was the glue that held the early TT efforts together. As Dora acknowledged, Emily was her best friend as well as a remarkable Theosophical teacher, writer, and editor. She stayed in the background, but did a great deal to ensure that the groundwork by Fritz and his colleagues in education could be applied to health care professions. Emily wanted to ensure that the bedside nurse have access to new theories in science to understand what it means to be healthy. She was open-minded and often advocated for others with humor and a light touch; at other times her advocacy was accompanied by an adamant look with arms akimbo.

Emily was one of few people who corrected Dora when she was intent on a certain line of action. Unlike those who made an icon of Dora, Emily could disagree with her. It is largely to Emily's credit that Dora graciously said on many occasions, "I stand corrected." John Sellon stayed in the background, but was well aware of Dora's independent temperament. He quietly provided counsel to the very end of Dora's life. He served as a steady supporter of Dora's efforts to encourage and organize what he described as "good people doing good work."[26] Their son, Michael, a talented artist, illustrated Janet Macrae's book *Therapeutic Touch: A Practical Guide*. He continues to serve on the board of Pumpkin Hollow Farm, where he was resident manager for a number of years.

Along with his brothers, Michael helps to ensure that the work begun at Pumpkin Hollow Farm continues to grow and develop.

Dora persevered with a lot of help from others. In healing, she accepted that miracles are relatively rare. More often patience and perseverance are required. In her view, significant and suddenly integrative healing involves synchronicity. She respected the complexity of karma, which she associated with synchronicity, and she said, "It's a subject we don't know." Ordinary people are not omniscient, and it is not easy to know who might be helped by healing. However, Dora often knew intuitively that a particular patient would especially benefit. "Oh yes, I've had forecasts; I've had that very often but you see, nothing surprises me. . . . Like this MS patient [Jean Marquis], she was in a desperate state, but she came [for healing treatments] twice and her life is totally changed. She phones me all the time to thank me. I think, the moment I touched her I felt that I could help her, and it has really proved it."[27]

One of the cards Dora received at Christmastime included a photo of Mrs. Marquis surrounded by what appears to be a dozen grandchildren. She wrote, "Thanks to you, these children have a grandmother."

It is impossible to know how much further Dora might have developed her ability to heal if she had not been elected president of the Theosophical Society in America in 1975. She accepted the top administrative position in the national organization and left Port Chester with some of her belongings. At TSA headquarters in Wheaton, Illinois, she faced the work at hand. She continued to teach several workshops on Therapeutic Touch each year and occasionally lectured on healing at conferences. She also started a healing group at headquarters that met regularly and provided consultations to people who came to see her for an "interview" or "healing."

Chapter Ten

President of the Theosophical Society in America (1975–1987)

Dora was seventy-one years old when she entered a very demanding period of her life: her tenure as president of the TSA. She said that she had not intended to work at the national level, but several associates urged her to seek the office. The main factor in her decision was her devotion to the Theosophical Society, coupled with keen interest in bringing the same vitality to the national level that she and others had created in the New York Theosophical Society. Her experiences in the New York lodge and at Indralaya and Pumpkin Hollow Farm had been, in effect, a pilot study for her efforts as president.

From her experience in the lodge and the camps, Dora was well prepared in some ways for a leadership role at a higher level. In other areas she had much to learn: finance, building maintenance, publishing, marketing, and complex public relations associated with over a hundred lodges and study centers. Since her teenage years when she "chose the Theosophical Society," she had done every conceivable volunteer job for the TS. She had also learned from some of the best leaders in the Society. She knew that she did not always agree with other Theosophists, nor was she expected to. The mission of the Society is broad, and uniformity of view and behavior is not part of its purpose.

Despite the Vietnam War, there was an overriding sense that the Theosophical Society as a whole had been founded in the United States because this country is associated with religious freedom, equality, and the pursuit of happiness. The civil rights and antiwar movements raised many questions. Among young people in particular, there was restlessness but also a sense of searching for happiness greater than that afforded by material comfort. The War against Poverty raised awareness that one's happiness has little relevance when huge segments of the population remain hungry and oppressed. The Theosophical Society in America turned one hundred years old the year Dora took office, and there was a sense of purpose and wary optimism among members, Theosophists in general, and people in the United States.

The Theosophical movement in the United States had its share of difficulties. It had not entirely distanced itself from the early interest in psychism as reflected in Ouija boards and levitating tables. The Second World War had a damaging effect on relations among scholars and other thoughtful individuals nationally as well as among nations. That was followed by the McCarthy era of the 1950s, which had a detrimental effect on the free expression of ideas.

New members or potential new members to the TS were confused by the various Theosophical groups and the lack of exchange among those organizations, although they professed to strive toward brotherhood. The Sanskrit terminology and related concepts that captivated Theosophists in the '20s demanded more time to master than many members could afford.

Dora and Fritz had traveled across the country in 1926 to participate as Mrs. Besant ceremoniously placed the cornerstone of the Rogers building at headquarters. Fifty years later, the grand building and its gardens were magnificent. And Dora discovered that they required a lot of maintenance, if not restoration. Among the staff at headquarters, instead of a sense of camaraderie, cooperation in undertakings, and shared resources, there were often disagreements and misunderstandings, rivalry, and mistrust.

To Dora, the Theosophical Society was much more than a network of individuals who met for discussion over cups of tea. Theosophists participated in discussions as enjoyable and challenging efforts toward self-development. They kept people from being dry and self-absorbed. Moreover, the groups and camps were laboratories in which to build a sense of cooperative community. They were nodes in a large network of altruism that spread across the country. Groups around the country meditated together and sent goodwill to the devas of the region, the land, and the people. These efforts helped fulfill an important part of the Society's mission of cultivating brotherhood.

Although many people see meditation as a withdrawal from earthly responsibilities, Emily Sellon emphasized that in no way is it an escape from the world. Instead, meditation is an activist effort. It helps to solve the problems of increased anxiety and enables practitioners to gain insight and energy in order to benefit others.

In Dora's view, the Theosophical Society existed to help the Masters uplift humanity. In a 1955 address, she said:

> They cannot be brought back into the vortex of personal relationships. The Theosophical Society is useful, and it will only remain useful if we, the members, are dedicated to that ideal of humanity, and realize that we must be willing to be the agents of karma for the Masters in carrying out their work. When you know the Masters, you cannot help but be devoted to them but they do not want us to worship them. The Theosophical Society was not meant to be a religious organization.... It will not fulfill its destiny if we unconsciously

treat it like a church. . . . Devotion is a fine thing, but the Masters require a very great deal more.

We have to feel with the Masters that sense of being colleagues engaged in a great work together. . . . The great thing which comes if you meditate on the Master is an ability to be unafraid to do, to act, to work, and to experience. Think of how you can help. If you get "hide-bound," if you get set or enclosed in rigid ideas, if you get into a permanent state of status quo, then you will slowly close the gateway between yourself and the Masters. . . . We must not remain static because the Masters must work through us and the Theosophical Society.

If you once get the feeling of what the Masters are, don't talk about it, but live it. Dedicate yourself . . . to the idea of serving the Masters, trying to do their work through the Theosophical Society. Then, from moment to moment, when the opportunity comes, you will take it. Don't have a lot of preconceived ideas. Keep open. Then, whatever is put before you, any kind of work, you will be able to take it in the right way. You will be able to realize that it can be an important experience, and if you are dedicated to understanding something about the Masters then you will become what I call a Theosophist. There are thousands of members of the Theosophical Society, but there are very few Theosophists.[1]

Dora's role as TSA president was to serve the members (who numbered 4,218 at the end of 1976) as well as a public that increasingly sought the resources of the TS. Her duties included participation in the general council of the international TS in Adyar. She was responsible for the forty-acre campus in Wheaton, which included housing for some of the staff, a bookshop on campus, and the Theosophical Publishing House. She also served as chairman of the publishing house and editor in chief of the journal *The American Theosophist*. A radio committee produced the Quest series, aired by forty radio stations. As part of the Theosophical Research Institute, she was peripherally involved with the publication of a journal published three times a year. Her administration also produced special editions of *The American Theosophist*. Each of these explored a single topic in depth with a collection of articles by authors from diverse disciplines.

Dora served four three-year terms from 1975 to 1987, and was eighty-three years old when she retired. (Following her tenure, the board reduced the maximum number of presidential terms to three.) During the twelve years she was in office, there was a tremendous increase in the number of young people who traveled to India, Africa, South America, and other parts of the world in search of traditional cultures that had maintained cohesive communities. Interest in the religions of Asia and the Middle East increased. The culture was beginning to shift away from the view that technology would solve the world's problems, and there was increased interest in ecology and spirituality. It was an exciting time to be president of the Society.

Three years after Dora took office she wrote, "We have had a steady increase in our membership in the last three years and the age of our members who are joining the Society is much younger."[2]

Dora's first term followed an interim president, Ann Wylie, who stepped in after Joy Mills left to become the international vice-president in Adyar. It was easier for Dora to follow an interim president, even though some momentum may have been lost. The personable Joy Mills was well loved and had been a TS lecturer for many years. She was also knowledgeable, dedicated, and dynamic as a president. Joy Mills's administration had created a two-story modern building on one of the perimeter streets of the campus of the TSA headquarters, known informally as "Olcott." Today the Mills building houses the Theosophical Publishing House, Quest Book Shop, and staff living quarters on the second floor. The publishing house was well positioned in a niche market that was growing at that time, as were the retail efforts at Quest Book Shop.

Dora inherited fiscal realities that were challenging but likely no surprise to her. Her term coincided with a thirty-five percent increase in total expenses for headquarters operations over a five-year period. That compared with an only sixteen percent increase in net membership dues. There were also periods of recession and inflation during the '70s. Dora may not have been able to change the batteries in her transistor radio or drive a car, but she had both feet on solid earth. She wasted little time getting appraisals in Manhattan and Chicago for jewelry, furniture, and artwork that had been donated to the Society. Instead of preserving antiquated fixtures that served little purpose, she and the TS board members approved the sale of certain goods: they needed to liquidate assets for operational expenses and did not want to tap the investment trust.

Dora was businesslike and serious of purpose. Those who were stolid and staid would not have liked to serve on staff during Dora's terms in office. It seems that hardly a stone was left unturned. During her first year in office a questionnaire was mailed to members asking what changes they thought should be made in the policies of the Theosophical Society. Some of the changes that were made were in anticipation of the introduction of computerized systems in several of the administrative departments. A printing press was installed in the basement of the Rogers building (the main building on the Olcott campus), and a staff person was trained in its operation.

In 1976, the year after Dora took office, she formed an energy committee that initially included Dorothy Abbenhouse, Floyd

Kettering, and the Leenhouts, the architectural team that had designed a wing to expand the library. She found individuals, largely from the membership, with expertise in various areas who were willing to volunteer for the committee as well. They surveyed various means to increase energy efficiency and conserve energy at headquarters. They also considered relocating headquarters and offered four possible alternate locations around the country.

Dora wrote to one of the committee members, Lillian Leenhouts: "We all liked the sketch you sent us about how to conserve energy. It is posted on the board and I lecture the staff every week on how to close doors, etc. Slowly we will get these ideas into more permanent action. . . . . I have found that buying some heavy mica sheets and fixing them to the windows on the outside is also very helpful. . . . We are also in the process of buying heavy curtains for the auditorium which we will keep drawn all of the time, and we are investigating how to insulate the windows there."[3]

A new roof had just been put on the Rogers building, and they were in the process of researching options for insulating it. Those changes sound small-minded, but many of the windows, for example, were not of standard dimensions and leaked cold air during the winters. The auditorium on the top floor was hot during the summer, even with insulation in the roof, but another twenty-five years passed before air-conditioning was installed. Dora did not significantly improve the infrastructure, though the determination was made to maintain headquarters at that location. Part of the reason was the cost for relocation, but a great deal of the decision had to do with members' attachment to the Rogers building in particular. The beautiful Olcott Library and the elaborate mural in the foyer would be difficult to duplicate.

The energy committee assessed weather patterns and projected changes in climate and the availability of resources. They created a root cellar and started a small orchard. They looked at grey-water systems and the Clivus Multrum waste disposal system, greenhouses for food production, future water availability, and alternate heating and cooling systems, including solar and wind generation. There was significant interest in attempting to become self-sufficient in food production. Food costs were rising at about ten percent a year for staff. Of the forty acres, about half of it was tillable, and there was discussion of farming it.

The report produced was far ahead of its time in its assessments. It said that resources needed to be efficiently utilized and additional sources of revenues needed to be generated. The new Mills building was deemed to be a well-located asset on the property that required little maintenance compared to the Rogers building, dating from 1926. Overall the report indicated that Dora's administration needed to be very frugal and very creative. The TS lacked the start-up costs for some of the recommendations, such as food production to support self-sufficiency. As a result, while some renovations were undertaken, goals such as solar power and self-sufficiency in food production are still unrealized to this day.

Many of the staff members lived at headquarters. Of the board members, Dora was the only one who lived at Olcott. The others were spread all over the country. Ann Wylie, who had become the national vice-president, had moved to Ojai. In 1976 she agreed to attend the general council meeting in Adyar in Dora's place. Dora had a number of new staff members and wrote, "I feel I have to mind the fort here and cannot go." Dora was quickly making it clear that she lacked a "go along to get along" style.

For example, her letter to Ann Wylie shows that she was dubious about a proposal to build an "English-teaching school for the more affluent" at Adyar. The plan had been proposed by Radha Burnier, the niece of Rukmini Devi Arundale (a close friend of Dora's since the Australia years). The Society was to contribute the capital investment, and Damodar Gardens on the Adyar campus was the selected site. Dora wrote: "The deficit in Adyar is terrific, but Radha is very set and I am sure that she will carry her weight there with so very few people present. I personally feel the Society has really to take care of its deficits and not do so much reckless spending. This of course applied to us too."

Radha Burnier became president of the international TS in 1980 after the sudden death of John Coats. Dora said that she had a good relationship with Radha, whom she had known since 1925—which says a lot about diplomacy and patience on both their parts.

Fortunately, there were no difficulties in the TSA that resulted in conflict and distancing on Dora's part, as she had threatened if the international board intervened. As for the proposed school in Damodar Gardens, it is now over thirty years old and is thriving. Moreover, the affluent students are involved in community service and development projects for the underserved. Despite her reluctance to support large capital expenditures in Adyar, Dora supported the Adyar Day annual fundraising campaign. After all, Fritz had proposed it after his return in 1922 following his five years in Adyar. He felt that TSA members would generously support the Society's mission by contributing money to the international headquarters.

Dora finally published one book, *The Real World of Fairies*, during her presidency and two more books before the end of her life. Nevertheless, even as computers were introduced into many of the departments at headquarters and the Theosophical Publishing House, she never became computer literate.

Dora protected herself against wasted energy. For example, she had an extraordinary habit of hanging up the phone when she was finished speaking. That often left the person with whom she conversed speaking into a dead phone line. Her nephew, Nicolas, enjoyed the competition: how often could he hang up before she did? He rarely won.

Dora was in her late seventies and early eighties during her presidency and had to be selective about how many events and conferences she could attend. In a letter to the general secretary of Kenya, she indicated that neither she nor anyone from the American Section would be able to "travel the distance to attend the 60th Anniversary Celebration of the Nairobi Lodge."[4]

Similarly, in 1978 she asked Seymour Ballard from Puerto Rico whether he thought it was important for her to attend that year's Inter-American Congress in Argentina. "I have not participated before," she wrote.[5] Despite her reluctance, in 1979 Dora and Emily Sellon both attended the sixth Congress. Dora even gave two extra talks: on healing and on the Masters. Although Emily had not been on the program, she presented a talk on meditation. The federation's report indicated a "spirit of solidarity at work . . . the Inter-American Federation has become a well-knit, cooperative group of working members, capable of carrying forward a long-range program such as its publication venture."

The conference was not a case of all work and no play. On the last evening, "a series of impromptu and hilarious take-offs" selectively poked fun at the English-speaking guests—including John and Betsan Coats, Emily Sellon, and Dora. The report described the skits as "imitations which certainly brought out all the little personal idiosyncrasies."[6]

Another person who, like Emily, could stand firm with Dora was Lakshmi Narayan. She epitomizes the selfless Theosophical worker but is also someone who does not mind leaving the office behind at the end of the day. After working for seven years at Adyar, she moved to the United States so that she could be closer to her son, daughter-in-law, and grandchildren. She had met Dora a year earlier when she was assigned to assist her during her Adyar visit. Dora made mistakes in some of the staff she hired at headquarters, but when she hired Lakshmi to work at Olcott, she made an excellent choice. Twenty-nine years later, Lakshmi still works as librarian in Krotona. Lakshmi offered a few words about Dora:

> In March 1985, I moved to the American Section HQ of the TS in America as Librarian of Olcott Library—for which Dora Kunz was responsible. I did not have a green card to work, nor the finances to meet with the health insurance or room and board. All of this Dora accepted and helped me. I applied for the green card, when Rosie Escudero, Dora's secretary, once head of Philippines Embassy in Seattle, helped me apply.
>
> Dora kept a close eye on me and would walk into the library and ask me what I am doing. She seemed stern but was very kind and concerned about me. She took me to movies and other outings with Jeff Gresko who had other portfolios besides being her chauffeur. I am ever grateful for this good life despite its ups and downs.[7]

Willamay Pym, who also served at Olcott during Dora's presidency, described the Olcott Library as "a very fine reference library that has been used by non-Theosophists because it's open to anyone who wants to come in and use it. In fact they can join the library without being members of the Theosophical Society."[8] Dora encouraged the acquisition of new books, videos, and tapes on a range of subjects during her tenure. Surprisingly, one finds a number of titles on the religious culture of Native American groups among the collection. Books written for nonscientists on modern physics and a new philosophy of science were some of the additions that were made during Dora's tenure. A book written by Dr. Mary Rocke, who was so helpful to Dora during her teenage years, is located in a special collections room upstairs.

Dora lacked administrative experience at the level of president, but she certainly had no illusions about the Theosophical Society and the other Theosophical organizations in the United States. These organizations include the TS itself, based in Adyar, with its American headquarters in Wheaton (sometimes called the TSA-Adyar). There is also the Theosophical Society (Pasadena), which traced itself back to a group called the Universal Brotherhood and Theosophical Society, founded by Katherine Tingley in 1898. In 1909, the United Lodge of Theosophists was started by Robert Crosbie. Another group, the Arcane School, was founded by Alice and Foster Bailey in 1923. Alice Bailey had been a member of the TSA-Adyar, as well as a member of the Esoteric School (ES). She had also been the editor of the journal of the ES at that time, the *Messenger*.

Dora had been first-hand witness to some of the conflicts and difficulties among these groups during her fifty years in the United States. Rather than magnifying old issues, she preferred to keep sight of the primary goals, while recognizing that the conflicts were not going to disappear without concerted effort over a long period of time. Dora's role as president was to discover more about the problems, their roots, and the various factors involved. Her job was to explore competing needs and demands and what might be accomplished over the short and long term. Just as she discriminated about what she would and would not support, there were limits to how much change others would support—or even tolerate.

Dora cared about the Theosophical Society as a whole, of course. But one of her strengths was that she personally knew and cared about people from lodges and other Theosophical groups all over the country. She had visited many of the lodges around the country since 1925, and she understood the wide range of interests among the members of the organization and other Theosophical organizations.

Dora did not always make decisions that turned out well. Sometimes she took risks in hiring, and there were occasionally staff members who were clearly unable to function well in the headquarters environment. On one occasion Dora wrote to Ann Wylie that she had to choose among two candidates for a position on the board, and her choice turned out to be problematic. Within a year, she wrote that the person she selected "is in a mood to bring trouble to every part of the [American] Section and he is already distorting whatever he heard from the Board meeting." She was far from passive in that situation, because her letter to the board members reiterated her view.

> Whatever has been discussed in the Board meetings if it's talked about with the staff, produces waves of unrest and anger. . . . It is up to the administration to carry out the decisions of the Board and not for the Board to initiate these decisions with any member of the staff. . . . Please do not talk about resolutions with regard to headquarters or any part of the Section until they are carried out by the administration.[9]

Even though it does not require clairvoyance to notice workplace problems, Dora's use of the phrase "waves of unrest and anger" indicates that her assessment was partly based on her clairvoyance. Her memo indicates that she made a clear distinction between the administration and the nonadministrative and support staff.

Dora did not dwell on problems. After devoting little more than a paragraph to this item, in her characteristic quicksilver manner she described a gala open house as a success. Over 350 people attended, including about one hundred members of the Society from around the country. She said, "We had gorgeous weather. . . . Karole Kettering and Margaret Montgomery did a wonderful job and several people joined the Society on the spot."[10] She saw no need to give more attention than necessary to disruptive issues when there was much positive action as well.

Dora may well have encouraged an exodus of many older members of the Society who had taken up residence in the Rogers building at headquarters. She was not sentimental; there was work to be done and she clearly imposed her view that Olcott was the headquarters of a national organization. To say she "cleaned house" is harsh, but records indicate that there were many going-away parties during her first months in office. By Christmas of both her first and second years in office, there were so many new staff that she stayed on campus instead of flying back to Port Chester or going to India for the TS's general convention. In a letter written to Ann Wylie a little over a year after she assumed office, Dora listed the staff in each of the positions and wrote, "As you can see, you would not recognize Olcott at this moment! I think we have a very nice bunch of kids with us right now. They are willing, eager and have such a nice attitude. The atmosphere is so very much nicer. But I am staying here because we now have to really make every-body work together as they are so brand new."[11]

During her first year in office, Dora was in New York City for the Centennial World Congress of the Theosophical Society, which had been founded in 1875. It was fitting that she should have begun her term at the dawn of a new century for the Society and that her efforts were centered in the United States, where the Society was founded. Dora and her colleagues did their best to ensure that the TSA was reinvigorated and reimagined for the start of the second century.

Boris de Zirkoff was a Secret Doctrine scholar, the last living relative of Madame Blavatsky, and a friend of Dora's. He lived for many years at the Point Loma Theosophical community in San Diego, edited Blavatsky's Collected Writings, and created the periodical *Theosophia*. De Zirkoff wrote, "It is evident . . . that the Second Century in the history of the Movement is opening with great promise—a promise of solidarity, mutuality, and increasing strength of spiritual and intellectual ties."[12]

Those who planned the World Congress in New York City, largely John Coats and Joy Mills, the president and vice-president respectively of the international Theosophical Society, set the stage for that promise to be realized. Dora's work in the TSA could not have been framed better. She was one of over 800 delegates who attended. John Coats made an appeal to members of various Theosophical organizations, including the Adyar Theosophists, "to heal some of the misunderstandings that have existed for far too long between the many Theosophists who, each in his or her own way, are conscientiously serving the great ideal. We should, as men and women of sound common sense and good will, help that 'poor orphan Humanity' which is so vastly more important than ourselves."[13]

During the centennial Dora had her first opportunity as president to write a rebuttal to the editors of a national publication. An article in the November 24, 1975, issue of *Newsweek* included what was described by one of the World Congress participants as a "disconcerting and unjust attack on Madame Blavatsky."[14] On the other hand, a *New York Times* article published on the fifth day of the centenary celebration referred to the delegates as "students of truth." The article said that the delegates represented the spirit of New York City itself as open to people of all different backgrounds.

Dora defended Blavatsky, one of the Society's founders, against unjust attack. Nevertheless, she was objective when she talked with members of the Society about Blavatsky. As she said in another context:

> The one thing in which she was totally—could I say "impersonal"—was her dedication to the Master. But in daily life she must have been very difficult to live with. There is no doubt she must have been extremely trying to live with. But that devotion—and the Masters to her—were the great reality to which she devoted her life. . . .
>
> To her the Masters were completely real. She called her Master "The Boss." She kicked very often; she resented it very often—what had to be done.
>
> She had a very difficult life. She was accused of many things. . . . She was tremendously maligned.
>
> She was a medium in that—through her—this phenomenon could take place. She had devoted friends. She was a person who was impetuous in many ways. . . . She died having found Mrs. Besant and after writing *The Secret Doctrine* which is certainly a monumental task. . . . That doesn't mean that every work in *The Secret Doctrine* necessarily needs to be the gospel. Everybody can make a mistake finally and particularly with her temperament. I think the tremendous philosophy is true but I wouldn't be surprised if there were mistakes. . . . Think of all she did.[15]

Dora cannot be given sole credit for the significant attempts during her presidency to bring various Theosophical groups together for open dialogue. John Coats was instrumental in supporting such efforts. He wanted members to be welcome at one another's lectures and other meetings, and he sought her help in that matter.

Coats proposed a committee of members of different Theosophical groups that would best be formed in the United States. He suggested that it meet "from time to time when convenient. . . . A discussion around a table would not commit anyone, but could lend itself to understanding of each other's problems, and if followed by a lunch or dinner, all could be relaxed and at ease with one another, and this always helps." In a 1975 letter to Boris de Zirkoff, Coats said that Dora was organizing his tour in America in the summer of 1976 and that he wanted to have an exploratory meeting while there. "There are different points of view and we have to accept that they have existed, and try to understand why. But they should not in any way, prevent us from leaving the past to take care of itself and going ahead freely into the future."[16]

Another important achievement of Dora's presidency was the expansion of the TS's prison outreach program. Its inspiration can be traced back to H. M. Stokes from Washington, DC, in the early twentieth century. Stokes was a chemist and president of the American Chemical Society, as well as a member of the Oriental Esoteric Society. He started a magazine in 1911, *The Oriental*, devoted to prison reform. Inspired by Stokes's efforts, Annie Besant started a prison program of her own.[17] Fritz Kunz, influenced by Mrs. Besant's program, lectured in prisons as a volunteer during most of his adult life. Partly because of what Dora jokingly described as her "experience in prison," and thanks to key members who took interest, her administration expanded the program.

Correspondence, and occasionally literature, went directly to prisoners from the national headquarters. Increased numbers of books from the Theosophical Publishing House were donated to prison libraries. Dora often told students about a prisoner who, she believed, had changed remarkably during imprisonment and that he had worked hard to do so. That same prisoner helped others after his release. She said that in his case and a few others, Fritz served as a character reference, because he saw that radical change is possible even in a challenging environment.

Edith Karsten, who worked closely with Dora at headquarters, said that Dora preferred to teach young adults and adults rather than children. Even so, Dora's joy, playfulness, and friendliness seemed to attract children to her. Sometimes at Indralaya or Pumpkin Hollow Farm a toddler who had never seen her before would go running into her arms without prompting. Later in her life when she had the pressures of the presidency behind her, she loved to play with children. When she played, she expressed a childlike joy and exuberance and seemed unaware of her physical limitations in her late eighties and nineties.

Dora helped children she treated or through counseling their parents, but she devoted herself almost entirely to helping adults and developing new curricula in adult education.

Many times during the last decade of her life Dora said that she wanted to help sensitive children in particular. She also thought that there were more sensitive children being born, and she began to identify some ways to help them early in life.

During her presidency, she also wanted to start a school on the Olcott campus for young children. A proposal was prepared, and the board purchased a house adjoining the Olcott campus with the intention of creating the school there. In the end, it was determined that the school would have demanded more resources than could be justified, and the project was shelved for several decades. Some dreams were not realized.

Another innovation failed to stand the test of time. Dora thought it was helpful for the staff to have time away from headquarters, so she moved the Summer School and National Convention from the headquarters in Wheaton to Lake Geneva, Wisconsin. This change occurred early in her tenure and lasted until she left office. At that time, for financial reasons the decision was made to return the activities to headquarters. It was also much easier for those who flew to Chicago to take a limousine to nearby Wheaton than to find their way to Lake Geneva, some sixty miles away.

Dora loved to be in gatherings in natural settings, and the TSA board may have indulged her love of nature to some degree. She recognized that the harmony of the group was improved when people all slept and shared meals in the same location. The campus of George Williams College in Lake Geneva fostered the relative informality that Dora preferred for discussion groups and presentations. She followed *Robert's Rules of Order* during business meetings, but for Theosophical discussions she preferred less formality. Pontificating and posturing bored her. Although she loved discussion and—as a Theosophist since birth—was undeterred by complex subject matter, she preferred to work in the informal environments of Pumpkin Hollow Farm, Indralaya, and Lake Geneva Summer School. At Lake Geneva she could feel she was one among many rather than an administrator or hostess.

At the lake one imagines that she enlisted the help of the water fairies and higher orders to lift the energies of weary participants or those who were ill. In most cases, that would have occurred quite naturally, especially where there were children and others who feel joy in nature. Everyone stayed in one of the simple cabins, and there was a piano for her grandson and others to play while there. There was entertainment or campfires in the evenings, and people dressed up in the evenings, as they did at Pumpkin Hollow. The women often wore floor-length skirts or dresses, which also served to keep mosquitoes away.

Dora thought participants had the best of both worlds at Lake Geneva. The natural environment allowed participants and their children and grandchildren to swim, boat, play volleyball, and dress comfortably. On the other hand, participants with the finest intellects could tackle challenging issues and topics undistracted by restless children. Since the sessions were largely for members, there was free discussion concerning issues within the Society as an organization. The last evening was traditionally devoted to fun—musical entertainment and improvisational skits and spoofs.

Dora often lectured on healing and Therapeutic Touch during her presidency. She started a weekly healing group at headquarters, as she had at the New York Theosophical Society, and she and Erik Peper authored a series of articles on healing under the auspices of the Theosophical Research Institute. For the most part, however, she limited her healing work during those twelve years. At the same time, under Dolores Krieger's guidance, Therapeutic Touch took on a life of its own. The Nurse Healers–Professional Associates became an international organization and developed curricula for beginning, intermediate, and advanced practitioners. Dora and Dolores continued to offer annual Invitational Healers' Workshops at Indralaya and Pumpkin Hollow Farm, and Dora participated in the annual Nurse Healers–Professional Associates conferences as well.

While Dora was president, she encouraged staff to study so that the concepts they shared and the language used reflected the modern world. In her effort to modernize the language of Theosophy, she discouraged members from using confusing terms or language from the turn of the twentieth century without defining those terms. Similarly, she discouraged nurses and other professionals from using medical or technical terms at headquarters, Pumpkin Hollow Farm, and Indralaya.

More than a few of her Therapeutic Touch students helped her with research during her presidency and enabled her to develop her expertise in certain areas. Mention has been made of some of those people, but there were many others Dora knew from her "healing work" who generously taught at the camps or headquarters. A nurse named Michelle Moran moved to Olcott and was instrumental in the production of a series of videotapes that explored various Theosophical concepts. Sue Wright, another nurse, had mastered videotaping and took time off from her work each summer for ten years to act as Dora's assistant at Pumpkin Hollow Farm. Janet Macrae taught Therapeutic Touch at the NYTS for nearly two decades. Marie Jenkins, a nursing faculty member at Sacramento City College, facilitated a healing group in Sacramento for many years. Some of Dora's students who studied healing became active members of the TS, while others remained nominal members.

Dora spoke of her contribution thus:

> I think my "medical work" is bringing the Theosophical teachings to hundreds and hundreds of nurses who learn Therapeutic Touch. They also come to our camps and pick up Theosophical ideas. . . . It has—officially—nothing to do with the Theosophical Society, but it was founded in a Theosophical camp and we still have workshops there. It has thousands of nurses now joining, and it has made a contribution to the United States. And I think I did that; I can take the blame for it or whatever it is.
>
> The Theosophists have no idea about this. . . . I mean it's interesting, if you picked a member anywhere, they wouldn't know about Therapeutic Touch and that we have really made a contribution. . . . Karma is what I talk about often; I talk to the nurses about it because they ask, "Why does a person have cancer?" . . . Karma is really something we teach the nurses

because it really helps them. It really means something because now they think it's an accident, an accident of God or whatever it is. . . . A lot of Theosophical ideas are permeated in the nursing profession, therefore, and I think that's good.[18]

Dora's strengths included her knowledge of the various aspects of the organization's purpose. She had special sensitivity to what could realistically be expected of her staff and others. But her actions were perceived by some of the staff as intrusive. She had a tendency to drop by their offices, look over their shoulders, and go through papers on their desks.

Both Edith Karsten and Willamay Pym had known her much of their lives from Indralaya. Willamay was the national secretary for a year and then worked at Olcott in another capacity for two more years. Edith Karsten was the national secretary for eight years. Both of them had raised children and had retired from their careers when they moved to Wheaton. Willamay Pym retired as registrar at a community college and had a great deal of autonomy in her work. She was quite frank in her assessment of Dora's management abilities.

> To quote her son, she had practically no administrative ability. Having been an administrator myself and then going back and working for her, I concurred with that. She had so many valuable things to contribute, but a real understanding of administering the Society was not one of them. I found working with Dora a very good lesson in flexibility. I had run my own operation for about fifteen years for the college. And whereas I had a boss, he did practically nothing as far as my operations were concerned unless I needed help or asked him.

But working for Dora—when I first went back I started a project which she'd given me, had it probably two-thirds of the way through and she said, "No I don't want it that way." So I went back and started over again. Flexibility was the rule as far as working with her is concerned.

I felt that a good portion of my time—of the three years there—was as a buffer between Dora and the staff. She had the feeling that if a person was there she could use that person any way she wanted to. And if the department to which he or she was attached was not in as great a need as another place, she was just as apt as not to say, "Oh well, we can put so and so over here"—whether [or not] it was anything that that person was qualified for or interested in. So I spent a lot of time smoothing ruffled feathers and trying to explain to the staff that Dora's strong points so far outweighed the others that we just had to be patient and work with it.[19]

Edith Karsten's observations concur with Willamay Pym's: that Dora could be a micromanager.

Dora was the boss. No matter what office I held, I had to get permission from her. . . . We had to work on it together. Now she was a strong leader. I was her secretary for many years but I wasn't her secretary for more than fifteen minutes. I was just there for her to send me when she did a lot of traveling and public lectures—all over. I was there to keep things running smoothly when she was gone. . . . I tried to hold things together. . . . Because when she got back, everything had to be in order. She relied on me to be just sitting in the chair, but any business that came up [during her absence] had to be transferred over to her.[20]

On one occasion when Dora's behavior caused friction at head-quarters and staff members expressed particular unhappiness, her old friend John Sellon flew from New York to meet with her. He later said that the two of them sat down together and that he told her very frankly that if she wanted to have a staff, she had to allow each of them to do his or her work. Dora accepted his suggestions, and the staffing crisis was averted.[21]

When she was eighty-seven years old and looking back, Dora said of her presidency, "I guess maybe I was bossy but I went to every department twice a week and I knew whatever they were doing. I personally got involved in every department." The Quest Book Shop is located in the Mills building on the Olcott campus, just a few hundred yards from the Rogers building. Dora later said about it, "If I disapproved of a book I'd make them take it out, because if it was unutterable junk, I wouldn't have them sell it."[22]

Nonetheless, according to Edith Karsten's recollections, Dora's sensitivity also contributed to astute decisions regarding person-nel. "She could see how things were going to blend together; more, the personal traits of the person. She seemed to know how it would be, and it usually turned out she was right."[23]

Dora was altruistic, loving, and compassionate, but she had a habit pattern that was brusque and caustic. At a Wainwright House seminar, she had given the example of a negative habit pattern. The person she described could very well have been herself: "A person would like to be nice or loving to somebody. But instead of say-ing something nice, something sharp sometimes comes out. Unconsciously."[24] If she felt strongly about something or had to make a decision, she tended to find solitude in nature, or she medi-tated. That, along with lecturing and treating patients, helped keep her from making blunt remarks. She often seemed unaware that she had said something rude, but if confronted, she was apologetic.

Rude remarks occurred more often during the last decade and a half of Dora's life. She worked very hard as the president of the Theosophical Society and may have experienced periods of strain. She also had an episode of very low blood pressure from cardiac dysrhythmia when she was in her early eighties that may have contributed to mild dementia. That and mild hearing loss may have added to strain from a demanding travel schedule and administrative responsibilities. One of her friends said that she was bossy at times but that this did not happen when Fritz was alive, implying that he had a moderating effect on her. Dora did not express rancor or malice; she did not manipulate or make scenes. She just made occasional rude remarks. Dora's students who knew and loved her for decades accepted her. Others left to find other teachers.

Renee Weber explained that there was "Upper Dora" and "Lower Dora" and that Upper Dora was funny, compassionate, and generous with her insights. Another friend, Margot Wilkie, passed Dora's rude behavior off as her way of letting go of accumulated tension. Dora was more sensitive than most people and also had many more demands for her attention than most people experience during their seventies, eighties, and nineties.

Dora maintained a demanding schedule as president of the Theosophical Society, but she did not see her work as a burden. For one thing, it enabled her to meet people that she would otherwise not have known. One of the people she admired the most was Tenzin Gyatso, the Fourteenth Dalai Lama. The Theosophical Publishing House had published his book *The Opening of the Wisdom-Eye* in 1966, and it was around that time that Dora met him in New Delhi.

In 1981, at Dora's invitation, the Dalai Lama came to speak at Olcott. He had visited the United States and Canada two years earlier, so this was not his first visit to North America. He was accompanied by a small entourage. It included his translator, Jeffrey Hopkins, who was a professor in the Buddhist studies department at the University of Virginia. Radha Burnier traveled from Adyar for the Dalai Lama's visit. He had visited Adyar on three occasions, the first in 1956, and the second and third shortly after he escaped Tibet in 1959.

Dora and the staff had never hosted someone who was in effect a head of state. Security was necessary for the head of the Tibetan government-in-exile. There were multiple briefings regarding security issues for the staff and volunteers involved in his visit. An around-the-clock police presence in the Rogers building was also required, as was a police escort whenever the entourage left the compound. Despite all these procedures, the Dalai Lama's visit was relatively uncomplicated.

During his stay, the Dalai Lama gave a teaching outdoors at Olcott, as well as a public talk at Wheaton North High School. His teaching at Olcott, "Universal Compassion and Global Crisis," spoke to hatred and anger as well as the presence of nuclear arms in the world. He said that in terms of creating compassion and kindness, he viewed himself not as a Dalai Lama or a Buddhist, but as a human being. He also viewed the listeners not as Americans or Westerners or Theosophists but as human beings. Whether one is rich or poor, educated or uneducated—these, he said, are all secondary.

> The time has come. We should think at a deeper level, on the human being level. Express from that level and appreciate or respect [that] others are sameness of human being. We must build a closer relationship: mutual trust, mutual understanding, mutual respect, mutual help. Build from that basis in respect of what is culture, what is philosophy, what is religion, what is faith. All human beings are the same: human being. So, each

human being has the same responsibility for all mankind. The conclusion is that at this time we should think of all human beings as your brothers, sisters. And you should be concerned with other people's benefit, other people's suffering. Compare other people's benefit and your own benefit. Even [if] you could not sacrifice your own entire benefit, you should not forget other people's concern. So we should think more about all mankind's future and benefit.

Someone asked, "What is the real reason for meditation?" The Dalai Lama replied:

There are two kinds of meditation. One is for developing calm-abiding of the mind and the other is for developing special insight. For the development of calm-abiding of the mind, one channelizes the mind. At present our mind is too much scattered. Once it's scattered, the force is limited. Channelize like water, becoming forceful. So that's the purpose of that kind of meditation. Special insight is to investigate about nature, reality.

Another question posed was, "What specific things can Westerners do in the next ten years to bring about the changes you speak of, that is to say, universal brotherhood and sisterhood?" He replied, "That is a difficult question; I don't know. I think it is your responsibility—you Westerners' responsibility. Everybody agrees that it is something necessary, something important. Now how to follow upliftment about this idea? We all have the responsibility to think and investigate and try, try, try."[25]

Dora walked with the Dalai Lama all around the large property in Olcott and through many of the peaceful gardens. They walked in silence most of the time. When asked what he had said to her during those times, she responded, "If you want to know the truth, he asked me a lot of questions." She later told a friend that he had less ego than anyone she had ever met. She also mentioned that she could see that he was what she called "fully functioning":

> If a person is sensitive or if they are healing, they develop more strength in the different levels of consciousness and also their intuition develops. . . . I think that would be using all the levels of consciousness and would make a person develop intuition. At that moment, if one is clairvoyant, particularly what shines out or becomes more developed is this chakra in the middle of the forehead. One uses the different chakras if one does all these things in meditation. The Dalai Lama is fully developed in that way; he uses all his chakras because he meditates all the time.[26]

Despite these feelings, Dora was not willing to budge when members of his entourage requested that meat be served to them at Olcott. She said that she did not care if anyone ate meat away from the campus, but it had never been introduced there.

Long after his visit, Dora continued to speak of the Dalai Lama with great admiration and respect: "Yes, I thought he was a wise man. The Dalai Lama has made the most impression on me."[27]

Another man who left a powerful impression on Dora was Father Bede Griffiths. She and Renee Weber traveled to his Saccidananda Ashram in Shantivanam, Tamil Nadu, in January 1983, while Dora was in India for the TS international convention.

Father Bede was two years younger than Dora and, though he had left England when he was forty-nine years old to live in India, his Oxford accent remained. Renee Weber interviewed him over the course of several days for her book *Dialogues with Scientists and Sages*. According to her description of him, aside from his devotion to Christianity, nothing else in his appearance or lifestyle bespoke England.

> Tall and lean, almost gaunt, his muscular frame reflects the years of hard toil under the Indian sun. . . . Fr. Bede wears the saffron *kavi* of the Hindu holy man and goes mostly barefoot. . . . Security, he says, has been the ruin of the religious life and of many monasteries. . . . Fr. Bede feels strongly that the members of the community must live as the local Indians live and this, together with his commitment to primordial Christianity, dictates their lifestyle of extreme simplicity. The ashram is almost self-supporting. It raises rice in its own rice-paddy, coconuts, vegetables, fruit and milk, and is helped by contributions from visitors on meditation retreats who want to pay for their stay. The ashram charges nothing, so there is no fixed income. Fr. Bede says that they live from month to month, sometimes from week to week, and adds that "this is the way it should be."

Father Bede had arrived in India with what he thought was necessary to his life but soon discovered that he did not really need chairs or even silverware. The ashram had narrow beds of stone, and, according to Renee Weber, "the vegetarian meals are eaten Indian style, without utensils, on the floor of the simple dining hall, and though ample they are simple to the point of austerity."[28]

Dora also admired the way Father Bede introduced elements of Hinduism into his services, even though he was a devout Benedictine monk. As she later put it, "He has a Christian ashram where he tries to bring the Hindu ideas of religion and combine them with studying the Christian faith. I visited this ashram and what I thought was very remarkable was how close the villagers feel. There does not seem to be any division, from what I observed, between the simple villagers all around it and the people in the ashram. And I thought this was a beautiful thing to behold."[29]

In August 1983, Father Bede came to Olcott and, along with Kenneth Vaux, spoke on the interface between Christianity and other faiths. Dora did a taped interview with Father Bede, and he also spoke with the Olcott staff. Father Bede's words at this event show how he understood unity and diversity.

> We very much want to create an Indian Christian tradition. Not just Christianity but a Christianity that India can open itself to. What the Hindu, the Buddhist, the Jain, the Sikh—all the religions of India—have to say. So that gradually we have this convergence. . . . We don't want simply to merge everything into one but to see how the one mystery—the divine mystery— manifests itself in different ways, in different traditions. And they're all interrelated and they all have this unity behind them. . . .
>
> Because we are unities, we are psychosomatic spiritual unities, each of us experiences the one reality in a different way. And I think these differences are important and beautiful. We're not meant all to merge into one. We're each to bring a unique mode of experiencing the one reality. They sometimes describe it as the one light shining in many mirrors, and each reflects it and reflects it in a slightly different way. So that the beauty of creation is the One manifesting himself in the many and the many recognizing himself in the One.
>
> So early in the morning at dawn and at sunset we have this solitary meditation. And to me that is more fundamental.

That is the point where we go beyond words; we go beyond thoughts and we try to enter into the unitive experience of dwelling in the heart. So that is the point of meeting. Everybody is capable of meditating at that depth, but I think we must recognize that until we reach that level of the consciousness experience, no real meeting in depth will take place.[30]

In his interview with Renee Weber, Father Bede elaborated:

There is a second aspect to this; in order to be spiritually free one must not be attached to anything. One may use things but one must not be attached to them. To live in a very simple life-style is one of the best means of learning this detachment. In India, partly because of the climate, one is able to live in almost incredible simplicity, and I have found that this is a wonderful way to attain to inner freedom and joy. This has taught me that the elaborate system of material conveniences built up in the West is not necessary for the real enjoyment of life.

I think if you live in peaceful surroundings related to the natural world it gives you a balance and a harmony in your life, and in your whole relation to people and to God. . . . We should emphasize decentralization and more human communities. To create a community which is living in harmony with its natural environment is fundamental. With regard to human relationships, it is best to have a comparatively small face-to-face community, where people know one another. So these are the conditions I feel are necessary for the growth of humanity and for the experience of the reality of the spirit of God in one's life. . . . Then you are open to the divine and you can experience it day by day, hour by hour in your life.

Living close to nature is very important. For me the great discovery in India is the discovery of the sacred. In India everything is sacred: the earth is sacred; food, water, and taking a bath are all sacred, a building is sacred. . . . From the earliest times men and women all over the world lived in this sacred universe, whether it was the Australian Aborigines, the American Indians, the tribal people of Africa; they all sensed a sacred living universe of which humans are a part. And this divine power, whatever name it is given, penetrates through the earth, the water, the air, and through your own being. . . . Only now in the last fifty years, are we recovering the sense of the sacred.[31]

Dora brought in other remarkable speakers to Olcott. Many "scientists and sages," to use the words from Renee Weber's book title, taught there during her presidency.

Another significant achievement during Dora's presidency was the development of the Theosophical Research Institute (TRI). The Masters had predicted that science would be the language of the time, and the international Society had supported research at the highest levels, as evidenced particularly by Mrs. Besant and Leadbeater. In the United States there was a Theosophical research group in New York as well as one at the national level. Fritz had been part of those efforts, especially regarding the meeting of East and West and the confluence with modern physics. Such research, until relatively recently, received little support in traditional academic institutions. The TRI brought together scientists and other scholars from diverse fields.

The Society's increased support for research efforts during Dora's terms in office was not limited to healing phenomena. She drew on the considerable resources among the membership for this purpose, but if outside expertise was necessary to move lines of enquiry forward, Dora invited public speakers to Olcott to help enrich the dialogue. That was not unique to her administration, but she had access to a great range of very knowledgeable people largely because of Fritz's foundation and *Main Current in Modern Thought*.

Dora had support from capable scholars from a number of fields: the chemist Ralph Hannon; the physicist Ravi Ravindra; and E. Lester Smith, the English biologist who was the codiscoverer of vitamin B-12. Renee Weber and Erik Peper were among the associates who advanced ideas on healing and other topics. Emily Sellon brought her knowledge of relevant scientific advances, Theosophical literature, and the direction of research in recent years.

Ralph Hannon, a professor at Kishwaukee College in Malta, Illinois, was the chairperson of the TRI. He participated in many of the conferences and seminars at Olcott in addition to convening regular meetings of the committee.

In 1980 the TRI held two science seminars. The first was "The Holographic Model of the Universe" with Ravi Ravindra, Renee Weber, and Marilyn Ferguson, editor of *Brain/Mind Bulletin* and author of *The Aquarian Conspiracy*. The second seminar, with Fritjof Capra and Renee Weber, was entitled "Space, Time, and Consciousness."

These were exciting times: the scientific basis for what Dora called "healing at a distance" was becoming recognized through the concept of non-locality in quantum physics. Physicists reported that if twin subatomic particles were separated, the behavior of one particle exactly matched the behavior of the other, no matter what the distance was between them. That finding supported the hypothesis— made by Leadbeater and Besant and other early Theosophical authors—that thoughts and feelings affect people nearby and have the potential to affect others at a distance. Dora's healing too is based on the nonlocal effects of positive thoughts, compassion, and goodwill directed toward someone in need.

In December 1980, Dora supported the publication of *The Extrasensory Perception of Quarks*, a unique book by a physicist in England named Stephen M. Phillips. Dora had been following his research and wrote to Ralph Hannon in April 1978 saying she arranged for Henry Margenau of Yale University to evaluate Phillips's thesis and formulas. She also enlisted scholars associated with the TRI to evaluate the validity of Phillips's mathematical formulas. In December 1979, Dora accompanied Renee Weber to London and met with Phillips. Making her clairvoyant assessment, Dora commented on his intense concentration and pronounced him a "remarkable young man."[32]

Leadbeater and Mrs. Besant had begun clairvoyant research on atoms almost one hundred years earlier, in 1885. Their findings were published many years later as *Occult Chemistry: Clairvoyant Observations on the Chemical Elements*. Dora said that the scientific community ridiculed them terribly for the work.

Before Phillips's work, scientists had not been able to correlate *Occult Chemistry* with modern physics and chemistry, according to Dora.[33] Phillips posited that Leadbeater affected the subatomic particles by slowing them down for psychic observation. Many of the things Besant and Leadbeater described were later corroborated by science. For example, as Phillips's work showed, they described several isotopes (elements with atoms containing extra neutrons) before isotopes were known to science. They also discovered that geometrical configurations of atoms corresponded to the position of elements in the Periodic Table of Elements.

Dora took particular interest in Phillips's book, though she knew it would appeal to a very small audience. The technical aspects of reproducing the diagrams were challenging, and she remained attentive to every step of the process. She wrote to the board in September 1980, "Stephen Phillips is here, and we are very busy getting the *ESP of Quarks* ready for press. There is a lot involved in this and keeps me very busy. Phillips will stay in the United States till end of October or first week of November."[34] Dr. E. Lester Smith, a Fellow of the Royal Society in England, wrote the foreword. In 1999 Phillips published another book: *ESP of Quarks and Superstrings*.

Another scientist whom Dora got to know was the respected physicist David Bohm. Bohm was remarkably courageous and innovative even as a young physicist. He lived most of his life as an expatriate after his security clearance had been revoked as a result of the McCarthy hearings in the 1950s. After retiring from the University of London as a professor of theoretical physics, Bohm continued to live in London until his death from heart failure in 1992. Dora met him through Renee Weber, who had known him as a fellow student of Krishnamurti.

Bohm and Dora became friends, and he seems to have felt that he could drop in on short notice at Olcott. During these visits, one staff member recalled, Bohm must have stayed just long enough to meet with Dora, because he caught a taxi to the airport before most of the staff were aware of his arrival.

It was common for Dora to protect a person suffering from fatigue. She provided a good excuse to be antisocial by ordering the person to avoid talking with people and go to his or her room and rest. She sounded just bossy enough that she was rarely refused.

Dora was very thoughtful and helped many people, not just those who visited headquarters but also those who wrote. Some of the letters, sent from members and nonmembers, asked for specific advice about meditation, psychic experiences, or intuitional experiences. Dora responded personally to many of the letters. Some seemed to indicate that the writer struggled with mental health issues; others were sent from prisons; some describe psychic experiences; and some describe experiences of a more subtle, intuitive nature. Handwritten letters with spelling errors that filled the back and front of several pages of lined paper were given individualized responses as if the writer were a longtime member of the Society and a brother or sister. When a person sought help, Dora felt that there was an opening and an opportunity to help the person change. Whether letters were answered by Dora or another member of the staff, she did not want to miss an opportunity to help someone.

The letters, along with Dora's responses, give insights into her counseling ability and the careful way in which she reached toward the best in each person. Dora had her limits; Edith Karsten reported that she was soundly scolded by Dora after giving out Dora's phone number while she was on a lecture tour to a member who sounded urgently in need. If Dora did not believe she was likely to be of help, she would respond politely and briefly and, if she was on the phone, would then hang up abruptly in her usual style.

One of Dora's letters was to a young man who sought her help about unsettling experiences during his explorations with someone he described as a fraudulent spiritual teacher. He had mentioned his religion and she encouraged him to rely on that faith as a source of strength.

> I am sorry to hear that you feel you are being controlled by other people, and particularly through your chakras. I am at least glad to know that you are not doing any automatic writing, meditating or other occult activities; this is a healthy abstention. No person should be controlled by anyone else. It is important that you do two things. One, if this is permitted by your Church of Christ, burn incense before going to sleep

and say to yourself, "I believe in the Lord Christ and I want the force of His love to go through me and keep me safe."

Second, try to feel strong and whole within yourself and with this thought, no evil powers can get to you. If you belong to a Church of Christ, you could wear a cross around your neck and this would remind you that you are attuned to the power of Christ. I think the symbol of the cross is very protective against evil influences. Don't be afraid, because it is a negative feeling and causes a weakened state. Fear only encourages this phenomena. We will think of you and try to help you from here. I do hope that you will gain the strength to be fully yourself.[35]

Looking back on her years as president, Dora said, "I opened the door of the Society for a lot of things when I was president." She was referring to the incredible teachers, researchers, musicians, artists, filmmakers and religious leaders who led seminars, gave public lectures and concerts, and taught classes and special programs. She opened the door for others to reimagine new curricula and share their expertise in other ways.

If Dora's administration at Olcott introduced considerable innovation, it was because some of the changes, such as computer systems, had become a matter of course. Nonetheless, the changes to the education department and the Theosophical Research Institute were her greatest achievements as president. During the same period, the Theosophical Publishing House produced many new books, including the *ESP of Quarks*. That she was in her late seventies and early eighties when she and her administration accomplished the changes indicates that the decline of intellectual creativity during aging may very well be a product of one's environment. Olcott was full of vitality, and Dora thrived.

Chapter Eleven

Dora's Last Decade
(1987–1999)

Dora retired after twelve years at Olcott. Unlike many people who retire and rarely see their former colleagues, Dora did not step back from participation in the Theosophical Society. After she moved back to Washington state, she began to attend Wednesday evening members' meetings at the lodge on Seattle's Capitol Hill, and often attended public meetings as well. Every other Thursday evening, from late September through May, she held her healing group. It was well attended, and she always returned home with an announcement of how many doctors there were to help her, even when nurses outnumbered physicians. Her son, John, was active in the Society during those years and served on the boards of the Seattle lodge and Krotona in addition to being Northwest regional representative on the board of the national TSA. He and his wife, Aino, and their two children had sold their house in Port Chester and moved to Seattle in 1978.

Dora continued to teach several workshops at Indralaya and Pumpkin Hollow Farm each year. At both Indralaya and Pumpkin Hollow nearly a hundred health care professionals and patients participated in the Invitational Healers' Workshops. Many of the participants returned year after year, and there was a feeling of harmony and shared learning among participants. There was a very cheerful and peaceful feeling in the groups, even though many of the patients were very ill. For many, it was the only opportunity they had during the year to hear Dora or Dolores and to see one another. Many of them had little time off from demanding jobs, and participants often rested in between sessions.

Dora's good friend Dr. Bengtsson still lived in Ossining, where she had spent all but her college years. Her niece often accompanied her to Pumpkin Hollow Farm for the Healers' Workshop. At other times Dora instructed her most trusted nurses to assist Dr. Bengtsson and to ensure that Dr. Bengtsson's cabin was warmly heated on chill evenings.

Dora did not slow down until her weakening heart finally forced her to do so. She was committed to teaching and helping patients, as well as the professionals who helped her develop new approaches to treating a number of health conditions. When teaching, Dora included insights, not only about health challenges, but about greater social and economic conditions. She suggested that there would be economic challenges. She commented on the general anxiety and suggested that people continue to practice her healing meditation, particularly in large cities. She continued to read a daily paper and discussed current issues with John Sellon and others.

Dora was keen to learn, because she could then apply what she learned to help someone who sought her help. Along with Erik Peper, she did some follow-up research on some of the patients who attended Pumpkin Hollow Farm and Indralaya. But there was little funding for research, and the Theosophical Research Institute she had championed at headquarters in Wheaton had largely lost its funding. Since then there have been no similar follow-up studies on those who studied with her, particularly during the early years.

With Dolores Krieger's guidance, the Nurse Healers–Professional Associates International supported some research, but many of the professionals who assisted Dora in advancing her ideas did so on their own time and without monetary compensation.

A great number of Dora's students continue to contribute in innovative ways to nursing, medicine, social work, psychology, psychiatry, and other fields. Many people have extended Dora's work by incorporating elements of her approach into their own work in a variety of settings. Some of them acknowledge her contributions, and for many others, her ideas seem to glimmer from the pages of their writing. She was ahead of her time, and many of her concepts, lacking adequate research and development, remain controversial.

After Dora retired as president, she began treating people with AIDS and people who were HIV positive. Her patients did not report miraculous elevations of their T-cell counts or spontaneous remissions. But many patients found a new community of caring people at the camps and at her Seattle healing group. Some of her patients taught her a great deal about what it is like to be young and terminally ill. During the early years of HIV, young gay males were disproportionately affected by the disease, but over the years Dora treated a few heterosexual women who were HIV positive. She learned about HIV and AIDS largely from working with patients alongside a physician or a nurse who specialized in the field.

When an interviewer suggested that it must have been oppressive to be dealing with nothing but illness and sickness and death, Dora responded, "I'm detached." She did not try to deny that HIV, during the early years, was "a death sentence." She did her best, she said, even as her patients became sicker and sicker. "My mother was a much more loving girl. My lovingness [sic] is practical. My mother hasn't [sic] always had to deal with such terrible sicknesses.

I have seen thousands of extremely, terribly sick people. In one way I have seen more AIDS people, even now, than a lot of doctors in small towns. There's no doubt about it, I have dealt with a tremendous lot of sickness and that's the difference. The big healers do nothing else but heal and do [public] speaking."[1]

Dora counseled patients one by one. For those who were open to new ways of perceiving themselves and life, she suggested that there is a more subtle self than the physical body, the intellect, and the emotions. She encouraged identification with the inner self and would say at the most profound moment of her guided meditation, "I am that peace."

While cancer and AIDS research led to sometimes remarkable recoveries that extended people's lives and enhanced their quality of life, Dora continued helping in the way she had for most of her life. She continued to avoid "big words," as she referred to philosophical concepts and principles and Sanskrit terms. She spoke in a simple and clear way. "At all times you must say, 'I have an illness.' You must not say, 'I am that illness,' because if you have, then you block the healing energy." Dora persevered during a time when life-threatening illnesses seemed to be increasing faster than effective treatments. Central to her approach was the idea that each person is unique. The wrong choice of words or thoughts can lead the patient to reject help, and an opportunity to be of benefit is lost.

As Dora suggested, the healer helps to create integration of the personality and the inner self. She said, "If they're open to it, if they don't identity with the sickness, I'm telling the patients to just let go of everything, to relax completely; feel as well as you can. That's all I'm asking when I'm treating the really sick ones."[2]

She was often attentive to members of her audience who were very ill or had disabilities that affected their functioning. Regardless of the title of her lecture, she found ways to share stories. She motivated; she gave hope; she counseled people to accept death as part of life. And she laughed a lot. She was very calm and quiet inside and projected peace to those who were the most ill. She encouraged "her nurses" to do the same. Everyone laughed a lot in the midst of all the suffering and death.

One unsung heroine about whom Dora frequently spoke was Nabeela George, a friend from Port Chester who had post-polio syndrome. Nabeela had endured over a dozen surgeries throughout her life, and she had lived with pain since childhood, as Dora said, "every day of her life." Despite that, and despite the fact that she depended upon a wheelchair for mobility, she became an accomplished painter and took interest in the world around her. Dora often spoke of another woman who was homebound. Because she was cheerful, outgoing, and took interest in them, the neighborhood children often visited her on their way home from school. Neither of these people identified with her physical disorders.

Another individual who influenced Dora was Dan, a tall, elegant man in his forties who was dying of AIDS despite the new medications. He was part of Dora's Seattle healing group and one of the Indralaya patients for many years. When his care became too much for his elderly mother to handle, he moved to a facility that had nurses around the clock. During the last six months of his life, Dan often attended Dora's healing group on Capitol Hill with his morphine pump tucked beside him in the wheelchair. He was cheerful and gracious when Dora visited him. She was mystified by one of her visits with him because she had assumed that he would ask about dying and how to prepare for death. She described his situation thus:

> My friend Dan . . . is dying from AIDS. He absolutely will not accept it. He's deteriorating. He can't walk. He can't use his

fingers. But he says he is going to be cured. He is in a hospital now. They do everything for him because he is completely helpless. Though to this day I try to prepare him for dying—nothing doing; he's going to get cured.

I don't think so, but I may be wrong. I'm not wishing him anything, but he is not too [well]. He's fighting it off. He's wanting to keep alive with all that pain and getting the medicine and not being able to do anything. But he wants to live. He will not admit he's going to die. He comes to my healing group even. I do my best for him; we all do our best for him. His decision is not to die. I should think I would be glad to go, myself, if I was in a similar [situation]. I wouldn't [like it] at all; let me tell you. I have done my best, my absolute and complete best [for him].

The nurse who is in charge of one of the hospitals here, she took me there and she sat by him. We both agree there's nothing we can do. . . . I treat him and I reduce his pain [but] that's not curing him and I tell him that. He must do it his own way, mustn't he? He doesn't want to die. How he can want to live is beyond my understanding.

I'm trying to help these people. . . . You see, death to me, being a Theosophist—life and death and believing in reincarnation—makes me have a different point of view.

Other people denied death; it is not uncommon among people who die in the prime of their lives and people, even Theosophists, who die in this American culture. Preparation for death helps. When Dora was a very young child, her mother took her across Java by train and allowed her to sit quietly beside her grandfather's bed. He was very ill with cancer, had a large bandage on his neck, and could only sip liquids. That experience helped prepare Dora for her own death.

Dora spoke about the way she prepared those who were very ill and how some of her nurses helped patients and their families during the patients' last weeks of life.

> Lots of people ask me, "How do I die?" I say, "Take it easily and let go"—and go. I think of the relatives. Lots of our nurses do it that way; they bring their children and everybody to the death bed and they kiss them goodbye [and say] that Granny or somebody "will be there with you and we love you and we want you to go." And they kiss them, and are there and send them with love.
>
> That's what many nurses do with the children and they say it's a beautiful experience because they know they go with the concept that Granny, or whoever it is, will be with them. They say it's a lovely experience. Lots of nurses have done it with their children and their parents. And they say, "We are so happy that we believe it because we aren't crying. We are happy that they are released and that we love one another. The children feel that dying is just a nice thing for her."
>
> They say it's beautiful. I've never seen it myself, but from the letters I get from my nurses, that's what they write, that Therapeutic Touch has made such a difference in their own relations [with] their parents or whoever died, and even the children. They felt that.[3]

The son of one of Dora's nurses attended Pumpkin Hollow Farm with both his parents. His father had retired from the State Department and had not known his son was gay until he was diagnosed as HIV positive. For several years before the young man died, he counseled high school students in the mid-Atlantic region about how to avoid the disease. He was another of Dora's unsung heroes, as were his parents, who supported him in every way possible.

Many of the gay men who came to Indralaya and Pumpkin Hollow Farm during those years had caring partners and families and good social networks. But there were others whose families had abandoned them—not because they were ill but because they were homosexual. Dora mentioned to a weary nurse that fatigue comes more from contending with "unsolvable social problems" day after day than from working long hours with those who are ill.

In response to those who had strained relationships with family members, Dora said that people are brought together in life because of past karma. Some people have been friends and teachers, children or parents in previous incarnations. She counseled people to think of those with whom they have difficult relations and to project goodwill. Each person is unique; for some people it is difficult to project love if the relationship with the person is complicated. Dora said that people think they are supposed to love their parents when sometimes there has been abuse. In those cases, counseling them to feel love only makes them feel guilty that they cannot. Counseling them to feel forgiveness introduces what she called an "unequal relationship" and dualism. Instead of forgiveness, she focused on what could be done in the present and how that could shape more positive outcomes in the future.

> Sometimes we've had very difficult relations with our mother, father, [or] God knows. But you say, "Why have I been brought together with them?" It's something to work out. If you can see that it's karma from the past and this is a way of working it out—if you can see it that way, you see it differently.
>
> In my healing I've had people send "goodwill"—I don't say "love"—towards that person. They all say one thing. If they

really do it, at the end of three months, they have no more hatred. The funniest thing is, often the people [with whom they had difficulties] telephone and the thing [the resentment] is broken.

If you carry on these tremendous [resentments], you're bound by other people. But you can break that tie forevermore if you can substitute [resentment with] extending "goodwill." You work out the karma, particularly if they respond.

I think it affects the people on the other side. I think it makes a tremendous difference in life because many people have said they have a completely different [outlook] if they can feel friendly and not tied to a person. They say they feel free. That's what they feel.

People have a thought; they build a thought-form. If you hate somebody for twenty years you build a thought-form of that person and you really send it to that person. That [hatred] you build in your mind and [then] if you dislike somebody else, it also strengthens your dislike to that person. If you can break it, you're really free. If you are doing the sending and don't expect anything, mostly after three months or four months, there is a response—an "easierness" [sic]. You break your bonds. It takes time.[4]

Dora said over and over again, "We can change." She worked with groups to help people experience harmony in a group. She worked with individuals. She said at the workshops that she took responsibility for the patients; she was not just there to teach others. She had the commitment of a leader, a teacher, a healer, and a social activist. She tried one approach and another until she found what helped a particular patient. She asked patients to tell her about their problems; she did not want them to be passive.

She enlisted their efforts, often even when she perceived changes before the patient did. That was part of the healing process: helping to change the passivity that is often learned in health care institutions.

Dora did not set out to change the health care system; she said in one interview that it was not her job to effect changes in hospitals. But she did influence the health care system by helping hundreds and perhaps thousands of health care professionals to perceive their worlds and their relationships a little differently. If a nurse recognizes that at some level she is interdependent with others, she is motivated to take responsibility for her emotions and train her mind to be calm, centered, and steady. If one nurse on a unit avoids being emotionally reactive and sends thoughts of quiet and peace to someone who is angry or fearful, that has a tremendous positive effect on the environment. The person does not have to accept the ideas of rebirth, karma, or even Therapeutic Touch.

In regard to different religions, Dora said, "the healing energy they draw on is one and the same." She contrasted a theistic religious view with a nontheistic, "impersonal" view. Dora used the term *impersonal* as a result of the influence of field theory and Asian philosophical traditions. In addition, she said, "I have had, in many ways, a good scientific training, so I'm used to making things impersonal. But a lot of people think of God or Jesus." She and Dolores Krieger designed Therapeutic Touch so that it could be taught anywhere in the world: to a Hindu, a Catholic, a Muslim, or a Buddhist. She said, "We can go in any country in the world. Therapeutic Touch isn't based on the belief of God. The Catholic nuns use it, but they put God in it. God bless them; what do I care?"

Because Therapeutic Touch does not presuppose a single religious viewpoint, it was controversial among some fundamentalist Christians in the United States. Bill Wilson's use of the term

Higher Power in the Alcoholics Anonymous movement had been similarly controversial.

In a discussion with Dora, the German writer Peter Michel observed that in Europe a healer may say that he works with a personal entity he calls "the angel of healing" or a "master of healing." In those cases, Dora replied, "I think there may be contact from the astral [psychic] world. There are people on the other side [who help]. Some of them are images [thought-forms] but some of them are really people on the other side in the astral plane."

By contrast, Dora said that Kathryn Kuhlman drew on the universal healing field, even though Kuhlman was "very religious and talked in terms of God. It's more impersonal than thinking of Jesus." She added: "I'm thinking of God from my scientific background and Theosophy, as a universal force for the whole world. It seems universal to me. . . . Theosophy accepts every religion. . . . So that has been fortunate. That has been really a great help. Anybody who tells me any belief, I accept it within reason. I can understand it's their background, [and it] doesn't have to be mine."5

In 1997, when Dora was ninety-three, she was invited to tea at the home of Kathi Kemper, a pediatrician who lived in Seattle at that time. Kathi had helped Dora for a number of years at the Seattle healing group and in subsequent years at Pumpkin Hollow Farm. Kathi's other guest that day was Dr. David Eisenberg, a physician well-known for his research on complementary and alternative medicine. In an expansive moment, Dora made one of her classic gestures with arms outstretched and sent her cup flying. She hardly missed a beat, despite Kathi's sudden pallor.

The following year Eisenberg published research in the *Journal of the American Medical Association* indicating that the popularity of complementary and alternative medicine in the United States has increased dramatically in recent years. In 1997, about 30 percent of health care dollars were spent by consumers on alternative health care. Americans made an estimated 629 million office visits to complementary therapy providers and spent an estimated $27 billion out of pocket on complementary care. Furthermore, 82 million adults in the United States routinely used complementary medical therapies to treat their most common medical conditions.[6]

In an online newsletter announcing a new Harvard division on complementary medicine, Eisenberg noted that "there has been a tendency to marginalize complementary and alternative medicine in mainstream medical institutions. Despite dramatic increases in federal funding for research as well as increased patient interest, far too little data currently exists on safety, efficacy, and mechanisms of action of commonly used complementary and integrative therapies." He and his associates studied medical aspects of complementary and alternative medicine as well as legal, ethical, and economic implications. As mentioned in the previous chapter, the National Institutes of Health were instrumental in funding those and the efforts of other researchers.

Even before Dora died in 1999, there were signs of change. The concept of energy fields was acknowledged by the North American Nursing Diagnosis Association (NANDA) in 1994. "Energy field disturbance" was recognized as a nursing diagnosis so that nurses who offer Therapeutic Touch can do so in response to their assessment of this disturbance. Their charting may then indicate the patient's response to the treatment and plans for other nursing interventions.

This interest on the part of mainstream medicine does not mean that Therapeutic Touch will receive any more research funding than it has in the past. Currently there is a shortage of nurses, particularly of those who are qualified researchers. Among them, those who have what Dora called "the moral courage" to undertake research on Therapeutic Touch are few. Therapeutic Touch, usually categorized as a "bioenergetic" modality, is not as easy to research as something like herbal therapy. Many challenges remain.

Fundamentalist Christians in the United States were at the forefront of a group who sought to undermine the efforts of nurses to practice Therapeutic Touch. During the 1980s, the Christian right organized a successful campaign against what they perceived as "cults," and they selected Therapeutic Touch as a focus for their vitriol. The attacks culminated in the publication of research by a nine-year-old girl in the *Journal of the American Medical Association*. Emily Rosa, the youngest person to have ever had a peer-reviewed article published in a medical journal, did a study that assessed the ability of a group of Therapeutic Touch practitioners to determine whether the hands of the subjects were present or absent behind a screen. A significant number of the Therapeutic Touch practitioners' reported findings did not correlate with the presence of the subjects' hands behind the screen. As a result, the young researcher concluded that claims of the effectiveness of Therapeutic Touch are groundless. The Emily Rosa study, as it was called, got a lot of attention in the press, in journals, and on television and radio across the country. *A New York Times* article, however, noted that Emily's parents and helpers on the project were her mother, Linda Rosa, a registered nurse who had been campaigning against TT for nearly a decade, and Larry Sarner, chairman of the National Therapeutic Touch Study Group, an anti-TT organization.[7]

During this controversy, Dora received phone calls and articles from Dolores and others who kept her informed. The nurses and physicians in her Seattle healing group also phoned her about the negative media coverage. Some of them had radio interviews during the time there was organized opposition to Therapeutic Touch to present a balanced perspective of the challenges of research. Dora said about those who developed and promoted the Rosa study, "They don't like us. . . . They're entitled to their opinion."

The conservative backlash against Therapeutic Touch made it difficult for professionals to practice in work settings and increased doubts among patients. Nevertheless, Therapeutic Touch is one of the most successful of the alternative modalities in terms of its integration into orthodox health care settings. At the same time that healing was being challenged, in response to consumer demand, the National Institutes of Health increased support for research on alternative and complementary therapies. Researchers are exploring the issues that the Rosa study and others highlighted. There are still many unknowns about healing, the role of the mind in the placebo effect, and the ability to effect healing in others.

Larry Dossey is a Dallas physician whose book *Healing Words: The Power of Prayer and the Practice of Medicine*, published in 1993, explored prayer and distance healing. He knew Dora from their participation in conferences together. In 2003, four years after her death, he published an article in *Alternative Therapies in Health and Medicine* that suggested an alternative hypothesis for the success of TT:

> I am a fan of Therapeutic Touch (TT) and am intrigued by how it may work. This question—the mechanism of TT—is what the controversial 1998 study by Rosa et al tried inadequately to address. TT practitioners are correct in saying that an energy field exists around human bodies. This is hardly controversial; it can be measured with conventional devices that detect electromagnetism and heat. However, the contention that TT works by removing alleged imbalances

and blockages in the human energy field is hypothetical, a conjecture that has not been proved. An alternative hypothesis is simply that the conscious intention of the practitioner is the primary factor in TT, as seems the case in nonlocal, remote healing. In any case, the bottom line is that currently no one knows the mechanism of TT, despite evidence for its clinical effects. Should TT be abandoned because we don't know how it works? Surely not. Many therapies in conventional medicine are widely used despite their unclear mechanisms of action. General anesthetics are an example. Some therapies were used for centuries before we understood how they worked, such as aspirin, colchicine, quinine, and citrus fruits for scurvy.[8]

Some researchers who analyzed Therapeutic Touch and the effects of TT operationalized it by breaking it down into a series of steps such as "centering," "assessment," "intent to help and heal," and "modulation of energy." This operational definition was supposed to confer validity. Renee Weber responded to the suggestion this way:

If you restrict your scientific methods too narrowly to operational definitions, especially where biological or psychological systems are concerned, you're going to rule out much that contemporary scientists accept in practice. Rigidly construed, operationalism says that the meaning of a statement is its method of clarification. This is not acceptable to philosophers of science or to scientists today. Modern physics makes use of a lot of non-sensible objects. If you require operational definitions, I don't know what you're going to do with black holes, the big bang theory, and self-consciousness, for instance.

Weber recommended another approach: "It may be too early to impose a precise definition on the energy involved in therapeutic touch. At the beginning, the best you can do is get some kind of working consensus so that you at least adopt a similar vocabulary. Then you allow data to pile up. Only much later do you interpret them and pin things down. This is what happened, essentially, in the history of physics."[9]

Marie Connell-Meehan added her reservations about quantitative research: "I'm not sure that it's appropriate to do experimental studies of any sort. What you are looking at is individual and unique, a feeling that's going to help people, and experimental designs don't tell us what's unique. They tell us a general kind of thing that's common to everybody. What's going to be most therapeutic depends on the individual person, so I think a phenomenological approach is most appropriate."[10]

Today Therapeutic Touch may very well have entered the next phase of its development. It may be time to take the step that Weber suggested and analyze and interpret the data that have accumulated. Videos of Dora's patient sessions could be analyzed. Several projects that involve systematic transcription of her lectures are in process and will contribute more data. To do justice to Dora's contribution to health care and healing and to develop her work into the future, these efforts would be timely. Larry Dossey's suggestion of nonlocal effects, made both in his 2003 article quoted above and in his 1993 book *Healing Words*, requires attention, since it avoids introducing religion into the health care system.

Nevertheless, according to Janet Macrae, "Therapeutic Touch lost its momentum after the JAMA [*Journal of the American Medical Association*] article."[11] Forward movement requires recognition that there are fallow periods in endeavors and that effort is required to overcome stagnation. The Theosophical Society is uniquely placed to lead such a renewal of interest in these exciting areas of enquiry. Since Therapeutic Touch involves the "therapeutic use of self," qualitative research methodology needs to be reconsidered. It makes little sense to trivialize phenomenological research and then cite the lack of quality research as a reason to prevent patients from having Therapeutic Touch as a complementary health care option.

For those who stepped back from Therapeutic Touch, there has still been a helpful maturation in the process of understanding the application of modern physics in nursing and other professions. There are ways to understand Therapeutic Touch as an expression of the spiritual aspects of health care. It is too much to expect that a Christian or a Hindu or a Native American or anyone else should leave his religious perspective at the door. "Intent based on faith" may be another concept that warrants investigation.

Despite Dora's achievements during the last decades of her life, she still had many interpersonal issues to work out. She had to contend with the fact that she was aging and that she could no longer keep pace with her younger colleagues. She never talked about dementia, but she often mentioned that her memory for names in particular had declined. She announced on some days, "I'm dumb today" and expected a little less of herself on those days. On other days she denied that she had any physical limitations. She would insist "I'm an independent girl" while she carried her laundry up steep basement stairs.

"Everything dies," Dora said to her students. "Stars die. Trees die." The deaths of several of her close friends helped her prepare for her own death. Emily Sellon died in 1993 at age eighty-three from cancer, and her death was a tremendous loss. Dora treated her before and after some of her chemotherapy treatments, but Dora only visited Rye for a short time during the summers. Emily's illness was unexpected: she meditated, exercised, had a healthy vegetarian diet, and was so full of energy. Dora said that it never occurred to her that she would outlive Emily. Otelia Bengtsson died two years later, at age ninety-seven. For the four years after Bengtsson's death, Dora continued to stay in Rye with John Sellon when she flew east to teach at Pumpkin Hollow Farm.

The other huge loss that Dora suffered was around her ninety-second birthday, when she lost the good relationship she had had with her son, John, and his wife, Aino. There were so many stresses and strains in the Kunz household in Seattle that Dora offered to move out of her apartment adjoining the main house where John and Aino lived. She was a realist, and she understood the dynamics. She had had many discussions with Erik Peper over the years that were helpful. But she felt she could best serve the situation by getting out of the way. As was her custom, she was practical and selfless in the situation.

In April 1996 Dora left for Pumpkin Hollow Farm, as she often did in the late spring. But that year, before leaving, she went through her personal papers and threw away as much as possible. As she had for many years, Sue Wright flew out to spend the summer with Dora in New York and act as her personal assistant. She was surprised that Dora seemed at loose ends about where she would live in the autumn. She had always been the picture of confidence, but she was psychologically wobbly that summer. Nonetheless, Dora taught workshops and during those hours was clear and stable.

In August of the same year, Dora decided to stay with her nephew Nicolas and his wife, Kirsten, in Seattle. She arrived from New York a month later with her suitcases and a few boxes of belongings. Soon after, her desk, a TV tray, and a photo album were brought from her apartment. She focused on rebuilding a new life for herself independent from John and his family. Though she rarely saw them, she did see other family members, particularly five of her brother Harry's children, who lived in the Seattle area. Dora had said to her students that it is largely through relationships that karma is worked out, and that was her own challenge.

She still laughed a lot. In 1995 Dora was asked what stood out as remarkable to her from her years as president of the TS, and she responded, "Nothing is remarkable anymore."[12] She also said very occasionally, "Nothing shocks me anymore." She had counseled so many people from all over the world for so many years. During a visit to Seattle's Burke Museum of Natural History, she was asked if it was difficult to clairvoyantly view the Native American artifacts from a thriving culture that had been allowed to dwindle. "Sweetie Pie," she said, "I work with cancer and AIDS patients and *that's* difficult."

At age ninety-three, Dora said, "I'm not retiring. I see lots of sick people, and I give lectures etc. I travel; I go to California. I will this summer too: New York, everywhere, California, everywhere. I will speak. Whenever I'm asked, I speak to a place but I don't think that I want to go to a lot of conferences."[13] She knew that she was slowing down, and two or three years before her death, she started to prepare her students for the idea that she not going to live forever.

In 1999 Dora discussed life after death with an interviewer. He had read Leadbeater's book *The Other Side* and was particularly curious about its description of the after-death experiences of an alcoholic who has no way to satisfy his craving. Dora agreed with the description but took exception to the helplessness portrayed. She said that there is also help for overcoming difficulties in the after-death state. She did not view the after-death state as a physical location but as a state of consciousness. She understood life and death as a part of a totality. For a period of time after death, she believed, the emotions and lower mental consciousness cohere, and that seems to be the time an alcoholic has difficulty. The same would be true of those with other kinds of strong desire or hatred or other afflictions.

> People who are drunk all the time, they do feel lost without all that. They are unhappy very often because there is no way they [can] get drunk. So they have to get used to a different way of life etc. It takes time—I mean, if you have a real drunkard [and] not just a person who drinks just a couple [drinks]. If you're a drunkard and you go off drink, you have a bad time. It's something like that [in the after-death state]. I worked with Alcoholics Anonymous and I know something about drunken people.[14]

The interviewer quoted an author who said that there is no negativity in the after-death state. Dora responded, "What is negativity, sweetie? There are 'bad things' on the other side. What's the matter with you?" She was implying that 'bad things' include mental afflictions such as desire, jealousy, hatred, and such. A person who has a habit pattern of strong craving for alcohol, for example, has no immediate cessation of the mental and emotional continua at the time the physical body dies. Dora saw things clearly, without wishful thinking. She perceived negative habit patterns as tenacious. Change in consciousness occurs, however. We can change. Positive habit patterns can replace negative habit patterns to create a new way of life.

Dora continued to use the old-fashioned term "the other side" in reference to the after-death states of consciousness. It was easier for people to think of a veil between life and death than to understand the concept of fields of consciousness or the principle that consciousness is a nonmaterial continuum. Most people think of a human being as merely a physical body made up of chemical processes. Hence it is hard for them to understand Dora's perspectives. She responded to questions about what helps a person in the after-death state:

> Mostly they have somebody who has died before them. They will be there probably to think about—and be—with them. Now, with regard to a lot of people [who experience the death of a loved one], what they do is they scream and they yell and they are very unhappy. It makes the people on the other side [who have recently died] feel helpless because they can't [mentally] get through to them. For both, it is a difficult time. Does that sound sensible?
>
> Slowly, I think, the people on the other side get used to the things which are totally different. Some things are very much like the physical plane and they are levels of consciousness which some people stay in a long time. . . . Some people have extravagant minds and they haven't made up their minds [about the meaning and purpose of life] and they can experience all sorts of exciting things.[15]

Dora's interest during her long life had not been limited to merely having a series of exciting experiences. She shocked one of her young students into looking at life differently when Dora said that her own purpose in life was not to have fun; she had a greater purpose and she was firmly rooted in it.

Dora shared the concept of rootedness with students during her final years. Rootedness seemed to help her to weather the changes associated with aging. She associated rootedness with faith in one's spiritual purpose, and Dora perceived the spiritual as primary. Belonging to a particular family, community, land, or ethnicity was secondary. For her, this quality was personified by her

Dutch-Javanese grandmother, about whom she had said in a discussion at Pumpkin Hollow in 1979: "She could accept any civilization. She died in India finally; it didn't make any difference where she was. Rootedness has to do with a feeling of destiny or a place in life in which you can give. My grandmother had rootedness without having any particular place in the world."

During the same conversation, Erik Peper said, "If I think of the younger generation with no sense of rootedness, they are out of contact with their own internal destiny. How can a person search or get access to their own internal destiny? What is their reference to 'Who am I?' Many of the nurses and my students struggle with this. Periodically, I struggle with it, as well as many people I know."

Dora had her own answer: "That is from our complex civilization. . . . The farmer inherited his farm and he accepted his destiny. Now people have so many choices and they have no feeling for anything. They are not even rooted in a family." But she went on to say, "In rootedness comes a sense of place for you to act upon if you accept responsibility."[16]

Universal responsibility develops from rootedness and compassion, and that is not the path for many.

Dora was fortunate in having relatively minor health problems. She took only two daily medications. But when she was in her early nineties, she had an episode of back pain that was so severe that she could not get out of bed. She was successfully treated with two cortisone injections, the second of which improved the pain so that it never recurred to the same extent. Dora remained incredibly active until the last year of her life. Despite osteoarthritis and advanced age, she always felt that she could give. At ninety-five, she was unwilling to accept the fact that her old body could no longer keep up with her willingness to give and to teach. She pushed herself to teach the Invitational Healers' Workshop at Indralaya. She refused a cardiac workup when she returned, but appeared to be suffering acute heart failure. She was weak but comfortable, and as she had indicated in an interview, she had no intention of staying alive if she "couldn't do anything." To her, that meant being able to teach. Dolores Krieger phoned her, and they discussed the Invitational Healers' Workshop in Pumpkin Hollow Farm. But Dora would never fly back to New York again.

When it was finally clear that she could not teach anymore and that her heart was very weak, Dora gradually limited what she ate, reducing her intake to just a few sips of coffee with milk. She had made her decision.

In an interview four years earlier Dora said, "Older people when they die, some of them die very peacefully because they know they're at the end of their life and they slowly [withdraw]."[17] That was exactly how Dora died. She slowly withdrew over the course of about a month and died at 1:17 a.m. on August 25, 1999. She was ninety-five years old.

About a month after Dora's death, her nephew and his wife took half of her ashes to Pumpkin Hollow Farm, where they were put into the ground on the hill overlooking the waterfalls. A small, simple community memorial service had been planned. There was no music, just "the trees all around," as Dora said during meditations in the grove. The air was crisp and clear and carried hints of autumn. John Sellon was not well enough to attend the service. He died the following year.

On October 13, 1999, there was a larger service organized by the nurses who had been part of her healing group at the Seattle Theosophical Society. To accommodate the group, it was held in the Unitarian Church in the Wedgwood area of Seattle. Hein van Beusekom agreed to officiate and flew up from Krotona. Heidi Lewalder played the harp. That same day there were memorial services held for Dora at the New York Theosophical Society and at Olcott in Wheaton. Later that autumn, John Kunz spread the other half of Dora's ashes in the woods at Indralaya. That "seemed sense," to use her own expression; so much of her adult life had been devoted to the two camps, Pumpkin Hollow Farm and Indralaya. She left a bequest for each of them and a smaller one to the Theosophical Society in America.

Dora van Gelder Kunz affected the lives of thousands of people through her books, lectures, seminars, workshops, and meditation and healing treatments. A few tributes to her after her death may perhaps best serve to illustrate the regard, the esteem in which she was held. From James R. Lassen-Willems:

> Dora seemed small and fragile. She was, instead, a powerful presence with an acute wit and an outrageous honesty. . . . She never pretended to be anything except what she was—a very bright and gifted human being. . . . I have never met anyone except maybe Beatrice Wood who is able to look (not just act) like a young woman, even a girl, at one moment, and seem, in the next, to be the veritable expression of Mother Wisdom.

From Neila Campbell:

> I realize that every day of my life I use something Dora taught us all. When I'm working with clients, I think of these teachings as "Dora's pearls" which are the many strategies that help people to find their way "home" to themselves. Every morning my husband and I begin the day with the meditation we learned from Dora: she is woven into the very fabric of our lives. There's no way to lose her, she lives on in the way

I perceive my world, my attitude towards others, and in my desire to serve.

From Anna Lemkow:

Dora, as many of us well know, was always on call for one's personal consultation (incidentally, always free of charge). When I approached Dora, she glanced at me briefly and then, with head thrown back and laughing merrily, exclaimed, "You have the most fashionable disease in America— hypoglycemia!" I subsequently checked the accuracy of her diagnosis by visiting a doctor and undergoing tests. Dora proved right.

From Renee Weber:

Meditating in Dora's presence expanded one's space and consciousness. One became far more clear about what mattered and what didn't, and it helped one embrace one's own "dharma." When Dora affirmed my feeling about teaching, she heightened my joy. Beyond that, one felt centrally understood by her, and loved despite one's frailties.

From Diane Eisenberg:

Dear Dora opened a new door to my life that I would have never expected and I've been thankful ever since. It took me a long while after the healing sessions, but the message I received within was to offer Service to others. That was the most meaningful message I've ever received and I'm so glad to be able to serve at the Theosophical Society in America.

From Sue Wright:

> She could be an extraordinarily private person. I don't think
> any of us know how much she really did know and understand
> about the visible and invisible worlds around us. I believe she
> understood human behavior better than most psychologists.
> She probably understood natural law and energy better than
> many physicists and scientific methods better than most
> researchers I know. . . . I could hear her talk about the same
> subject a dozen times and each time hear something new and
> relevant to my situation at the moment.

From Joy Mills:

> It is so often said that no one is irreplaceable, but of Dora that
> can be and must be said, for the truth of the matter is that there
> is no one who can take her place. But her laugh will linger on,
> and we will hear it in memory's ear and we will see in memory's
> eye that quirky turn of her head with that inimitable smile,
> that sparkle of the eyes. And we will go on loving her, for one
> could not help but love her. And perhaps, just perhaps as a
> very practical girl, she is setting things right in the astral world!

From Clarence Pedersen:

> Dora schooled me, healed me, but most particularly, she
> refreshed me with her total integrity. She was one of the most
> honest people I have ever met, a quality that gave her rare
> talents such universal credence.

From John Kern:

I began going to Pumpkin Hollow when in Cambridge in the summers . . . even before I started work at MIT after my undergraduate degree, and through the close associations which developed there found myself asked to join NYTS research projects, attend meetings at the Kunz's home where I enjoyed her wonderful Indonesian cooking, and all in all felt myself an integral part of their gaggle of card-carrying far-out Theosophists. My wife Ann joined the group even before our marriage as I recall it and we almost called Hillandale Road our second home.

From John A. Sellon:

My wife, Emily, and Dora developed a most loving relationship, that of "best friends." On page 62 of Emily's book, *The Pilgrim and the Pilgrimage*, you'll find the sort of words that she would have liked to have said relative to Dora, had she survived her. I quote this for you:

"The essence of an incarnation, is perfume, is an intangible quality that is never lost. That essence, that fragrance, comes from the trials and the tribulations that the individual undergoes in incarnation. It is that human being's offering to the whole of life, to the world, and to all other people. It is never lost. That achievement, that accomplishment is the individual's mark of growth and enlightenment, but is also the individual's contribution to the whole."

From Betty Bland:

> Yet, with all her obliviousness to social convention or surface feelings, her focus would turn on a dime bringing all compassion to bear on counseling and healing a person in need. Long after her pointed questions and healing thumps ended, her "victim" would still be processing the life-changing experience.

From Erik Peper:

> Dora had the most remarkable, superb ability to extract out a person's self-image. . . . I think she was a true scientist in her own way, in a very nice way. . . . She didn't speculate if she didn't know. . . . She was the best mentor I ever had. As a personal influence, Dora has been remarkable.

Indeed, a most unusual person.

Notes

Chapter 1

1. Constant R. van Motman, *De Familie Van Motman: 1600–2006* (Amsterdam: Uitgave Stichting van Motman Familiearchief, 2006).

2. Nicolas van Gelder, recollections of discussions with Bet van Motman during the 1950s. Interview with Frank Chesley, Seattle, WA, 2011.

3. Dora Kunz, interview with Frank Chesley, Seattle, WA, 1996.

4. C. van Hinloopen Labberton, *The Wayang or Shadow Play as Given in Java: An Allegorical Play of the Human-Soul and the Universe* (Bandoeng, Java: De Uitgevers Trust Jamur Dvipa: 1912). Theosophists during the late colonial period in Java helped invigorate traditional arts. During the early twentieth century, however, growing recognition of a shared Muslim identity among many non-Europeans in the islands contributed to criticism. Theosophical literature often referenced Sanskrit rather than Arabic and lost appeal in the decades leading to the revolution and the creation of Indonesia.

5. Dora Kunz, interview with Frank Chesley, Seattle, WA, 1996.

6. Berth A. Peppeard, "Fairies, Real Fairies, Are Playmates of this Little Girl: Dora van Gelder Has the Most Sport with Water Sprites; Spies Elf in Harvard Botanic Garden," *Boston Herald*, June 19, 1927.

7. Ibid.

8. Dora Kunz, interview with Frank Chesley, Seattle, WA, September 2, 1997.

9. Melanie van Gelder, recorded by John and Aino Kunz, March 10, 1966, Ojai, CA. Kunz Archives, Olcott Library, Wheaton, IL.

10. The name "Esoteric Section" was changed to "Esoteric School" during the early twentieth century so as not to be confused with the various national Sections of the Theosophical Society, such as the American Section, the Indian Section, the Australian Section, and so on. Members of the Esoteric School must hold concurrent membership in the Theosophical Society associated with Adyar. However, the organization's governance is independent from that of the Theosophical Society, and it is considered an independent organization.

11. Dora Kunz, interview with Frank Chesley, Seattle, WA, 1997.

12. Ibid.

13. Dora Kunz, meditation workshop, Pumpkin Hollow Farm, Craryville, NY, 1992.

14. Dora Kunz, meditation workshop, Pumpkin Hollow Farm, Craryville, NY, 1993.

Chapter 2

1. Dora Kunz, interview with Frank Chesley, Seattle, WA, 1997.

2. Dora Kunz, interview with Nicolas van Gelder, Seattle, WA, 1991.

3. Dora Kunz, interview with Frank Chesley, Seattle, WA, 1997.

4. Ibid.

5. Dora Kunz, "Reminiscences of Early Leaders of the Theosophical Society" (lecture, Theosophical Society in America, Wheaton, IL, 1985). Olcott Library, #1970.

6. Dora Kunz, interview with Frank Chesley, Seattle, WA, 1997.

7. Kunz, "Reminiscences of Early Leaders of the Theosophical Society."

8. Dora Kunz, conversation with the author, Seattle, WA, 1998.

9. Kunz, "Reminiscences of Early Leaders of the Theosophical Society."

10. Dora Kunz and Fritz Kunz, "Reminiscences of Annie Besant and C. W. Leadbeater" (lecture, Theosophical Society in America, Wheaton, IL, 1967). Olcott Library.

11. Kunz, "Reminiscences of Early Leaders of the Theosophical Society."

12. Dora Kunz, interview with Frank Chesley, Seattle, WA, 1997.

13. The United States, with a population of about 97 million, suffered relatively fewer casualties: 53,000 deaths and 204,000 casualties.

14. C. W. Leadbeater, "Messages from the Unseen," *The Australasian E.S.T. Bulletin* 17 (October 1922): 205–218. In Joseph E. Ross, *Krotona in the Ojai Valley* (Ojai, CA: Ojai Printing and Publishing, 2009) 4: 241–258.

15. Dora Kunz, interview with Frank Chesley, Seattle, WA, 1997.

16. Dora Kunz, interview with Nicolas van Gelder, Seattle, WA, 1991.

17. "Invisible Helpers" was the topic of a lecture presented in Chicago's Steinway Hall by C. W. Leadbeater in 1902 and the title of a book by him first published in 1896. His thesis is that, through altruistic intention, one who wants to be of service and has the necessary conditions can help counsel others while his body sleeps at night. He describes what was called "astral travel" in the early twentieth century and practiced in parts of Asia.

18. Dora Kunz, personal correspondence to "Nadine Butler," Port Chester, NY, November 14, 1952. Personal files of "Nadine Butler's" daughter, Seattle, WA.

19. Dora Kunz, interview with Frank Chesley, Seattle, WA, 1997.

20. Dora van Gelder, "The Angels of the Lord," *The Liberal Catholic* (1924), 18–19.

21. Kunz, "Reminiscences of Early Leaders of the Theosophical Society."

22. Dora van Gelder, "Clairvoyance: What It Reveals," unpublished manuscript.

23. Ibid.

24. Dora van Gelder, "Fairies," *Theosophy in Australia*, September 1, 1924: 186.

25. Anna Kamensky, correspondence, *Theosophy in Australia*, August 1, 1922: 504.

26. Dora Kunz, interview with Nicolas van Gelder, Seattle, WA, 1991.

27. Dora van Gelder, "The Young Theosophist," *Theosophy in Australia*, March 1, 1924: 1090.

28. Karel van Gelder, *The Ideal Community: A Rational Solution of Economic Problems* (Sydney, self-published, 1922), 6.

29. Ibid., 11.

30. J. J. van der Leeuw, *The History and Work of the Manor*, unpublished manuscript.

31. Ibid.

32. Clara Codd, *So Rich a Life* (Pretoria, South Africa: Institute for Theosophical Publicity: 1951), 288–89.

33. Dora Kunz, interview with Frank Chesley, Seattle, WA, 1997.

34. Dora van Gelder, *Christmas of the Angels* (Wheaton: Theosophical Publishing House, 1921), 4–5.

35. Dora Kunz, conversation with Renee Weber, John Kunz, and Erik Peper, Craryville, NY, August 8, 1979, morning session.

36. Ibid.

Chapter 3

1. Dora Kunz, conversation with John Kunz, Renee Weber and Erik Peper, Pumpkin Hollow Farm, Craryville, NY, August 1979. The name of the osteopath is not known, but there are records of a blind osteopath who worked in Glendale in that era.

2. Ibid.

3. Sidney Field and Peter Hay, *Krishnamurti: The Reluctant Messiah* (St. Paul, MN: Paragon House, 1989), 23.

4. Robert Norton, *The Willow in the Tempest* (Ojai, CA: St. Alban's Press, 1990), 77, 80.

5. Dora Kunz, interview with Frank Chesley, Seattle, WA, 1997.

6. Kunz, "Reminiscences of the Early Leaders of the Theosophical Society."

7. C. W. Leadbeater, supplement to *The Australasian E.S.T. Bulletin* 14 (October 1928), 291.

8. Dora Kunz, interview with Frank Chesley, Seattle, WA, 1997.

9. Ibid.

10. *The New York Herald Tribune*, "Girl Who Believes in Fairies Says She Sees Them Frolicking in Central Park," April 10, 1927.

11. Peppeard.

12. [Illegible signature], correspondence from an editor at *The New York Herald Tribune* to Mrs. Ernest Sellon, Rye, NY, March 31, 1927.

13. Beatrice Wood, *I Shock Myself: The Autobiography of Beatrice Wood* (San Francisco: Chronicle Books, 2006), 77–78. Annie Besant received an honorary doctorate and was referred to as "Dr. Besant" occasionally.

14. Ibid., 92.

15. Fritz Kunz, 1927 pocket travel diary, personal collection of Nicolas van Gelder, Seattle, WA.

16. John Kunz, interview with Frank Chesley, Seattle, WA, January 21, 1997.

17. Kunz, "Reminiscences of Early Leaders of the Theosophical Society."

18. Ed Abdill, "Notes on Fritz and Dora Kunz," unpublished manuscript, Kunz Archives, Olcott Library, Wheaton, IL, 2010.

19. Kunz, "Reminiscences of Early Leaders of the Theosophical Society."

20. Dora Kunz, interview with Frank Chesley, Seattle, WA, June 7, 1997.

21. Ibid.

22. Kunz, "Reminiscences of Early Leaders of the Theosophical Society."

23. John Kunz, interview with Frank Chesley, Seattle, WA, June 5, 1997.

Chapter 4

1. John Kunz, interview with Frank Chesley, Seattle, WA, June 5, 1997.

2. Michael Sellon, interview with the author, Seattle, WA, September 30, 2010.

3. Ibid.

4. John Sellon, conversation with Nicolas van Gelder, Rye, NY, 1998.

5. Michael Sellon, interview with the author, Seattle, WA, September 30, 2010.

6. Dora Kunz, interview with Peter Michel, Rye, NY, April 26, 1995.

7. Aino Kunz, conversation with Kirsten van Gelder, Seattle, WA, December 5, 2011.

8. John Kunz, interview with Frank Chesley, Seattle, WA, January 21, 1997.

9. Dora Kunz, "Health Session with Patient, Sue." Transcript of research notes by Erik Peper, Berkeley, CA, December 5, 1980. Used with permission of Erik Peper.

10. Ibid.

11. Otelia Bengtsson, discussion with Kirsten van Gelder (then Kirsten Williams), Ossining, NY, 1986.

12. As early as 1922, Dr. Cooke and a colleague had presented on the classification system of "hypersensitiveness" in the allergic response: Arthur F. Coca and Robert A. Cooke. "On the Classification of the Phenomena of Hypersensitiveness," *The Journal of Immunology* (1923), 8: 163–182. Presented at the annual meeting of the American Association of Immunologists, Washington, DC, May 1, 1922.

13. Otelia Bengtsson, conversation with Kirsten van Gelder (then Kirsten Williams), Ossining, NY, 1986.

14. Ibid.

15. Dora van Gelder [Kunz], *Conscious Use of the Aura* (New York: Anchorite Press, n.d.), 3.

16. Ibid., 4.

17. Ibid., 5, 6.

18. Dora Kunz, "Clairvoyance: Its Value and Limitations" (lecture, New York Federation of the Theosophical Society, New York, November 11, 1935).

19. Dora Kunz, "The Human Aura: Paintings by Juanita Donahoo Done under the Direction of Dora van Gelder" (unpublished document, 1936), 2.

20. Dora Kunz, *The Personal Aura* (Wheaton, IL: Theosophical Publishing House, 1991), 44–45.

21. Ibid., 61, 63.

22. Ibid., 20–21. In the discussion of personal uniqueness entitled "The Effects of Karma," Dora wrote, "We are all born with a basic emotional pattern, or with the possibility of developing certain emotional qualities, as I shall try to show in discussing the auras of children. In this connection, it is impossible to ignore the question of karma (the effects of past action), which sets the boundary conditions of human life. These conditions are not cast in concrete, because karma can work itself out in many ways and on many different levels. Nevertheless, it establishes certain predispositions which a person will have to cope with during life, and these are clearly represented at the level of the emotions."

23. Ibid.

24. Dora Kunz, interview with Peter Michel, April 25, 1995, Rye, NY. Used with permission of the interviewer. Geoffrey Hodson was born in England in 1886, so he was a contemporary of Fritz rather than of Dora. He became involved in the Theosophical Society after World War I and, though he lived much of his life in New Zealand, he was a lecturer for the Society until his death in 1984. *Fairies at Work and Play* was published in 1925, *The Brotherhood of Angels and Men* in 1927, *The Inner Side of Church Worship* in 1930, and *Clairvoyant Investigations of Christian Origins and Ceremonial* in 1977.

25. Kunz, *The Personal Aura*, 125.

Chapter 5

1. Dora Kunz, letter to Carolyn Swanton, 1982? The letter included the following observations, "I knew Mr. Bragdon very well from 1927, I believe, until his death. . . . I saw him frequently, when we would meet for tea with a great mutual friend, Mr. Arnold Sprague, every year. And while I was president of the Society in New York he gave many lectures for the New York Theosophical Society."

2. Claude Bragdon, introduction to Dora Kunz, *The Real World of Fairies* (Wheaton, IL: Theosophical Publishing House, 1977), xii.

3. Claude Bragdon, *Merely Players* (New York: Alfred A. Knopf. 1929). Dora's maiden name is under the chapter heading in parentheses even though she was married in 1927, two years prior to the book's release. Dora used her maiden name during different times in her career as well as "Dora van Gelder Kunz." Bragdon refers to her as "Dora," rather than as "Mrs. Kunz" or "Mrs. van Gelder" throughout the chapter, and that remained Dora's preferred mode of address for her public life.

4. Bragdon, *Merely Players*, xii.

5. John Kunz, interview with Frank Chesley, Seattle, WA, 1997.

6. Kunz, *The Real World of Fairies*, 101.

7. Ibid., 1–2, 10.

8. Ibid., 13.

9. Dora Kunz, draft of a letter to Loren Wheeler for an article in *The American Theosophist* on the sixtieth anniversary of Pumpkin Hollow Farm in 1997.

10. Emily Sellon, from the videotape "Pumpkin Hollow Farm Fiftieth Anniversary: 1937–1987"; Pumpkin Hollow Farm, 1987.

11. Nicolas van Gelder, conversation with John Sellon, Rye, NY, 1997.

Chapter 6

1. Dora Kunz, interview with Peter Michel, Rye, NY, April 25, 1995.

2. Dora Kunz, "The Role of Karma in Life" (lecture, Theosophical Society in America, Wheaton, Illinois, 1986).

3. Dora Kunz, interview with Peter Michel, Rye, NY, April 26, 1995.

4. F. L. Kunz, "Editorial Summary: The Proper Study. . . ." *Main Currents in Modern Thought* 6, no. 4 (Winter 1949), 59.

5. The Nationaal-Socialistische Beweging, a Dutch pro-Nazi political party that frequently assisted the Germans in seizing Dutch Jews.

6. Nicolas van Gelder, recounting the story told to him by Harry van Gelder in 1964 in Vancouver, Canada, Seattle, WA, 2010; Nicolas van Gelder, "The van Gelders" (unpublished manuscript, 2010), 14.

7. Harry van Gelder, correspondence to Karel and Melanie van Gelder, July 21, 1945.

8. John Kunz, interview with Frank Chesley, Seattle, WA, 1997.

9. Arthur van Gelder, correspondence to Karel and Melanie van Gelder, various dates, 1945.

10. Sally Cheriel, unpublished biography of Chandran (Chad) Cheriel.

11. Joy Mills, *One Hundred Years of Theosophy: A History of the Theosophical Society in America* (Wheaton, IL: Theosophical Publishing House, 1987), 127.

12. Dora Kunz, interview with Frank Chesley, Seattle, WA, December 29, 1997.

13. Ibid.

14. Dora Kunz, interview with Frank Chesley, Seattle, WA, January 27, 1998.

15. Ibid.

Chapter 7

1. Elaine Peterson, e-mail correspondence with the author, Seattle, WA, November 22, 2009.

2. Dora Kunz, interview with Frank Chesley, Seattle, WA, February 25, 1998.

3. Dora Kunz, interview with Peter Michel, Rye, NY, April 25, 1985. Transcript used with permission of Peter Michel.

4. John Kunz, interview with Frank Chesley, Seattle, WA, July 16, 1998.

5. Dolores Krieger, interview with Frank Chesley, Rye, NY, February 19, 1997.

6. Dora Kunz, interview with Frank Chesley, Seattle, WA, February 25, 1998.

7. Wainwright House, *Second Spiritual Healing Seminar*, October 3–5, 1954 (Rye, NY: Wainwright House Publications, 1955), 39.

8. Wainwright House, *Second Spiritual Healing Seminar*, March 1954 (Rye, NY: Wainwright House Publications, 1955), 41.

9. Ibid., 41.

10. Ibid.

11. Ibid., 42.

12. Ibid.

13. Dora Kunz, "Report on a Healing Given to a Patient," Wainwright House, *Third Spiritual Healing Seminar*: 35–36.

14. Wainwright House, *Third Healing Seminar*, 39–40.

15. Dora Kunz, interview with Peter Michel, Rye, NY, April 26, 1995.

16. Wainwright House, *Third Healing Seminar*: 12.

17. Dora Kunz, interview with Frank Chesley, Seattle, WA, September 2, 1997.

18. Wainwright House, *Third Healing Seminar*, 14.

19. Ibid., 15.

20. Ibid., 16.

21. Ibid., 24.

22. Ibid., 25.

23. Otelia Bengtsson, conversation with Kirsten van Gelder, Ossining, NY, September 1986.

24. Wainwright House, *Third Healing Seminar*, 14.

25. Wainwright House, *Third Healing Seminar*, 20.

26. "B. J.", phone conversation with the author, Portland, OR, 2010.

27. Wainwright House, *Fifth Spiritual Healing Seminar*, October 8–10, 1956 (Rye, NY: Wainwright House Publications, 1957), 41–45.

28. Wainwright House, *Fifth Healing Seminar*, 45.

29. Wainwright House, *Fourth Spiritual Healing Seminar*, June 24–26, 1955 (Rye, NY: Wainwright House Publications, 1956), 69–70.

30. Wainwright House, *Fourth Healing Seminar*, 73.

31. Dora Kunz, "Founders' Day Keynote Address," Theosophical Society in America, Wheaton, IL, November 17, 1980.

32. Dora Kunz, interview with Frank Chesley, Seattle, WA, January 22, 1999.

33. Olga Worrall, Wainwright House, *Fourth Healing Seminar*, 67.

34. Wainwright House, *Fourth Healing Seminar*, 75.

35. Ibid., 74–79.

36. Ibid., 91–93.

37. Ibid., 99–100.

38. Dora Kunz, interview with Peter Michel, Rye, NY, April 27, 1995.

Chapter 8

1. John Kunz, interview with Frank Chesley, Seattle, WA, January 21, 1997.

2. Dolores Krieger, interview with Frank Chesley, Seattle, WA, June 26, 1997.

3. Their session was recorded by John Kunz; also present were Emily Sellon and Dolores Krieger. Karagulla recalled in her book *Breakthrough to Creativity* that Dr. Bengtsson was present, but her voice is not heard in the recording.

4. Shafica Karagulla, *Breakthrough to Creativity: Your Higher Sense Perception* (Santa Monica, CA: DeVorss, 1967), 33.

5. Dora Kunz, conversation with Shafica Karagulla, Port Chester, NY, 1956.

6. Dora Kunz, interview with Frank Chesley, Seattle, WA, April 1, 1999.

7. Dora Kunz, interview with Frank Chesley, Seattle, WA, January 22, 1999.

8. Karagulla, 39–40.

9. Ibid., 108.

10. Dora Kunz, conversation with John Kunz, Renee Weber, and Erik Peper, Pumpkin Hollow Farm, August 1979; part 2, 3.

11. Wainwright House, *Third Healing Seminar*, 23.

12. Dora Kunz, interview with Peter Michel, Rye, NY, April 26, 1995.

13. Ed Abdill, "Notes on Fritz and Dora Kunz."

14. Dora Kunz, interview with Frank Chesley, Seattle, WA, September 25, 1998.

15. Dora Kunz, in conversation with Erik Peper, Renee Weber, and John Kunz, Pumpkin Hollow Farm, Craryville, NY, August 8, 1979.

Chapter 9

1. Shafica Karagulla and Dora van Gelder Kunz, *The Chakras and the Human Energy Fields* (Wheaton, IL: Theosophical Publishing House, 1989), 93–94, 175–178.

2. Dolores Krieger, interview with Frank Chesley, June 26, 1997.

3. Martha E. Rogers, *An Introduction to the Theoretical Basis of Nursing* (Philadelphia: F. A. Davis, 1970), 90–91, 101–102.

4. Gay Gaer Luce, interview with Frank Chesley, Mill Valley, California, 1997.

5. Karagulla and Kunz, 42–43.

6. Ibid., 116.

7. Dolores Krieger, interview with Frank Chesley, Rye, NY, May 19, 1997.

8. Cookie Jurgens, interview with Kirsten van Gelder, Portland, OR, August 12, 2009.

9. Renee Weber, "Compassion, Rootedness and Detachment: Their Role in Healing: A Conversation with Dora Kunz." *The American Theosophist* 72, no. 5 (1984), 132–141. Reprinted in Dora Kunz, ed., *Spiritual Aspects of the Healing Arts* (Wheaton, IL: Theosophical Publishing House, 1985), 294.

10. Dora Kunz, ed., *Spiritual Healing*, 294–295.

11. Weber, in Kunz, ed., *Spiritual Healing*, 295–298.

12. Dora Kunz, discussion with John Kunz, Renee Weber, and Erik Peper, Pumpkin Hollow Farm, Craryville, NY, part 2, 3.

13. Janet Macrae, *Therapeutic Touch: A Practical Guide* (New York: Alfred A. Knopf, 1988), 7.

14. Janet Macrae, "Therapeutic Touch as Meditation," in Kunz, *Spiritual Aspects of the Healing Arts*, 277.

15. Dora van Gelder Kunz, *The Personal Aura* (Wheaton, IL: Theosophical Publishing House, 1991), 182.

16. Dolores Krieger, interview with Frank Chesley, Rye, NY.

17. Renee Weber published the article initially in *Revision: A Journal of Knowledge and Consciousness* 2, no. 2 (summer-fall 1979). It appeared in Marianne D. Borelli and Patricia Heidt, eds., *Therapeutic Touch: A Book of Readings* (New York: Springer, 1981), 13–39, and in *Spiritual Aspects of the Healing Arts*, 21–43.

18. Ibid., in Borelli and Heidt, 14–15.

19. Dora Kunz, interview with Peter Michel, Rye, NY, April 27, 1995.

20. Ibid.

21. Dora Kunz, interview with Frank Chesley, Seattle, WA, December 29, 1997.

22. Nelda Samarel, interview with Kirsten van Gelder, Ojai, CA, September 21, 2009.

23. Ibid.

24. Ibid.

25. Karagulla and Kunz, 41.

26. John Sellon, interview with Frank Chesley, Rye, NY, May 14, 1997.

27. Dora Kunz, interview with Peter Michel, Rye, NY, April 27, 1995.

Chapter 10

1. Dora Kunz, "Masters on the Path" (lecture, Philadelphia Lodge of the Theosophical Society, Philadelphia, May 8, 1955).

2. Dora Kunz, letter to Bruce Campbell, November 28, 1978.

3. Dora Kunz, letter to Lillian Leenhouts, October 25, 1976.

4. Dora Kunz, letter to Kiran H. Shah, October 30, 1978.

5. Dora Kunz, letter to Seymour Ballard, November 7, 1978.

6. Emily Sellon, "Interamerican Conference, March 24–31, 1979." *The American Theosophist* 67 (June 1979), 210.

7. Lakshmi Narayan, interview with Kirsten van Gelder, Ojai, CA, September 17, 2009.

8. Willamay Pym, interview with Frank Chesley, Seattle, WA, June 4, 1997.

9. Dora Kunz, letter to the members of the board of the Theosophical Society in America, July 20, 1978.

10. Ibid.

11. Dora Kunz, letter to Ann Wylie, September 20, 1976.

12. Boris de Zirkoff, "World Congress of the Theosophical Society," *The Eclectic Theosophist* 32 (January 15, 1976), 1.

13. John Coats, "A Message to the Centenary World Congress," *The Eclectic Theosophist* 32 (January 15, 1976), 2.

14. Richard A. Sattelberg, letter to the editor, *The Canadian Theosophist* 44 (July–August 1963), 61.

15. Dora Kunz "On the Early Leaders of the Theosophical Society" (lecture, Theosophical Society in America headquarters, Wheaton, IL, November 17, 1980).

16. John Coats, letter to Boris de Zirkoff, 1975.

17. Jerry Heijka-Ekins, interview with Kirsten van Gelder, March 11, 2011.

18. Dora Kunz, interview with Peter Michel, Rye, NY, April 26, 1995.

19. Willamay Pym, interview with Frank Chesley, June 4, 1997.

20. Edith Karsten, interview with author, Portland, OR, November 3, 2009.

21. John Sellon, conversation with Nicolas van Gelder, Rye, NY, 1998.

22. Dora Kunz, interview with Nicolas van Gelder, Seattle, WA, 1991.

23. Edith Karsten, interview with Kirsten van Gelder, Portland, OR, November 3, 2009.

24. Wainwright House, *Third Healing Seminar*, 37.

25. Tenzin Gyatso, the XIV Dalai Lama, "Universal Compassion and Global Crisis" (lecture, Theosophical Society in America, Wheaton, IL, 1981).

26. Dora Kunz, interview with Peter Michel, Rye, NY, April 27, 1995.

27. Ibid.

28. Renee Weber, "Sacred Simplicity: The Style of the Sage; Father Bede Griffiths," in Weber, *Dialogues with Scientists and Sages: The Search for Unity* (New York: Routledge and Kegan Paul, 1986), 157–58.

29. Dora Kunz, introductory remarks for lecture by Bede Griffiths, "Interface between Christianity and Other Faiths," Theosophical Society in America, Wheaton, IL, August 1983.

30. Bede Griffiths, "Interface between Christianity and Other Faiths."

31. In Weber, *Dialogues with Scientists and Sages*, 160–61.

32. Dora Kunz, letter to Gregory Tillett, August 26, 1980.

33. Dora Kunz, letter to Ralph Hannon, April 7, 1978.

34. Dora Kunz, letter to TSA board, September 17, 1980.

35. Dora Kunz, letter to Dan R., September 12, 1978.

Chapter 11

1. Dora Kunz, interview with Frank Chesley, December 29, 1997.

2. Dora Kunz, interview with Peter Michel, Rye, NY, April 27, 1995.

3. Ibid.

4. Dora Kunz, interview with Frank Chesley, December 29, 1997.

5. Dora Kunz, interview with Peter Michel, April 24, 1995.

6. "Harvard Medical School Launches Division to Study Complementary Medicine; BIDMC Physician Appointed Director," Beth Israel Deaconess Medical Center Web site, July 11, 2008; http://www.bidmc.org/News/Around-BIDMC/2000/July/Harvard-Medical-School-Launches-Division-to-Study-Complementary-Medicine.aspx; accessed November 6, 2014.

7. Michael D. Lemonick, "Emily's Little Experiment," *Time*, April 13, 1998.

8. Larry Dossey, "Therapeutic Touch at the Crossroads: Observations on the Rosa Study," *Alternative Therapies in Health & Medicine* 9 (January 2003), 38.

9. Renee Weber, "A Critical Appraisal of Therapeutic Touch," reprinted in Catherine Caldwell Brown, *The Many Facets of Touch: The Foundation of Experience* (Skillman, NJ: Johnson & Johnson Pediatric Round Table Series, 1984), 164.

10. Marie-Therese Connell, "A Critical Appraisal of Therapeutic Touch," in Brown, 164–65.

11. Janet Macrae, interview with the author, New Hope, PA, March 26, 2011.

12. Dora Kunz, interview with Peter Michel, Rye, NY, April 26, 1995.

13. Dora Kunz, interview with Frank Chesley, Seattle, WA, December 29, 1997.

14. Dora Kunz, interview with Frank Chesley, Seattle, WA, January 12, 1999.

15. Ibid.

16. Dora Kunz, conversation with Erik Peper, Renee Weber, and John Kunz at Pumpkin Hollow Farm, August 8, 1979.

17. Dora Kunz, interview with Peter Michel, Rye, NY, April 27, 1995.

Bibliography

Books and Ephemeral Publications by Dora Kunz

Karagulla, Shafica, and Dora van Gelder Kunz. *The Chakras and the Human Energy Fields*. Wheaton, IL: Theosophical Publishing House, 1989.

Kunz, Dora [van Gelder]. "The Angels of the Lord." *The Liberal Catholic*, 1924. 18–20.

———. "Auras: Talk Given by Dora Kunz at Indralaya." Transcription dated August 8, 1957. Kunz Archives, Olcott Library, Wheaton, IL.

———. *The Christmas of the Angels*. Wheaton, IL: Theosophical Publishing House, 1921.

———. "Clairvoyance: Its Value and Limitations" (lecture, New York Federation of the Theosophical Society, New York, November 24, 1935).

———. "Clairvoyance: What It Reveals" (unpublished manuscript). n.d.

———. *Conscious Use of the Aura*. New York: Anchorite Press, n.d. Pamphlet.

———. "The Human Aura" (lecture, Pumpkin Hollow Farm, Craryville, New York, August 1955). Kunz Archives, Olcott Library, Wheaton, IL.

———. "The Human Aura: Paintings by Juanita Donahoo Done under the Direction of Dora van Gelder" (unpublished document, 1936).

———. "The Masters and the Path" (lecture, Philadelphia Lodge of the Theosophical Society, Philadelphia, May 8, 1955). Kunz Archives, Olcott Library, Wheaton, IL.

———. *The Personal Aura*. Wheaton, IL: Theosophical Publishing House, 1991.

———. *The Real World of Fairies: A First Person Account*. Wheaton, IL: Theosophical Publishing House, 1977.

———. "Reminiscences of Early Leaders of the Theosophical Society" (lecture, Theosophical Society in America, Wheaton, IL, 1985).

———. "The Role of Karma in Life" (lecture, Theosophical Society in America, Wheaton, Illinois, 1986).

————, ed. *Spiritual Aspects of the Healing Arts.* Wheaton, IL: Theosophical Publishing House, 1985. Reprinted as *Spiritual Healing.* Wheaton, IL: Theosophical Publishing House, 2005.

————. "St. Michael and the Angels" (lecture, Ojai, California, September 29, 1960).

Kunz, Dora, and Dolores Krieger. *The Spiritual Dimension of Therapeutic Touch.* Rochester, VT: Bear and Company, 2004.

Kunz, Dora, and Fritz Kunz. "Reminiscences of Annie Besant and C. W. Leadbeater" (lecture, Theosophical Society in America, Wheaton, IL, 1967). Olcott Library.

Kunz, Dora, and Erik Peper. "Fields and Their Clinical Applications," in Dora Kunz, ed., *Spiritual Aspects of the Healing Arts,* 213–261.

Related Works

Asher, Joseph. "A Rabbi Asks: Isn't It Time We Forgave the Germans?" *Look,* April 20, 1965, 84–94.

Bailyn, Bernard. *On the Teaching and Writing of History.* Hanover, NH: University Press of New England, 1994.

Berzin, Alexander. *Relating to a Spiritual Teacher: Building a Healthy Relationship.* Ithaca, NY: Snow Lion, 2000.

Besant, Annie, and Charles W. Leadbeater. *Occult Chemistry: Clairvoyant Observations on the Chemical Elements.* Revised edition edited by A. P. Sinnett. London: Theosophical Publishing House, 1919.

Besant, Annie, and C. W. Leadbeater. *Thought-Forms: A Record of Clairvoyant Investigation.* London: Theosophical Publishing House, 1901.

Blavatsky, H. P. *The Voice of the Silence.* Adyar, India: Theosophical Publishing House, 1889.

Bohm, David, and Mark Edwards. *Changing Consciousness: Exploring the Hidden Source of the Social, Political, and Environmental Crises Facing Our World.* New York: Harper Collins, 1991.

Borelli, Marianne D., and Patricia Heidt. *Therapeutic Touch: A Book of Readings.* New York: Springer, 1981.

Bragdon, Claude Fayette. *Merely Players.* New York: Knopf, 1929.

Cahill, Susan, ed. *Writing Women's Lives: An Anthology of Autobiographical Narratives by Twentieth-Century American Women Writers.* New York: Harper Collins, 1994.

Carrell, Alexis. *Man the Unknown.* New York: Doubleday, 1935.

Cheever, Susan. *My Name Is Bill: Bill Wilson—His Life and the Creation of Alcoholics Anonymous.* New York: Simon and Schuster, 2004.

Coca, Arthur F., and Robert A. Cooke. "On the Classification of the Phenomena of Hypersensitiveness." *The Journal of Immunology* (1923), 8:163–182.

Codd, Clara M. *So Rich a Life.* Pretoria, South Africa: Institute for Theosophical Publicity, 1951.

Collier, John. *From Every Zenith: A Memoir.* Denver, CO: Sage Books, 1963.

———. "No Feeble Will." Introduction to Philip Reno, *Taos Pueblo.* Denver: Sage Books, 1963.

Conan Doyle, Arthur. *The Coming of the Fairies.* London: Hodder and Stoughton, 1922.

Cooper, Irving S. *Methods of Psychic Development.* Chicago: Theosophical Book Concern, 1912.

———. *Theosophy Simplified.* Wheaton, IL: Theosophical Press, 1915.

———. *Reincarnation: A Hope of the World.* Wheaton, IL: Theosophical Press, 1979.

Crook, Edgar. *Vegetarianism in Australia: A History.* Canberra, Australia: International Vegetarian Union, 2008.

Dossey, Larry. *Healing Words: The Power of Prayer and the Practice of Medicine.* New York: Harper Collins, 1993.

———. "Therapeutic Touch at the Crossroads: Observations on the Rosa Study." *Alternative Therapies in Health and Medicine* 9, no. 1 (January 2003): 38–39.

Field, Sidney, and Peter Hay. *Krishnamurti: The Reluctant Messiah.* St. Paul, MN: Paragon House, 1989.

Fox, Matthew. *The Hidden Spirituality of Men: Ten Metaphors to Awaken the Sacred Masculine.* Novato, CA: New World Library, 2008.

Gomes, Michael. *The Dawning of the Theosophical Movement.* Wheaton, IL: Theosophical Publishing House, 1987.

Grad, Bernard. "Some Biological Effects of the Laying-on of Hands: A Review of Experiments with Animals and Plants." *Journal of the American Society for Psychical Research* (1965): 95–127.

Karagulla, Shafica. *Breakthrough to Creativity: Your Higher Sense Perception.* Santa Monica, CA: DeVorss, 1967.

Krieger, Dolores. *The Therapeutic Touch: How to Use Your Hands to Help or to Heal.* Englewood Cliffs, NJ: Prentice-Hall, 1979.

———. "Therapeutic Touch: The Imprimatur of Nursing." *American Journal of Nursing* 75 (1975): 784–787.

———. *Foundations for Holistic Health Nursing Practices: The Renaissance Nurse.* Philadelphia: J. B. Lippincott, 1981.

Krishnamurti, Jiddu. *Revised Report of Fourteen Talks Given by Krishnamurti: Ommen Camp, 1937 and 1938.* Hollywood: Star Publishing Trust, 1938.

Kuhn, Thomas S. *The Structure of Scientific Revolutions.* Chicago: University of Chicago Press, 1962.

Kunz, Fritz L. "On the Symmetry Principle." *Main Currents in Modern Thought* 22, no. 4 (March–April 1966): 92–96.

———. "The Metric of the Living Orders." In Henry Margenau, ed. *Integrative Principles of Modern Thought.* New York: Gordon and Breach, 1972, 291–364.

———. "Personalities from the Theosophical Society" (lecture, Eastsound, Washington, Indralaya, August 6, 1957). CD.

———. "The Reality of the Non-Material: The Consequences When Life and Man Are Put in the New Context of Field Physics." *Main Currents in Modern Thought* 20, no. 2 (December 1963). Reprinted in *Retrospective Issue: November 17, 1940–November 17, 1975,* 32, nos. 2–5: 16–23.

Leadbeater, C. W. *Clairvoyance.* Adyar, India: Theosophical Publishing Society, 1899.

———. *Invisible Helpers: A Story of Helping at Night the So-called "Dead" by Those Who Are Still in the Land of the "Living."* London: Theosophical Publishing Society, 1896.

———. *Man Visible and Invisible: Examples of Different Types of Men Seen by Means of Trained Clairvoyance.* London: Theosophical Publishing Society, 1902.

———. *The Occult History of Java*. Adyar, India: Theosophical Publishing House, 1951.

LeShan, Lawrence. *The Medium, The Mystic, and the Physicist: Toward a General Theory of the Paranormal*. New York: Ballantine, 1966.

Macrae, Janet. *Therapeutic Touch: A Practical Guide*. New York: Knopf, 1988.

Margenau, Henry, ed. *Integrative Principles of Modern Thought*. New York: Gordon and Breach, 1972.

Margenau, Henry, and Emily B. Sellon, eds. *Main Currents in Modern Thought (Retrospective Issue)* 32, no. 2 (1975).

Michel, Peter. *Charles W. Leadbeater: With Eyes of the Spirit: The Biography of a Great Initiate*. Translated by Elisabeth Trumpler, revised February 2012. Unpublished manuscript.

Miller, Henry. *The Air-Conditioned Nightmare*. New York: New Directions, 1945.

Mills, Joy. *One Hundred Years of Theosophy: A History of the Theosophical Society in America*. Wheaton, IL: Theosophical Publishing House, 1987.

New York Herald Tribune. "Girl Who Believes in Fairies Says She Sees Them Frolicking in Central Park," April 10, 1927.

Nicholson, Shirley, and Brenda Rosen. *Gaia's Hidden Life: The Unseen Intelligence of Nature*. Wheaton, IL: Theosophical Publishing House, 1992.

Norton, Robert. *The Willow in the Tempest*. Ojai, CA: St. Alban's Press, 1990.

Peppeard, Berth A. "Fairies, Real Fairies, Are Playmates of this Little Girl: Dora van Gelder Has the Most Sport with Water Sprites; Spies Elf in Harvard Botanic Garden." *Boston Herald*, June 19, 1927.

Peper, Erik. "You Are Whole through Touch: Dora Kunz and Therapeutic Touch." *Somatics* (1986/87): 14–19.

The Quest: Journal of the Theosophical Society in America. "Anniversary Congratulations," 87, no. 6 (1999): 230.

———. "Dora Kunz: April 28, 1904–August 25, 1999," 87, no. 6 (1999): 237.

Reno. Philip. *Taos Pueblo*. Denver: Sage Books, 1963.

Rhine, J. B. *Extra-Sensory Perception*. Boston: Boston Society for Psychic Research, 1934.

Rockefeller, C. Steven, and John C. Elder. *Spirit and Nature: Why the Environment Is a Religious Issue.* Boston: Beacon, 1992.

Roe, Jill. *Beyond Belief: Theosophy in Australia, 1879–1939.* Kensington, New South Wales: New South Wales University Press, 1986.

Rogers, Martha E. *An Introduction to the Theoretical Basis of Nursing.* Philadelphia: F. A. Davis, 1970.

Ross, Joseph E. *Krotona in the Ojai Valley,* 4 vols. Ojai, CA: Ojai Printing and Publishing, 2009.

Samarel, Nelda, Jacqueline Fawcett, Moira M. Davis, and Francisca M. Ryan. "Effects of Dialogue and Therapeutic Touch on Preoperative and Postoperative Experiences of Breast Cancer Surgery: An Exploratory Study." *Oncology Nursing Forum* 25, no. 8 (1998): 1369–1376.

Sears, Laurie J. *Shadows of Empire: Colonial Discourse and Javanese Tales.* Durham, NC: Duke University Press, 1996.

Sellon, Emily. "Fritz Kunz: May 16, 1888–February 13, 1972." *American Theosophist* 60, no. 4 (1972): 72–75.

———. "The Root of Being and the Process of Becoming." *The American Theosophist* 68, no. 9 (1980): 277–82.

Stern, Andrew. "Higgs Boson Coming into Focus Say Scientists." *Christian Science Monitor,* March 7, 2012.

Stevenson, Ian. *Children Who Remember Previous Lives: A Question of Reincarnation.* Charlottesville, VA: University of Virginia Press, 1987.

Sinclair, Upton. *Mental Radio.* Charlottesville, VA: Hampton Roads, 1930.

Smith, Justa M. "Enzymes Are Activated by the Laying on of Hands." *Human Dimensions, Approaches to Healing: Laying on of Hands* (1976) 5, nos. 1 and 2: 46–48.

———. "Paranormal Effects on Enzyme Activity." *Human Dimensions, Approaches to Healing: Laying on of Hands.* Buffalo, NY: Human Dimensions Institute (1976) 5, nos. 1 and 2: 49–51.

Taylor, Alastair. "Integrative Principles in Human Society." In Henry Margenau, ed., *Integrative Principles of Modern Thought.* New York: Gordon and Breach, 1972.

The Theosophist. "Rehabilitation" (January 1946), 179.

———. "Starvation in Java" (November 1945), 85–86.

Tillett, Gregory. *The Elder Brother: A Biography of Charles Webster Leadbeater*. London: Routledge and Kegan Paul, 1982.

Van der Post, Laurens. *Merry Christmas, Mr. Lawrence*. New York: Quill, 1983.

Van Gelder, Karel. *The Ideal Community: A Rational Solution of Economic Problems*. Sydney, self-published, 1922.

Van Gelder, Melanie. *The Object of Yoga*. Adyar, India: Theosophical Publishing House, 1944.

———. Unpublished document including descriptions of her father's business, education, and the family home. n.d.

———. Unpublished journal of travel in Europe beginning September 8, 1936.

Van Gelder, Melanie, and Karel van Gelder. "Van Gelder Grandparents." CD of recorded recollections about themselves. Ojai, CA, March 10, 1966. Kunz Archives, Olcott Library, Wheaton, IL.

Van Hinloopen Labberton, C. *The Wajang or Shadow Play as Given in Java: An Allegorical Play of the Human-Soul and the Universe*. Bandoeng, Java: De Uitgevers Trust Jamur Dvipa, 1912.

Van Hinloopen Labberton, Dirk. *Atta Sjrimad Bhagawad Gita: Labberton's Gita Transcriptie (voor Meditatie)*. Amsterdam: Uitgave van de Theosofische Uitgeversmu Amsteldijk, 1910.

Wainwright House. *Second Spiritual Healing Seminar*, March 1954. Rye, NY: Wainwright House Publications, 1955.

———. *Third Spiritual Healing Seminar*. October 3–5, 1954. Rye, NY: Wainwright House Publications, 1955.

———. *Fourth Spiritual Healing Seminar*. June 24–26, 1955. Rye, NY: Wainwright House Publications, 1956.

———. *Fifth Spiritual Healing Seminar*. October 8–10, 1956. Rye, NY: Wainwright House Publications, 1957.

Weber, Renee. *Dialogues with Scientists and Sages: The Search for Unity*. New York: Routledge and Kegan Paul, 1986.

———. "Philosophical Foundations and Frameworks for Healing." In Marianne D. Borelli and Patricia Heidt, *Therapeutic Touch: A Book of Readings*. New York: Springer, 1981. Also in Kunz, *Spiritual Aspects of the Healing Arts*, 21–43.

———. "Compassion, Rootedness and Detachment: Their Role in Healing: A Conversation with Dora Kunz." *The American Theosophist* 72, no. 5 (1984): 132–141.

Whorf, Benjamin Lee. *Language, Thought, and Reality*. New York: John Wiley, 1956.

Williams, Walter. *Javanese Lives: Men and Women in Modern Indonesian Society*. New Brunswick, NJ: Rutgers University Press, 1991.

Wilson Ross, Nancy. *Three Ways of Asian Wisdom: Hinduism, Buddhism, and Zen and Their Significance for the West*. New York: Simon and Schuster, 1969.

Wood, Beatrice. *I Shock Myself: The Autobiography of Beatrice Wood*. Edited by Lindsay Smith. San Francisco: Chronicle Books, 2006. Originally published, Ojai, CA: Dillingham Press, 1985.

Index

A

AA. *See* Alcoholics Anonymous
Abbenhouse, Dorothy, 248–49
Abdill, Ed, 195–96
abdomen, 211
active listening, 169
activism, 57–59, 245
Adam (cancer patient), 3–4
Adams, Miss, 164–65
addiction, 97
adrenal glands, 211–12
adrenalin, 150–51
Adyar (Theosophical Society
    headquarters), 29, 73–74, 88,
    246, 250–54
Adyar Day, 251
after-death states
    contacting people in, 28–29,
        41–46
    Dora on, 299–302
AIDS patients, 283–88
Al-Anon, 94–95
alcoholics, 299–300
Alcoholics Anonymous (AA),
    93–97, 290–91, 300
alcoholism, spiritual dimension
    of, 95
Allah, 230
allergy medicine, 98–99

alternative medicine, 208, 240,
    291–92, 294
*Alternative Therapies in Health and
    Medicine* (journal), 294–95
altruism, 20, 111, 192, 224, 245
American Journal of Nursing
    (journal), 231
American Society for Psychical
    Research, 147–48
American Theosophist, The
    (magazine), 247
amputation, 210
Andrews, Donald Hatch, 135
angelic kingdom
    Dora and, 21–22, 66–67, 119
    evolution and, 121
    humans and, 48–49, 121
    power of, 50
angels
    appearance of, 21–22
    in astral realm, 55
    as "crossovers," 121
    Dora and, 20–22
    healing, 48–49, 179, 291
    in Muslim culture, 22
    religious rituals and, 22, 48
    viewpoint of, 66–67
"Angel Who Wore Black Tights,
    The" (Beatrice Wood), 78–79

learning meditation, 6, 17
as lecturer, 89
lectures by, 262
management style of, 265–66
marriage to Fritz Kunz, 75–76,
    79–80, 82
memory of, 213
nickname of, 28
as parent, 86–87, 91–92
patient assessments by, 55,
    100–101, 109, 178–79, 208–9
as practical, 225
Pumpkin Hollow Farm and,
    125–29
as religious, 149–50, 158–59
research with Bengtsson,
    98–101, 108, 150–51
retirement in Seattle of, 281–83,
    297–99, 302–4
role in meetings of, 136–37
Sellon family and, 92–93
sexuality of, 122
shyness of, 27, 41, 53, 101, 149
teaching clairvoyance, 54–55
teaching meditation, 54, 63–64,
    93, 97–98, 141, 179
teaching style of, 214–16
terms used by, 9, 112–13, 160,
    262, 284, 300
as TSA president, 246, viii
as Upper Dora and Lower
    Dora, 267
use of maiden name, 146

as vegetarian, 27
work with after-death states,
    28–29, 41–46, 78, 132
worldview of, 20, 108
World War II and, 125, 131–34
Young Theosophists and, 57–60
Kunz, Fritz (husband)
    Adyar Day and, 251
    in California, 70–71, 75–76
    on centering, 229–30
    death of Nityananda and, 73–74
    family of, 82–83
    final years of, 199
    Indralaya and, 85–86
    integrative education and,
        143, 185
    Krishnamurti and, 53, 73–74, 76
    as lecturer, 76, 79–81, 87–88, 89
    marriage of, 75–76, 79–80, 82
    in New York, 91–92
    as parent, 86–87, 92
    periodical of, 133
    prison lectures of, 259
    Pumpkin Hollow Farm and,
        125–29
    Sellon family and, 92–93
    in Sydney, 52, 60, 64
    as vegetarian, 83–84
Kunz, John (son)
    birth and childhood of, 86–87
    death of father of, 200
    Dora and, 298
    on Dora as crossover, 121

Quest Books

encourages open-minded inquiry into
world religions, philosophy, science, and the arts
in order to understand the wisdom of the ages,
respect the unity of all life, and help people explore
individual spiritual self-transformation.

Its publications are generously supported by
The Kern Foundation,
a trust committed to Theosophical education.

Quest Books is the imprint of
the Theosophical Publishing House,
a division of the Theosophical Society in America.
For information about programs, literature,
on-line study, membership benefits, and international centers,
see www.theosophical.org
or call 800-669-1571 or (outside the U.S.) 630-668-1571.

To order books or a complete Quest catalog,
call 800-669-9425 or (outside the U.S.) 630-665-0130.

Related Quest Titles

The Chakras and the Human Energy Fields,
by Shafica Karagulla, with Dora van Gelder Kunz

Finding the Quiet Mind, by Robert Ellwood

*The One True Adventure: Theosophy and
the Quest for Meaning,* by Joy Mills

The Personal Aura, by Dora van Gelder Kunz

The Real World of Fairies, by Dora van Gelder

*The Secret Gateway: Modern Theosophy and
the Ancient Wisdom Tradition,* by Edward Abdill

Spiritual Healing, by Dora Kunz